Labor and Capital in 19th Century Baseball

# Labor and Capital in 19th Century Baseball

ROBERT P. GELZHEISER

*Foreword by* MARK ALVAREZ

McFarland & Company, Inc., Publishers

*Jefferson, North Carolina, and London*

796.357
632L

LIBRARY OF CONGRESS CATALOGUING-IN-PUBLICATION DATA

Gelzheiser, Robert P., 1955–
    Labor and capital in 19th century baseball /
Robert P. Gelzheiser ; foreword by Mark Alvarez.
        p.        cm.
    Includes bibliographical references and index.

    ISBN 0-7864-2169-X (softcover : 50# alkaline paper) ∞

    1. Baseball teams—United States—History—19th century.
    2. Baseball—United States—History—19th century.    I. Title:
Labor and capital in nineteenth century baseball.    II. Title.
    GV875.A1G45    2006
    796.357'64097309034—dc22                                    2005025350

British Library cataloguing data are available

Cover image ©1997 Wood River Gallery

Manufactured in the United States of America

*McFarland & Company, Inc., Publishers*
    *Box 611, Jefferson, North Carolina 28640*
        *www.mcfarlandpub.com*

To my father,
who played catch with me and
took me to Pittsburgh Pirates games,

and

to my mother,
who helped me to appreciate the
poetry of baseball and the importance of history

# Acknowledgments

Writing this book has been a fascinating personal journey that I would not have been able to complete without the generous help of many people. Despite spending countless hours in front of the computer screen, I am still a technological neophyte. I encountered numerous problems with software and hardware during the many years I worked on this book, and Ken Swain, Brian Dina, Professor Robert Pruzek, Fred and Toni DiMenna, Brian Kish, and Pat Hatcher all patiently came to my rescue on numerous occasions. Keith Gonnelly, my sister Professor Lynn Gelzheiser, my wife, Lynn Angela Gelzheiser, Nick Sedelnik, Gail Novaco, and Mike Roer all read the manuscript and provided me with valuable feedback. Professor Edward Sloan was my American labor history teacher and thesis advisor when I worked on my master's degree in history at Trinity College, Hartford, Conn. Professor Sloan is a superb teacher, first-rate scholar, and longtime baseball fan. Without his help, I would not have been able to write this book.

The library staffs of Trinity College and the National Baseball Hall of Fame in Cooperstown, New York, were also very helpful. I was also able to obtain much valuable primary source material from the Society for American Baseball Research collections, as well as much needed advice from SABR members. Over the years I have talked with Mark Alvarez, the author of several baseball books and the former director of publications for the SABR, on numerous occasions. He was always generous with his time, and he gave me much good advice.

It has been more than thirty years since I took American history from Mr. Richard Gribko at Roger Ludlow High School in Fairfield, Conn. He wove such a wonderful tapestry of stories during class each day that I often looked at the clock, hoping it would slow down. He helped me to develop my love for history, and for this I will always be grateful.

If my love of history started in Mr. Gribko's classroom, my love of baseball began much earlier on the sandlots of Fairfield. I am grateful that I grew up before computer games and the incessant need adults now seem to have to organize their children's lives around structured activities. Warm days in any season meant pickup baseball games with Joe, Pete, Tom, "Dino," Mark, Doug, "Buck," Tim, Rick, my brother Ed, "Millsy" and "Kal." Thanks to all of you. I know now that I will never get to play for the Pirates, but I put my share on the roof of the Visiting Nurses' parking garage, and the thrill of this is still with me. I am blessed to have had such a wonderful childhood.

I am grateful to my three canine friends: Einar, Maz, and Willie, who quietly stood by and gave me important moral support as I worked on this book. Finally, I would like to thank my wife, Lynn. She was supportive throughout this entire process. She typed the original manuscript, helped me to edit the book, and assisted me in countless other ways. Thanks, "Ziti." You are the "Babe Ruth" of wives.

Bob Gelzheiser
Fairfield, Connecticut
January 2006

# Contents

# Foreword
## by Mark Alvarez

Nineteenth century baseball was dynamic in every way. Rules changed, styles of play evolved, equipment developed, and the very nature of players and their relationship to the sport shifted. Over several decades it changed from an amateur game dominated by clubs of middle class gentlemen to a money game, from which the smartest owners and the most skilled players could make good livings. Amateurs still played, of course, in every corner of the country, and it was their devotion to baseball that made it the national pastime, but by the 1870s the professionals set the tone.

To me, the so-called Brotherhood War of the late 1880s and the establishment and ultimate failure of the Players' League of 1890 have always been among the most fascinating — and confusing — events in baseball history. Bob Gelzheiser here places them in the larger context of nineteenth-century American labor history, and in doing so sheds light on actions, reactions, and results that are otherwise impossible to understand. In the process he supplies a concise economic and social history of first decades of professional baseball. National League owners, Darwinian capitalists all, headed by Albert Goodwill Spalding, have always been relatively clear figures. But how about John Montgomery Ward and his colleagues in the Brotherhood? How about the players' putative allies, the money men who backed the Players' League? And how was it, not just vaguely, but in detail, that the Brotherhood "won the battle but lost the war?"

Bob has done the research and has the answers. Here they are.

Mark Alvarez was the Publications Director for SABR from 1992 to 2001. His baseball books include *The Official Hall of Fame Answer Book*; *The Official Baseball Hall of Fame Story of Jackie Robinson*; and *The Old Ball Game: A History of Nineteenth Century Baseball Up to the Founding of the National League in 1876*.

# Introduction

Ernie Banks, the former Chicago Cubs shortstop, once described baseball as a game that "ameliorates the classic polarization between the self-motivated individual and the collective ideology."[1] His description says much about the owner-player relationship that existed in the game until the mid–1970s. Though baseball is a team sport, individual performance is closely tracked by all, and the exact ways that it can be measured make baseball players likely candidates to be strong believers in the free market that, in theory, should give fair rewards based on their recorded statistics. Throughout most of the history of professional baseball, however, competitive forces have had little to do with how players have been rewarded. For most of the professional game's history, players were expected to drive themselves on the field to achieve their individual best, but they were collectively controlled by the game's power structure and rarely given a fair share of the revenues that they produced. As in other industries, in baseball the answer to this injustice was organization and collective action. Mr. Banks's "self-motivated individuals" would have to learn to act collectively off the field if they hoped to reap their fair share of the game's wealth.

The relationship between capital and labor in the last two decades of the 19th century was tumultuous. Events such as the violent railroad strikes of 1877 and the Haymarket bombing made corporate and middle-class America suspicious and fearful of organized labor. The Knights of Labor and the American Federation of Labor fought to ensure for their members a fair piece of America's growing economic pie, but in spite of their generally moderate demands and conciliatory posture, they were often attacked and mercilessly redbaited. This was the era of the trust, and most businessmen believed that only through control of the market could an industry survive. Corporations grew dramatically, swallowed up their rivals, and then regulated the supply and price of the goods produced and

3

the wages paid to the workers. Employers valued order, stability, and control above all else; organized labor was viewed as a threat to all of these.

To combat this hostile attitude toward labor, baseball players organized, broke from the established league, and formed their own Players' League. They believed that this rival league would make wages subject to market conditions and give players more mastery over their careers and industry. Although the League lasted only one year, it was a significant attempt by skilled workers to break from an established monopoly, gain more control over all aspects of their industry, and reap a larger portion of the revenues that they created.

This book explores the early history of professional baseball in the United States, the factors that contributed to the player rebellion of 1890, and the impact this rebellion had on the player-owner relationship in the decade that followed. Although the focus is the capital-labor relationship in the baseball industry, it is in the context of the overall capital-labor relationship in the country during the last decades of the 19th century. More specifically, the following questions are addressed: How did the movement to organize baseball players relate to the larger labor movements of this period? To what degree did baseball owners reflect the attitudes and actions of magnates in other industries? Can the player-owner relationship in baseball be viewed as a microcosm of the labor-capital affiliation that developed during this period, or was this an industry that was so unique that it has to be examined independently and was in no way reflective of a more general, national trend? Finally, how did the owners' victory over the players in 1890 affect the national pastime in the years that followed, and to what degree was this victory and the ensuing player-capital association typical of the labor-capital relationships in other industries after owners secured dominance?

Baseball is a topic worthy of such examination for a number of reasons. The game is a mirror of the great American dichotomy. The communal aspect of American society that dates back to John Winthrop's *Modell of Christian Charity* is represented in the intricate coordination required of teams to play defense. All must work together for a common goal, and rarely are individual players rewarded or extolled for their defensive prowess.

The individualistic and competitive side of America popularized in Herbert Spencer's *Social Statics* and by many Gilded Age capitalists is reflected when batters step up to the plate. Alone, hitters fend completely for themselves and then have their performance statistically recorded and closely scrutinized by fellow players, fans, and owners. Fan adulation and financial rewards are based largely on the degree of individual success.

American capital in the late 19th century claimed to be leading the nation to a new prosperity by emphasizing individual and corporate competition that would ultimately lead to increased production, productivity, wages and profits. In fact, the opposite was occurring. American corporate leaders talked of survival of the fittest, but really did all they could to reduce competition and control markets, prices, and wages. They quietly redefined the cooperative side of American culture, incorporating it in corporate policy instead of the community realm in which it had always existed. The good of the corporation mattered above all else. This often led to the destruction or annexation of competition, reduced wages, and increased prices often at a cost to communities, the environment, consumers, and labor. This trend extended into the baseball business, and its effects were more measurable than they were in other industries because baseball labor was more rare and its productivity easily and publicly measured. In ways corporate leaders did not like to admit, baseball was the quintessential American game. Not only did it reflect the great American dichotomy, but it also showed how necessary management believed that control of labor and markets was, and how willing they were to eliminate competition and extend control while extolling the virtues of the new corporate order.

It is essential to define certain ambiguous terms that are used in this book. *Capital* refers to those who have invested money in a particular industry and therefore control it. *Middle class* refers to individuals who are small capitalists: shopkeepers who control the profits that their businesses create; professionals such as lawyers; or white-collar, salaried employees of larger firms. Although the income and wealth of these individuals varied widely, their status in society was usually above that of employed skilled craftsmen or factory operatives. *Workers* refers to individuals who are employed by capital, are involved in the production process, and earn a wage. Generally, these individuals are employed in manufacturing. However, in a more general context, workers are producers of their industry's product and are under the control of capital or the middle class. In this context the baseball player is viewed as a worker. The skills and incomes of these individuals varied widely, but their status, although not always their wages, was below that of the middle class. Members of this class generally associated with fellow workers who performed the same tasks and generally defined themselves as members of a particular class. They often viewed capital as a natural adversary whose interests were diametrically opposed to theirs. This helped to create class unity and often led to organized attempts to gain higher wages or more control of their industry.

# 1

# The Origins of Professional
# Baseball in the United States

Baseball, the quintessential American game, evolved from the British game of rounders in the 1840s. Long before this, Americans and Englishmen had played numerous games with sticks, balls, and even bases. Soldiers enduring the harsh winter at Valley Forge played a game called "baste ball," and college students participated in similar contests as early as the 1780s. However, it was in the 1840s that the game that would become America's national pastime emerged. During this decade, baseball's rules were codified and its popularity grew.[1]

The first established baseball team was the New York Knickerbockers. Members of the Knickerbockers' baseball club initially played sandlot games among themselves. They used a set of rules devised by the club's founder, Alexander Joy Cartwright, in many ways similar to today's rules. By 1846, this loosely organized team became the Knickerbocker Base Ball Club of New York.[2] Club members paid a $2.00 initiation fee and $5.00 annual dues. Some of these dues were used to pay the $75 annual rent to use Elysian Field in Hoboken, New Jersey, which is still viewed by many as the birthplace of baseball.

Cartwright's club was not established just to play baseball. Team members were all from the middle class, 75 percent were of English ancestry, and most aspired to improve their professional and social status by joining the club. Team membership was based more on one's position in New York society than ability with bat and ball. The organization, like many of its day, was composed of men from society's elite and often kept its policies secret to outsiders. However, these policies were usually determined using democratic procedures.[3]

Early baseball was viewed as a gentleman's game. Fines of 25 cents were levied on individuals who questioned an umpire's call, 50 cents for

New York Knickerbockers (*left of umpire*) and Brooklyn Excelsior's (*right of umpire*) Base Ball Clubs were two of the earliest baseball clubs. The figure in the top hat in the center of this 1858 photograph is the umpire. The Knickerbockers were formed by Alexander Cartwright in the mid–1840s, and they are generally considered the first organized baseball club. The Excelsiors were a similar club formed in 1854. Members of both clubs were generally from the middle class, and games against rival clubs were often followed by a banquet or a dance. (Transcendental Graphics).

disobeying a manager's orders, and six cents for using profanity. Contests were arranged when one team sent a formal invitation or challenge to its prospective opponent and were usually followed by elaborate banquets and dances. Knowledge of etiquette and gentlemanly behavior were just as important as an understanding of the game.[4] Throughout the 1850s, baseball's popularity grew. More Irish and German immigrants began to play, and on some teams white-collar players lost their positions to more skilled blue-collar participants. However, when this occurred, white-collar club members almost always continued to manage the team, and until the Civil War, the organized game remained primarily amateur, genteel, and dominated by the white, urban middle class.

By the late 1850s, numerous baseball clubs had formed along the East Coast, in and around New York City, and as far west as Chicago, Cleveland, and St. Louis. Even some Californians were playing the game in the 1850s, having learned it from the Gold Rush-bound Alexander Cartwright. In response to this growth, several club leaders created a loosely knit organization in 1858 known as the National Association of Base Ball Players. The Association's founders did not intend to develop a well-defined league, and consequently, it never had strong leadership. Instead, they hoped to popularize and standardize the game, and they were successful at both.[5]

The Association standardized the Knickerbocker rules, helped organize new clubs, and created uniform sizes for balls, bats, pitcher's boxes, etc. Instead of awarding victory to the team that first scored 21 "aces" or runs, the standard game was made nine innings, with victory going to the team that scored the most runs. Although all of the teams in the organization were technically amateur, the rivalries that it created put an increased emphasis on winning and fielding the best team possible. Team travel became more extensive, the sporting press increased its coverage of games, and advertising became more common. All of these helped the game's popularity to grow. The National Association of Base Ball Players originated with only 25 teams, but membership grew to 50 in 1860, 97 in 1865, and 1,000 by 1869.[6]

The Civil War affected baseball in many ways. During the conflict, it became harder for many clubs to find an adequate number of quality players. As a result, some secretly paid skilled players to join their clubs. This often reduced club loyalty, but it paved the way to the professional game that would emerge after the war. In addition, ballplayers in both the Union and Confederate armies were dispersed throughout the ranks, and these individuals taught the game to many young men who were not familiar with baseball when they entered the military. At the war's end, these young men returned home baseball enthusiasts. This increase in the number of participants improved the quality of many of the contests and

Alexander Cartwright organized one of America's first baseball clubs and created the Knickerbocker rules, which helped popularize the game with America's middle class. Cartwright moved to California in 1849 and Hawaii in 1852, and he helped to popularize the game in both places. He was inducted into the Hall of Fame in 1938 (National Baseball Hall of Fame Library, Cooperstown, N.Y.).

increased the expectations of fans. Fielding got better, and in 1865 Arthur "Candy" Cummings developed the curveball. The "scientific game" had arrived.[7]

Baseball teams in the 1850s were often made up of players who had similar occupations. Artisans, shopkeepers, and clerks often organized teams. The Manhattans were made up of New York policemen; the Mutuals, firemen; the Phantoms, barkeepers; and the Metropolitans, schoolteachers.[8] As the number of teams grew, some teams began to have difficulty paying for increased travel, uniforms, parks, and equipment. Some clubs began to charge admission to watch games, and annual team revenues of over ten thousand dollars were not uncommon by the late

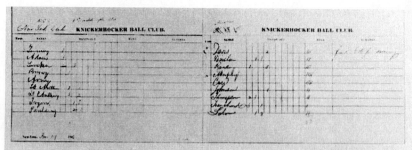

Sec. 1—The Bases shall be from "home" to second base 42 paces; from first to third base 42 paces equidistant.

Sec. 2—The game to consist of 21 counts or aces (runs), but at the conclusion an equal number of hands (outs) must be played.

Sec. 3—The ball must be pitched (underhand) and not thrown (freehand) for the bat.

Sec. 4—A ball knocked outside the range of first or third is foul. (If it hit inside but rolled out it was fair.)

Sec. 5—Three balls being struck at and missed and the last one caught is a hand (player) out; if not caught is considered fair and the striker bound to run.

Sec. 6—A ball being struck or tipped and caught either flying or on the first bounce is a hand out.

Sec. 7—A player running the bases shall be out if the ball is in the hands of an adversary and the

runner is touched by it before he makes his base, it being understood, however, that in no instance is the ball to be thrown at him. (He could also be forced out at bases.)

Sec. 8—A player running who shall prevent an adversary from catching or getting the ball before making his base is a hand out.

Sec. 9—If two hands are already out, a player running home at the time a ball is struck cannot make an ace if the striker is thrown out.

Sec. 10—Three hands out, all out.

Sec. 11—Players must take their strike in regular turn.

Sec. 12—No ace or base shall be made on a foul strike.

Sec. 13—A runner cannot be put out in making one base when a balk is made by the pitcher.

Sec. 14—But one base allowed when the ball bounds out of the field when struck.

*Top:* The 1845 Knickerbocker Rules were devised by Alexander Cartwright and became accepted throughout the United States. Section Six states that a batter is out if he hits a ball that is caught on one bounce. As players' skills improved, many argued that only balls caught on the fly should be outs. *Bottom:* Baseball at Fort Riley, Kansas, in 1870 — baseball became the most popular game in the United States military, and it was played by troops throughout the world (both from National Baseball Hall of Fame Library, Cooperstown, N.Y.).

The Civil War did much to spread the popularity of baseball throughout the United States. In this photograph, one of the first that shows baseball being played, Company H of the 48th New York Regiment stands at attention while other soldiers participate in a game, about 1863 (National Baseball Hall of Fame Library, Cooperstown, N.Y.).

1860s. Baseball was becoming an increasingly popular spectator sport, and some teams regularly drew three thousand fans to their games.

Admission fees had a profound impact on the game. Spectators who paid ten to fifteen cents to see a contest wanted to view the best performance possible. They were far more concerned with a player's ability than his professional or social standing.[9] Winning became more and more important; consequently, teams had to acquire the best players.

Often the best players were not artisans, businessmen, or club members, but graduates of the nation's sandlots. The sandlot game was growing in popularity. In 1856, a New York newspaper reported, "Games are being played on every available green plot within a ten-mile circuit of the city."[10] From these sandlots emerged highly skilled players which baseball clubs, anxious to win games and draw spectators, coveted. These players were often brought into a club specifically to play ball, and they were often secretly paid to play. They were usually not voting members of the club, and generally they did not participate in other club activities. These players frequently "revolved" or changed clubs, and often had little loyalty to the club they played for or the trade or profession of its members. Like craftsmen in other industries, they sold their skills to the highest bidder. Club directors did not view these players as social equals and tried to keep the "employed" players segregated from dues-paying club members.[11]

The gentlemanly standards of the day prevented teams from overtly paying these players. Instead, "ringers" would be given jobs at a club member's business or in local government or paid money in secret in order to attract them to a particular team. As early as 1860, Jim Creighton received money in secret from the Brooklyn Excelsiors to play, and by the late 1860s, most top clubs paid at least some players. These players would play with some of the less skilled gentlemen players, but it soon became evident that the more paid players a team had, the more successful the team would be.[12]

Gentleman clubs had a hard time attracting fans unless they played the game at a certain skill level. Practice became more important, but this took time and made it difficult for people who worked for a living to participate. This made pay for play more common. The new urban masses, uprooted from much with which they were familiar, needed something with which to identify, and this was often a local baseball team and its star player. However, this individual was often a baseball mercenary who "revolved" several times per season, and this negatively influenced fan loyalty and support.[13]

The number of professional players grew, and middle-class social clubs that excluded them quickly lost fan support. In an attempt to keep the game gentlemanly and amateur, the National Association of Base Ball Players passed a rule stating that any player had to be a club member for thirty days before he could play. This rule was generally ignored, but it was the first attempt at controlling player mobility and limiting the use of professionals.[14]

Newspapers reported on the best teams, and fan expectations for the local nine grew. Gambling, which would long be the scourge of the game, became more common, and fan behavior grew more rowdy and sometimes violent.[15] Slowly the game was becoming less reflective of the Victorian elite who had popularized it and more like the masses who were playing and watching it at an increasing rate.[16]

In the late 1860s, the Cincinnati Red Stockings Baseball Club fielded one of the best teams in the Midwest. Like many teams of the era, the Red Stockings were part of a social club whose members saw baseball as a means of increasing club status in the community. The team's success caused fan support to grow, and the admission fee paid by fans was an important source of club revenue. Hoping to maximize this revenue, the club borrowed $9,000 in 1868 and built a new baseball park. Many of the gentle-

The Cincinnati Red Stockings became baseball's first openly all-professional team in 1869. Under the leadership of manager Harry Wright, the team went 57–0 its first season, often attracted large crowds, and paved the way for the future professionalization of the game (Transcendental Graphics).

man clubs owned their own parks, but few were as elaborate or as costly as that of the Red Stockings.[17] To help pay for the park, the club announced that it would recruit and pay the best players available. Players would be asked to join the team regardless of their club status, hometown, or social standing. For the first time a baseball team was completely and overtly professional; its sole purpose to win games and make a profit. Baseball's professional era had begun.[18] (See Appendix 1: List of players, occupations, and salaries of Cincinnati Red Stockings.)

The man in charge of this first all-professional team was Harry Wright. Wright had been a fine player, but he was an equally skilled manager. He used $15,000 of the club's money to attract the best players. He then organized a series of games against the nation's best teams and took his team on the road.[19]

The Red Stockings were a huge success on the field. In 1869, they recorded 57 victories without a defeat, a record that has yet to be broken. (The team actually recorded as many as 70 wins, but Harry Wright only counted the 57 victories against NABBP clubs.) Crowd size varied, but total attendance for the tour was about 100,000 fans, and when they finally lost to the Brooklyn Atlantics 8–7 in 1870, over 9,000 people paid 50 cents each to attend the game.[20]

The success of the Red Stockings proved several things: A professional team would almost always outperform a club that was even partially manned by amateurs. (The Red Stockings later found this out when they attempted to reduce costs by having some amateur players on the squad and proceeded to lose more than half of their games.) Successful teams could draw large crowds even if team members were not "local boys" and played primarily for the money; skilled players could command high salaries since they would always be in short supply; and even successful teams did not necessarily make money. When the 1869 season ended, the Red Stockings' profits were minimal and the club's debts had not been reduced.

The advent of professional teams created a schism that still exists today. Paid players were viewed as employees and club managers as owners. Professional players, like workers in other industries, would often want higher wages and more control of the industry, and owners would want to keep wages low and maintain strict control over the industry and its work force.[21]

The limited financial success of the Red Stockings caused their owners to return the team to the amateur ranks in 1871. However, other clubs were intrigued by the idea of an all-professional team, and so by the end of the 1870 season, there were five all-salaried teams in the United States.[22] The emergence of professional squads created a dichotomy within the baseball community. The old order, which consisted of middle-class players on middle-class clubs who were out to prove their manliness, get some exercise, and socialize, could not compete on the field or at the gate with paid teams. It is unlikely that many wanted to. Professional teams were often dominated by working-class youths out to improve their social and economic lot, and most amateur gentlemen would not have wanted to play with or compete against such players.[23]

At the annual convention of the National Association of Base Ball Players in March of 1871, a split developed between the amateur and professional teams. Angered by their inability to compete with the professional nines, the amateurs walked out of the convention. The remaining representatives of the ten professional teams formed the National Association of Professional Base Ball Players (N.A.P.B.B.P.), the first all-professional league. The new league had clubs in Philadelphia, Boston, Chicago, Cleveland, Rockford (Illinois), Troy (New York), Washington, New York and Fort Wayne (later to be replaced by Brooklyn). It was loosely organized, had almost no central authority, and was not particularly successful. Each club made its own schedule, but league teams were supposed to play each league member three to five times, and the team with the most wins at the end of the season won a pennant. The league standardized playing rules, and these were generally also used by amateur teams throughout the nation.[24]

Managers like Boston's Harry Wright wanted to run teams as businesses. After the Association formed, Wright said to his players, "Professional ball playing is business and as such, I trust that you will regard it as such while the season lasts."[25] Most teams, however, were not well-run enterprises. To join the league, all a team needed to do was pay a 10-dollar entry fee. This meant

HARRY WRIGHT, Man'g. Philas

GOODWIN & CO. New York

Harry Wright was born in England but gave up cricket for baseball when he moved to the United States. He played for Alexander Cartwright's New York Knickerbockers and then founded, managed, and played center field for the Cincinnati Red Stockings, the first baseball team acknowledged to be all-professional. The Red Stockings went undefeated in 1869, and Wright continued to manage in the National Association and the National League from 1871 to 1893. He was elected to the Hall of Fame in 1953 (Library of Congress).

that many under-capitalized teams joined, and many of these could not afford the salaries, park rental fees, and travel expenses. During the Association's five-year existence, it had 26 different teams in 17 cities. Eleven would not last one season, and in 1872, five of the 11 teams folded before they had played all of their games. Only three teams completed all five seasons.[26]

Team ownership and control in the N.A.P.B.B.P. varied from franchise to franchise. As the league title suggests, players did have a degree of control. Many teams had player/managers who not only performed on the field but were in charge of finances, scheduling, payroll, and travel arrangements. The Association's president for two of its five years was James Ferguson, a former third baseman of the Brooklyn Atlantics. Some teams, like Wright's Boston franchise, were run by professional managers, and these teams were generally more profitable and successful on the field (Boston compiled a 71–8 record in 1875) and were generally unhappy with the league's weak central structure.[27] Team managers were expected to schedule games, organize travel and lodging, and watch over daily finances. Players sometimes performed these functions, but they rarely had the proper training and often did a poor job.[28]

Baseball was not yet big business, and this was reflected in the ownership of most teams. The elite disliked the idea of sport as business and still clung to Victorian ideas about the purity of amateur sport and the corruptive influences of money. For most, owning a professional team was unthinkable. Teams were usually owned by fledgling capitalists or blue- or white-collar workers, and often teams had more than one owner. In 1872, teams were owned by liquor dealers, attorneys, clerks, livery stable keepers, sportswriters, players and even political machines. (Early in his career, to help gain political support, New York's Boss Tweed helped to organize the New York Mutuals, who played in the N.A.P.B.B.P. from 1871 to 1875.)[29] Interestingly, many of the players from the N.A.P.B.B.P. emerged as the baseball leaders of the late 19th and early 20th centuries, and several of them became business giants.[30]

Baseball remained a risky business throughout the early professional era. Seventy-five percent of all 19th-century baseball teams went out of business within two years of their formation. Capital shortages, travel expenses, building costs or rental fees, poor fan support, and high player salaries were all factors in team failures. Because players were free to change teams as soon as their contracts expired, revolving was common, and team bidding for the best baseball talent drove up wages. Well-financed teams tended to pay the highest salaries, get the best players, attract the most fans and win the most games. Under-financed teams rarely did well on the field or on the bottom line. Their lack of capital made it difficult for them to keep their best players, win games and draw fans.

Often these poor teams were cooperatively run. Management could not afford to guarantee players a set salary and would instead pay them a share of the gate receipts. Players would also participate in other club tasks such as bookkeeping, ticket collecting, etc. Generally, this arrangement did not work well. Most teams that used it were poor, lost most of their games, and were not well supported. Also, their best players would often jump to clubs that offered guaranteed contracts with no extra duties.[31]

Revolving hurt team stability and made it difficult for fans to identify with some teams because their players changed teams frequently. The N.A.P.B.B.P., in an attempt to reduce player movement, passed a rule in 1873 that said a player had to give 60 days' notice before he left a team, but this rule was rarely enforced. Poorer teams insisted that this control over player movement was necessary, but wealthy teams, eager to improve their squads, quickly hired on prime players, regardless of what notice they had given their former teams.[32]

Revolving highlighted the fundamental difference between baseball capital and labor. Capital tended to be stationary, community-oriented, involved in local businesses and heavily invested in playing grounds. Players were mobile, in great demand, and often encouraged by the richest teams not to be loyal to their clubs so that it would be easier for them to sever their bonds and revolve to richer clubs. Often the more wealthy the team, the less control it wanted teams to have on players. Poor teams resented this, but could do little to stop it.[33]

Team payrolls averaged $15,000–20,000, and many players made more money than team owners.[34] Player drunkenness was common, and rowdy fans often drove away more respectable spectators. Management found it difficult to control players because the league had little central authority, and disciplined players would often jump to another team.[35] Competition was uneven, with the better financed and organized clubs usually winning. Wright's Boston team made money in spite of high payrolls because it was successful on the field, at one point winning four straight pennants, and was managed by one of the few men who understood the baseball business.

The most insidious problem that the league faced was gambling, and this would remain a dilemma for professional baseball throughout the 19th century.[36] Betting had plagued the game as far back as 1867 when Thomas Devyr, William Wansley and Edward Duffy of the New York Mutuals confessed to selling a game against the Brooklyn Eckfords in 1865. All three players were banned from playing, but were later reinstated by the N.A.P.B.B.P. Baseball pools were common in barber shops, billiard halls and tobacco stores. Gamblers bet on everything from the number of hits in a game to a contest's outcome.[37] Betting booths were often set up inside ballparks, and some teams were even owned by gamblers.[38] At one point, gambling was so rampant and the outcome of games so controlled that police installed signs outside of N.A.P.B.B.P. parks that said, "No Game Played Between These Two Teams Is To Be Trusted."[39]

Many fans began to question the game's integrity as it became apparent that many players were on the take. In 1875, the *Brooklyn Eagle* published a "Cheat's All-Star Team" which consisted of nine players and two substitutes. None of the players sued. Many fans believed that the most successful teams were the ones that were most adept at keeping their players off the take. In 1874, the *New York Herald* wrote of the Red Stockings:

> Above all, they invariably play to win. The latter cannot be said of all of the professional nines now contesting for a championship. Indeed to such a low ebb have the morals of so many professional players descended that no man can now witness a game between many of the clubs and be sure that both sides are striving to win. Gamblers buy up one or more players to lose a game and it is lost.[40]

Professionalization changed the way baseball was played. Winning, not gentlemanly behavior, now dominated players' thinking (at least the honest ones). Like skilled employees in other industries, players now became specialists at a particular position; teamwork and the execution of fundamentals were stressed, and the pace of the game quickened.[41] Working-class players tended to be less literate and less couth than their middle-class predecessors. Profane language, verbal and physical attacks on umpires, and disobedience to team captains were common.[42]

The professional game brought an end to many of social club teams. Not able to compete with the professional nines, the clubs soon lost fan support and died. After 1871, amateur and professional teams were officially separated, as they still are today. Although millions of amateurs continued to play the game, it was the professional teams that attracted the largest crowds, had the best players, and generally defined the game's rules.[43]

By the mid-1870s, baseball was the most popular sport in the United States. Despite this popularity, the professional game had encountered problems that it would have to overcome if it was to be a prosperous industry. If players had free movement and if the market determined their value, how could teams with less capital in smaller markets compete for players with richer teams in larger markets? Unlike other industries, machinery could not replace labor or increase productivity. The players were the baseball industry and were almost solely responsible for a team's success or failure on the field.

In the game's earliest era, players had a degree of control and were free to change teams as they pleased. However, as financial failure destroyed many organizations in the N.A.P.B.B.P., many capitalists began to believe that a new order was necessary in professional baseball that would control player movement, keep salaries down, profits up, and stabilize the industry. Players, it was believed, had to be kept out of the decision-making process and become strictly salary-earning employees. These changes would forever alter the owner/player relationship in professional baseball.

# 2

# The Development of the American Association and the National League of Professional Baseball Clubs: Baseball Becomes Big Business

William Hulbert was one of the people most responsible for making baseball a successful business. Hulbert was born in 1832 in Burlington Flats, New York, near where his game's Hall of Fame would one day be located. When he was two, his family moved to Chicago, which would soon become one of the nation's most baseball crazed cities. He was educated at Beloit College, and after he graduated, he found success in several business ventures. While still a young man, he got a position on the Chicago Board of Trade and then became a shareholder in the National Association's Chicago franchise. In 1875 he became a White Stockings executive. At the end of the 1875 season, Hulbert secretly lured star players Albert Spalding, Ross Barnes, Cal McVey, and Deacon Jim White from the Boston Red Stockings and Adrian Cap Anson from the Philadelphia Athletics to his Chicago White Stockings. Despite the fact that none of these players was under contract when they jumped to the White Stockings, Hulbert still faced expulsion from the league. This threat did not bother Hulbert. His plans were much more grandiose than winning the 1876 N.A.P.B.B.P. pennant.[1]

Hulbert was a businessman concerned with the instability of his industry caused by rising wages, low profits, alcohol, gambling, and a difficult-to-control labor force. In 1875 alone, half of the thirteen teams in the

N.A.P.B.B.P. did not complete their schedules. Hulbert feared that if such instability was allowed to continue, the baseball industry was doomed.[2] He believed that to be a viable industry, baseball's operation had to be based on true business principles. On February 2, 1876, Hulbert and a group of like-minded businessmen from Boston, Hartford, New York, and Philadelphia met at the Grand Central Hotel in New York. When the meeting was over, the National League of Professional Base Ball Clubs had been created.[3]

The group of founders believed that if baseball was to be a profitable industry, it would have to be structured and run as a "respectable and honorable" business. The new league would have to be completely independent of the N.A.P.B.B.P., whose owners the National League founders saw as "corrupt and feeble."[4]

A new industrial order was emerging in America, and people like Rockefeller, Pillsbury, and Vanderbilt were creating huge corporations run by skilled managers that reduced competition and controlled markets and labor. Cooperation, and not competition, was seen as the key element to a business's success.[5]

Hulbert was aware of this emerging order. He believed that the baseball labor force had to be controlled, competition for players had to be reduced, and prices had to be fixed. Most importantly, businessmen, and not players or unprofessional club managers, would have to run the league.

The National League consisted of eight teams that would play each other ten times per season.[6] Only cities with 75,000 people or more were to be allowed into the league (exceptions were made to this rule, especially if a city had an established record of supporting professional baseball), and teams were to have territorial rights extending five miles from the cities in which they played.[7] Ticket prices were set by the league, Sunday games were banned, and betting booths, oddsmakers, and alcohol were not allowed in the parks. Rowdy fans were ejected, and umpires were paid five dollars per game to ensure professional officiating.[8] In addition, each team had to pay annual dues of one hundred dollars to help finance league affairs.[9]

All of these policies were implemented to help make the baseball industry more respectable and profitable. Hulbert said shortly after the league's founding, "The National League was organized as a necessity to rescue the game from its slough of corruption and disgrace."[10] He later said that the new league hoped "to encourage, foster, and elevate the game of Base Ball and to make Base Ball playing respectable and honorable."[11]

Most of the league's pioneers believed that gambling and hippo-droming (the throwing of games) were "cancers" that had to be controlled if the game hoped to survive. Henry Chadwick, the dean of 19th-century sportswriters, had warned in 1876, "If ever professional baseball playing ceases to exist, the proper inscription to place on its gravestone will be: "Dead of Pool Selling." Chadwick went on to say, "The great bane of professional ball playing prior to the organization of the National League was the crookedness in the ranks brought about through the malign influence of pool gambling, the primary cause of all dishonesty in sports."[12] Respectability was deemed to be the key to the league's success. How the owners defined this and how they attempted to attain it would have a major influence on their relationship with players and fans for years to come.

Teams in the new National League were organized as businesses. Most

teams were owned by a few stockholders, and minority stockholders were usually ignored and often not even given a financial report.[13] Majority stockholders hired a team president, secretary, treasurer and board of directors.[14] The league appointed a five-man board of directors and league president and secretary each year. These men would oversee league affairs, make sure that teams adhered to league policies, and give out punishments to players and teams that deviated from the organization's dictates. The board of directors was chosen by lot, so all league owners had an equal chance at league control.[15]

William Hulbert was a Chicago businessman who owned the White Stockings of the National Association. Hulbert lured several star players, including Albert Spalding, to his team in 1876 and then formed the National League. He did much to legitimize the league and make it popular with prized middle-class patrons until his death in 1882. He was elected to the Hall of Fame in 1995 (National Baseball Hall of Fame Library, Cooperstown, N.Y.).

Morgan Bulkeley, former governor of Connecticut who would later serve in the United States Senate, was the first league president; however, Hulbert was the real driving force behind the league until his death in 1882.[16] The players were excluded from any say in league or team affairs and were often blamed for the professional game's previous shortcomings. The Spalding Guide, the organization's official publication, wrote:

... they seceded from the old Association and organized a reform movement under the auspices of the National League of Professional Base Ball Clubs— not "Players" but "Clubs" ... the method of purification of the professional system was then subjected to the hands of the officials of the new National League until professional ball playing was established on a respectable footing, and the game once more played in its integrity, was due entirely to the effects of the leading officials of the National League in the 1870s, which organization did not cease its war upon the "crooks" until the knaves were driven from its ranks....[17]

Teams usually employed between 50 and 75 people. These included scouts, ushers, policemen, ticket sellers, gatekeepers, refreshment boys, musicians, and fieldmen. Team managers were hired to oversee the day-to-day activities of the team such as park maintenance, travel, lodging arrangements, and payroll. The only player with any power was the team captain. He was expected to lead the team on the field, and all of the players were expected to follow his orders much like factory workers were expected to follow the orders of the shop foreman.[18]

Industrialization was increasing the class divisions in American society. Baseball reflected these divisions. The game had originally been played by the middle class for the middle class. As it became a business, the players became workers, and members of the middle class now owned the teams and watched the contests. They participated in the game less and less and increasingly played sports such as golf and tennis, which were exclusively for the rich.

One of the primary goals of the new league was to make professional baseball a respected form of gentlemanly, middle-class entertainment. Owners believed that rowdy crowds, alcohol, and gambling all contributed to the demise of the N.A.P.B.B.P. Attracting skilled tradesmen and people from society's upper classes would make the game more respectable and enable teams to charge higher prices. Hulbert commented, "The sole purpose of the league, outside of the business aspect, is to make it worthy of the patronage, support, and respect of the best class of people."[19] The *Spalding Guide* explained:

> There are two classes of the patrons of professional baseball grounds which club Presidents and Directors have their choice in catering to for each season, and these are, first, the reputable class, who prefer to see the game played scientifically and by gentlemanly exemplars of the beauties of the game, and second, the hoodlum element, who revel in noisy coaching, "dirty ball playing," kicking against the umpires, and exciting disputes and rows in every inning. The Chicago, Philadelphia and Boston Clubs in the League have laid out nearly $200,000 within the past two years in constructing their grounds for the express pur-

pose of eliciting the very best patronage of their respective cities. The Brooklyn Club has excelled in this respect in the American Association by constructing their grounds for a similar class of patrons. But all of the clubs have not followed this example, the majority committing the blunder of considering only the tastes and requirements of the hoodlum class apparently in catering for patronage. This is a great financial mistake. Experience has shown conclusively that it pays best to cater solely for the best class of patronage.[20]

Several policies were initiated to insure middle-class support. Ticket prices were set at 50 cents per game. This was comparable to the 25 to 75 cents charged to go to a play or the 50 cents charged to attend the circus or a lecture, but beyond the means of the average factory operative, who made about $1.34 per day in 1880.[21] Ballparks were generally constructed in middle-class neighborhoods, and this often made getting to games difficult for laborers.[22] Many teams lobbied to reduce the 50-cent ticket price in their communities because of competition from non-league teams, but these requests were almost always denied.[23]

Teams made a special effort to attract women to games. Owners believed that their presence would encourage men to act gentlemanly, prove to the public that league's games were respectable, and attract more men.[24] The *Spalding Guide* explained:

> Where the ladies congregate as spectators of sports, a refining influence is brought to bear which is valuable to the welfare of the game. Besides which, the patronage of ladies improves the character of the assemblages and helps to preserve the order without which first-class patronage cannot be obtained.[25]

Ladies' days were common, and many clubs had special sections that men could only sit in if accompanied by a woman.[26] Clubs also gave passes to clergymen, ostensibly to improve the game's image.[27]

Many owners believed that preventing workers from attending games would help ensure the league's survival. One of the Philadelphia owners explained, "the better class of people will not tolerate the antics of that class ... which does not know how to behave itself."[28] Hulbert reiterated these sentiments when he wrote, "You cannot afford to bid for the patronage of the degraded; if you are to be successful you must secure recognition by the respectable."[29]

For the most part, National League attempts to attract more affluent fans were successful. The *St. Louis Post-Dispatch* reported in May, 1883:

> A glance at the audience on any fine day at the ball park will reveal the presence of representatives of all respectable classes. Telegraph operators, printers who work at night, traveling men who go out on the road at nightfall, men at leisure ... men of capital, bank clerks who get

away at 3 p.m., real estate men who can steal the declining hours of the afternoon, barkeepers with night watches before them, hotel clerks, actors and employees of the theaters, policemen and firemen on their day off, strangers in the city killing time, clerks and mates, merchants in a position to leave their stores with a notice to the bookkeeper that they will not be back to-day, call board operators who need recreation after the experience of the noon hour, baseball players, semiprofessional and amateur; working men with the lame hand; butchers, bakers, candlestick makers, mechanics out on strike; lawyers in droves, an occasional judge, city officials ... the Mayor's private secretary, and last, but not least, doctors....[30]

Alcohol was forbidden in National League parks for several reasons. First, the coveted middle-class patrons were often native-born Protestants caught up in the temperance movement of the late 19th century.[31] Banning spirits would help to gain their favor. Alcohol was blamed for much of the rowdy fan behavior in the N.A.P.B.B.P., and National League magnates saw this as unacceptable. Prohibiting alcohol, owners believed, would help to give their league a respectable image and encourage society's "better element" to attend.

One of the more controversial measures employed by the owners to gain respectability was the banning of Sunday baseball. This was done to appeal to native-born Americans who were usually Baptists, Congregationalists, Lutherans, or Methodists and believed in the traditional Sabbath. These people viewed Sunday laws as necessary to protect public morals and safeguard religious sanctity.[32] Working-class immigrants tended to be Catholic, German Lutheran, or Jewish and believers in the "Continental Sabbath." They viewed their Sabbath as a day of rest and recreation, and believed that enjoying a ball game was not sinful. Since the magnates did not wish to encourage their attendance at games, they did not schedule contests on Sundays.[33] This made it almost impossible for most working-class people to attend games, since most worked ten to twelve hours a day, six days per week and were therefore at work when games were being played. Many National League owners fought to allow Sunday games, realizing that the crowds would be large. The fact that the league refused to allow play on the Sabbath shows just how important Protestant, middle-class support was to it.[34]

The attempts by owners to create a civilized atmosphere at the ballparks were not entirely successful. The crowds were never exclusively from society's upper crust. Fans still became rowdy, swore at umpires and each other, and often insulted players. There was so much animosity toward the umpires in Philadelphia that barbed wire had to be strung to protect them.[35] It is unclear whether the few workers who attended games were responsible for this rowdy behavior or if the middle-class patrons were not as genteel as management hoped they would be.

Workers did attend games in varying numbers, especially those who worked the night shift. However, poorly paid workers, for the most part, spent their limited free time in saloons or at vaudeville shows, the beach, or a public park. Not until the 20th century and the advent of Sunday games, larger parks with inexpensive bleacher seats, and eventually night games would National League baseball attract a large number of unskilled workers and other individuals from the lower echelon of the social spectrum.[36]

Black patronage was not uncommon in some cities. However, African players, such as Moses Fleetwood Walker, were officially banned from the game in 1890. This was done not only to calm bigoted players, but also to avoid offending middle-class patrons. As the industry matured in the late 19th century, black patronage became uncommon in most National League cities.

Overall, National League patrons in the 19th century were Protestant craftsmen, white-collar workers, or businessmen. These individuals had the resources to pay fifty cents for a ticket and flexible schedules that allowed them to leave work in the afternoon to attend games, which usually started between 2:00 to 4:00 p.m. They could also use an afternoon at the ballpark to discuss business with clients.[37]

Like capitalists in other industries, National League owners believed that their labor force had to be controlled. Many believed that the lack of management control over players was the primary reason for the failure of the N.A.P.B.B.P. Albert Spalding, one of the players taken by Hulbert when he formed the National League, later a team owner and successful businessman, argued:

> When players were gentlemen they could control the game, but when players lacked gentlemanly qualities they could not be expected to control the game. The problem with the N.A.P.B.B.P. was too much labor control and the gentlemen owners were taken advantage of.[38]

Spalding commented in 1879 that when the National League was formed, "It was, in fact, the irrepressible conflict between labor and capital asserting itself under a new guise."[39] He went on to say that the new league "put the life of the player in the hands of the organization that employs him."[40] These attempts by National League owners to control their patrons and workforce were indicative of what was happening in many American industries. Entrepreneurs throughout the nation worked hard to reduce the skills needed in the manufacturing process so that it would be easier to regulate the workforce. At the same time, advertising became much more sophisticated, and this enabled businessmen to tighten their hold on customers. Also, trusts and monopolies were created, and these allowed many industries to regulate the price and quality of their products.

But baseball players were in a uniquely powerful position. There was a limited supply of men with their skills and a growing number of businesses that needed them to win games and attract fans. They were more mobile than most other skilled workers and usually willing to sell their services to the highest bidder.[41] Players not only created the product of their industry, they *were* the product, and this made them extremely valuable.

Owners of teams in the fledgling league could not escape high wages. However, they could exert control over their workforce in other ways. Spalding wrote:

> Like every other form of business enterprise, baseball depends for results on two interdependent divisions, the one to have absolute control and direction of the system, and the other to engage in, always under the control of the executive branch, the actual work of production.[42]

Until 1879, National League owners were primarily concerned with controlling player behavior and not wage rates. Owners did not trust players, viewing them as socially no better than common laborers. Left to their own devices, owners argued, players would succumb to the same temptations that they had indulged in the now defunct N.A.P.B.B.P.: heavy drinking, rowdy behavior on the field, and game throwing. The new league's success, owners believed, was dependent on the public's perception of its integrity.[43] To insure public respect, stiff measures were needed to control players.

In 1877, the National League owners got their first chance to prove to the baseball public that they were serious about making the league worthy of their respect. That year, the league suspected that some of the Louisville players were associating with gamblers, which was against its rules. The league forced all of the team's players to allow management to examine all the telegrams they had sent. Management then concluded that Bill Craver, George Hall, Al Nichols, and Jim Devlin had thrown games and allowed rival Boston to win the pennant. The four players were banned from the league for life, and the Louisville team was moved to Milwaukee. The city would not get another franchise until 1892. This penalty was viewed as harsh in an era when gambling and its influences were common in most sports, but it demonstrated to the public and players that the owners were serious about keeping vice out of the National League. Despite these efforts, gambling continued to be a problem. Among themselves players often discussed gambling, and it was not uncommon for them to wager on games, although most of the evidence indicates that they would usually bet on their own teams to win.[44]

On the field, league players were expected to submit to the captain's authority "cheerfully," and insubordinate, ill or injured players were quickly dismissed.[45] Since substitutions were not allowed unless a player became seriously ill or injured, many players "played hurt" and developed career-ending injuries. Such individuals were soon unemployed.[46] Players were often required to pay petty fines or forced to perform non-playing functions such as ticket collecting or groundskeeping. They generally accepted any punishment that management gave them and performed these additional tasks because no grievance mechanism was available, and most of the players were young, poorly educated, and happy to be employed by the league.[47]

Until 1879, players continued to revolve at will and were often lured from competing leagues and teams with large contracts. Salaries varied depending on ability and position played, but they generally ranged from $1,500 to $3,000 during the 1870s, with "fielders" receiving the smallest average salaries and third basemen the highest.[48] Clubs could contact a player under contract and discuss a future contract as long as "the services to be rendered under the second contract were not to begin until the expiration of the first contract."[49] Some National League owners even paid players in competing leagues to play poorly so they would be released, allowing the National League team to sign them immediately.[50]

This system of "free agency" drove up wages and allowed players to determine where they would work. Even though players had this freedom of movement, the owners believed that their player-control policies were a success. As early as the spring of 1876 they claimed that they had made the game "clean" and rid it of gamblers and crooked players.[51] Being shut out of the administrative process and having their lives regulated during the playing season were acceptable to players, considering the high wages and mobility they had.

When the league was formed, regulation of ownership was deemed to be just as important as player control. Baseball was different from other industries because businesses (teams) competed and yet were dependent on each other. All franchises needed competition; consequently, one poorly run team could have a negative impact on all of the others. League standards had to be set, and all teams would have to be required to adhere to them. This would ensure the health of the teams and the league.

Not all teams abided by league policies, but those that did not were usually dealt with harshly. In 1880, Cincinnati found itself in last place and unable to attract fans. Desperate for revenue, the team started to sell beer, a favorite beverage of the town's large German population. They also began to lease their park to non-league teams that played Sunday ball. Unwilling to compromise on league policy, Hulbert and the National League Board of Directors expelled the team from the league.[52] Four years before this, the Philadelphia Athletics and New York Mutuals were expelled because each team failed to make its final road trip.[53]

The early success of some National League teams helped to destroy the N.A.P.B.B.P., but it also encouraged the formation of rival leagues. In October of 1881, the owners of the expelled Red Stockings and a group of businessmen met in Pittsburgh and created the American Association of Professional Base Ball Clubs.[54] The Association had teams in Cincinnati, Louisville, St. Louis, Baltimore, Pittsburgh and Philadelphia. Four of the six owners were brewmasters and saloon keepers, and one of their primary reasons for getting into the baseball business was to sell their products at the parks.

Christian Von der Ahe was typical of the new league's owners. Born in Prussia, he immigrated to the United States in 1863 and soon moved to St. Louis. Here he started a grocery business, successfully invested in real estate and a saloon, and became prominent in the Democratic Party. He observed the growing popularity of baseball and realized that money could be made selling tickets to games and beer to thirsty patrons watching the home nine. Many of the new league's owners wanted to market their games in the same manner, and it is not surprising that the American Association was dubbed the "beer and whiskey league" by its National League rival. The younger league also played Sunday games and only charged 25 cents admission to games.[55] Clearly the American Association had a different marketing strategy than its National League rival. Instead of discouraging working-class patronage, the Association did all that it could to attract proletarian patrons, hoping to fill its parks and sell lots of beer.

In response to the competition, some National League owners fought to reduce their ticket prices, and at the same time some American Association teams advocated raising their rates to their rival's level. In spite of these efforts, the Association continued to play 25-cent ball until its demise.[56]

The American Association was immediately attacked by such groups as the American Sabbath Union, the Sunday League of America, and the Women's Christian Temperance Union. It was branded by National League owners and some of its elite patrons as a "working-class league." Because of this, the new league was associated with the Democratic Party, which even then was viewed as more supportive of working men than its Republican rival. The National League continued to fight for the respect of middle-class Americans and continued to ban alcohol and Sunday games. It received the nickname "Republican League."[57] The American Association raided players from rival leagues and even hired players who had been expelled. It quickly became popular in most of its cities and played a caliber of ball not far below the National League. The new league was also a financial success. In 1882, all six of its teams made money, something the National League had never done.[58]

The success of the new league gave National League players more opportunities for mobility and helped to drive wages up. The directors of the National League continued to forbid ticket price decreases despite the competition from the American Association. The senior league was wedded to the idea that attracting civil, well-to-do fans was essential for long-term success, and league directors were not going to let the success of an upstart league change this. Years later the *Spalding Guide* summed up the different policies of the two leagues:

> There are two distinct methods of catering for base ball patronage in the professional arena, *viz*: that of the well-known method of the National League, and that which has characterized the American Association from its inception in 1882.... The League's rule of business always has been, first to prohibit the playing of Sunday games; also to prevent the sale of spirituous liquors on its club grounds, and to charge an admission of fifty cents to all of its championship contests.
>
> The Association rule is to admit of Sunday games; to allow the sale of liquor on its club grounds, and to charge but twenty-five cents admission to its games. There can be no compromise on this plain distinction. Clubs must cater either for grand stand occupants or those of the bleaching boards, and the latter plan requires the twenty-five-cent admission fee, Sunday games and "a license to sell liquor on the premises."[59]

The American Association was not the National League's only competition. The International Association of Professional Base Ball Players was founded in 1877. It fielded as many as 23 teams, three of which were in Canada, but it was never a serious long-term threat to the National League. Like the American Association, it charged only 25 cents admission, and visiting teams were guaranteed half the gross receipts or 75 dollars, whichever was greater. This was done to help balance out the league and guarantee poorer franchises a minimum sum of money per game. The league had numerous shortcomings. Its teams were scattered throughout the United States and Canada, so a balanced playing schedule was impossible. To join the league, clubs simply had to pay ten dollars; consequently, many teams were poorly capitalized and folded by mid-season. Also, revolving was common in the league, and this made it difficult for fans to identify with local nines. Many of its teams, including all of those in Canada, folded after the inaugural season, and the league ceased to exist after the 1878 campaign.

In 1883, St. Louis railroad millionaire Henry V. Lucas founded the Union Association. The twelve-team league, which began play in 1884, threatened the established order in several ways. Seven of its teams were located in National League or American Association cities, which ended the established monopolies in these locations. In addition, Lucas was opposed to the reserve rule (see Chapter 3), which meant that the Union Association's clubs could raid players from any of the nation's teams. Lucas's seemingly unlimited bankroll enabled him to build one of the best teams in the nation, and his St. Louis club won 94 of its 113 games in 1884. However, less capitalized teams lost many of their players to more wealthy franchises in different leagues, which hurt team and league stability. Also, Lucas's team was such a juggernaut that no pennant race developed, which reduced fan support. Only five teams completed the season, and the league folded after only one campaign.

Lucas remained in baseball. He bought the National League's Cleveland franchise and then moved it to St. Louis. The Union Association's players did not fare as well. Players who had jumped from the National League or American Association were

BROWN'S
CHAMPIONS 1886.
GOODWIN & CO. New York.

Chris Von der Ahe was the colorful and controversial owner of the American Association's and later National League's St. Louis Browns. Von Der Ahe, who became wealthy as the owner of a St. Louis saloon, loved beer, women, and baseball, and he made a fortune in baseball and real estate. His team won the American Association pennant from 1885 to 1888 and the "World Series" in 1886, and then moved to the National League when the American Association folded after the 1891 season. A declining real estate market, poor play by his team, a fire at his beloved Sportsman's Park, and debt forced him out of baseball in 1899 (Library of Congress).

blacklisted, and many others could not find employment after the league's demise because the number of baseball jobs in the United States was reduced.[60]

Independent teams and leagues flourished in the United States in the 1870s and 1880s, and most did not consider themselves to be "minor leagues."[61] Occasionally American Association and National League teams played teams from other leagues, and usually the games were competitive.[62] Eventually, both leagues passed rules that forbade their teams from playing non-league clubs within five miles of Association or League parks. One of the reasons for this ban was that games with non-League teams were often competitive, and the American Association and National League franchises were fearful of losing their status as the preeminent leagues in the nation.[63]

By the early 1880s, baseball was a firmly established business in America. In addition to the two "major leagues," a title given to the American Association and National League by their owners, there were at least fifteen other "minor leagues" with teams from Maine to California. Equipment was standardized and mass-produced, the sporting press had developed into an important source of free advertising, and box scores from the various leagues were printed each day in the nation's newspapers. Team owners developed additional sources of revenue. Peanuts and scorecards were sold during games, and telegraph companies paid clubs fees to transmit game information to bars and pool halls. The amateur game grew in popularity, and this created even more patrons for the professional contests.[64]

Despite this growth in popularity, the National League was not an immediate financial success. In 1876, seven of the league's eight teams lost money, and the following year, only one of the remaining six teams made a profit. In 1878, three of the original teams, Hartford, St. Louis, and Louisville, went out of business and were replaced by Providence, Indianapolis, and Milwaukee. During the league's first decade, it fielded between six and 12 teams per year in 21 different cities. Several teams folded midseason, and some lasted only one or two seasons.

Despite these difficulties, by the early 1880s, baseball had become a profitable business for many owners of major league teams. From 1882 to 1889 baseball attendance went up each year. In 1883 the American Association's Philadelphia, St. Louis, Cincinnati and Baltimore franchises reported profits of $75,000, $50,000, $25,000 and $10,000 respectively. The National League's Chicago franchise regularly paid stockholders dividends of 20 percent. From 1884 to 1888 dividends totaled $150,000, and in 1888 the team made a $60,000 profit. This happened despite the expenditure of huge sums to improve facilities. From 1884 to 1888 this investment totaled $600,000. Other National League teams also fared well. Detroit made between $7,000 and $12,000 in 1881. A year later Providence made $7,000, and although reports vary, the best evidence indicates that Boston made $48,000 in 1883. In total, National League teams made between $750,000 and $1,000,000 from 1885 to 1889. Such profits helped to finance the construction of large parks, which often led to an increase in attendance and revenue.[65]

Big-league baseball, at least by local standards, was now big business. The gentlemen owners of the N.A.P.B.B.P. had been replaced by aggressive businessmen who, like their counterparts in other industries, saw efficiency and control as essential to success. Success was now measured not only in the win/loss column, but on the bottom line.[66] The *Chicago Examiner* made this clear in 1888 when it reported:

> The Chicago Club is purely a money-making concern.... It is organized as any other corporation, by people of wealth ... who ... haul in such profits yearly as would make even bonanza kings envious.[67]

Baseball could be a risky business. Generally, the home team received 70 percent of all ticket revenue and 100 percent of the money received from concession sales.[68] How revenue was to be divided was often debated, and occasionally new formulas were introduced. In 1886, visiting clubs in the National League received a flat rate of $125, and this policy was changed again in 1887 when they received 25 percent or $150, whichever was higher.[69] Under any of these policies, the rich clubs benefited, because they could hire the best players, win the most games, and attract the largest crowds. Good attendance usually meant that they only had to give the visitors 25 percent of the gate, which left concession revenues and the remaining gate for them. While on the road, rich teams were guaranteed enough money to pay for expenses, which meant they would not have to dig into profits to pay for these trips.

Poorly capitalized teams could not compete with their richer rivals and often folded. Of the eight original National League teams, only two remained in 1890. A total of 23 teams competed in the league during this 14-year period. By 1889, the league schedule had been expanded from 70 to 140 games.[70] This increased potential revenue but also required teams to travel more. Less competitive teams were often out of the pennant race by midsummer and found it impossible to cover costs. These teams often folded during the middle of the season.[71] Like other businesses in the entertainment industry, baseball was greatly affected by the economy. The economic downturn of 1878 caused several teams to fold, and the 1880s were prosperous for professional baseball at least partially because of the strong national economy.[72]

Most National League owners lived in the same community as their team, and many owned additional businesses that benefited from a local baseball team. Spalding's companies published the National League's annual guide, manufactured much of the equipment used, and made and sold ticket turnstiles.[73] Other owners were also involved in the sporting goods industry, and several owned trolley lines that profited from the transportation of fans to and from parks.[74]

The formation of the National League in 1876 was a turning point for professional baseball. Unlike the N.A.P.B.B.P., the new league was determined to make players nothing more than paid performers who would not be involved in the management of the League. National League owners believed that the regulation of markets, prices, player behavior, and competition could help to insure profits. Although some teams did make large sums, the baseball business was still risky. Franchises often moved or folded, and this helped to undermine the public's confidence in the professional game. Players generally submitted to owners' demands because of the high salaries paid and the mobility that they had after their contracts expired. Eager to make baseball a more secure investment, owners would expand their control over players in 1879 and attempt to eliminate player-initiated movement. This would help to stabilize the industry, but it would also lead to a growing strain in the player/owner relationship. How players reacted to this strain would have a profound impact on professional baseball.

# 3

# The Player/Owner Relationship in the Mature Baseball Industry

During its infancy, the National League was unstable and unbalanced. Generally, the teams with the largest markets could afford the best players and dominate the league. This was an unsatisfactory situation, because even the best franchises needed teams that could compete with them on the field. Losing teams were often undercapitalized and could not keep their best players. This made them even weaker and was one reason they often folded. National League owners, like their counterparts in other industries, believed that the solution to this dilemma was to reduce competition for players and increase owner control over all aspects of their industry. They hoped that this would stabilize costs, create more competitive balance on the field, and thus draw more fans and increase revenues.

From its inception, this had been one of the primary goals of the National League. Markets had been clearly defined and protected. Ticket prices were set by the league, at first through gentlemen's agreements and later in the League Constitution. Rules and equipment had been standardized, giving the game a cohesiveness that it had lacked in the N.A.P.B.B.P. However, owners, especially those in smaller cities, believed that their industry's success could never be maximized unless they had total control over its greatest and most important resource, the players.

From 1879 to 1888, a series of policies was introduced to restrict player movement, behavior, and pay. These rules eventually extended beyond the National League to the minor leagues and helped to create a virtual baseball monopoly in the United States. The baseball industry thrived in the 1880s, but largely at the expense of the players. Not only were salaries controlled, but players were often expelled from the professional game and left unable to ply their trade.

League owners claimed that all of these rules were designed to make the game more competitive and stable and to "exact from players a more satisfactory equivalent for their services than has been the practice here to fore."[1] They argued that this stability would ultimately benefit owners, fans, and players, and therefore the players should cheerfully comply. But by the end of the 1880s, the players had been stripped of all their rights and, in the eyes of many, their manhood. Many were eager to change the system and enthusiastically joined the Players' League in 1890.

By the end of the 1870s, baseball had developed the star system that still exists today. Extraordinary players not only helped teams win, but they drew large, adoring crowds even when their teams were losing. However, many of these star players revolved regularly. This revolving affected the game in many ways. Star players were given large contracts, and even marginal players saw the free market drive up their salaries. Some marquee players frequently changed teams, and the owners claimed that this hurt fan loyalty and attendance. It also reduced the control that the owners had over their workforce.[2]

Since their league's inception, National League owners realized that the only way to insure standardization and regulation in their industry was through a league-initiated and enforced set of by-laws. This resulted in the creation of the League Constitution. The 1876 constitution made the first attempt at organized player control. Article V explained, "No club shall employ any person who has violated a provision of the constitution or who has been discharged, dismissed or expelled from any club belonging to the League. If any club plays such a player, it would be expelled from the League."[3] The constitution was expanded almost yearly from 1876 to 1879. During this period it was the sole mechanism for controlling players and defining their duties since there was no standard players' contract.

The 1877 addition to the League Constitution explained that players were to pay $30 annually for uniforms.[4] A year later an extensive section on the hazards of alcohol was added, along with a provision that teams that played Sunday ball would be expelled from the league.[5] The same year, the constitution forbade players from negotiating contracts during the season, as they had been able to do since 1876, but it also explained that any player who was cut or was a member of a team that folded could negotiate a new contract with any team.[6]

In September, 1879, Boston owner Arthur Soden organized a secret meeting with other league owners to discuss the revolving problem. The result of the meeting was the now famous reserve rule, which would become the backbone of the player/owner relationship in professional baseball until 1976 and would give the owners almost complete control over where a player played and how much he was paid.[7] (See Appendix 2 and 3: The reserve agreements.) The rule stated that any player who signed a contract with a National League team was automatically reserved by that team for the following season. Since players had to sign contracts before they could play, and since the contract bound the player to the team for an undisclosed sum of money for the following season, the player was, in effect, bound to the team that originally signed him for life. During the 1880 season, each team reserved only five players. Two years later the number of players each team could reserve was expanded to eleven. By 1887, all fourteen of a squad's players were reserved, ending all player-initiated team changes.[8]

The reserve rule affected professional baseball in several ways. First, it increased the sale value of players. Any player under contract was now the property of that club in perpetuity. The club could trade or sell him whenever it wished. Players had been sold prior to the reserve rule, but their value was limited because they could revolve as soon as their contract expired. Clubs now gladly paid huge sums for players because once they owned the contract, they controlled that player until he was traded, sold, released, or retired. Not since before the abolition of slavery had anyone had such control over another's labor.[9]

Bankrupt teams often sold off their players before they folded. After the 1885 season, Detroit bought the entire Buffalo club for $7,000 primarily to get the "big four": Dan Brouthers, Hardy Richardson, Jack Rowe, and Deacon White. The Buffalo team completed the season with sandlot players. That same year the Providence team, near collapse, sold its entire team to Boston for $6,600. Boston kept stars Charles "Old Hoss" Radbourn and Con Daily and then sold or released the remainder of the team. The most shocking sale of the decade occurred in December of 1886, when Mike "King" Kelly was sold by Chicago to Boston for the unheard-of sum of $10,000.[10]

Initially, owners tried to keep the reserve rule secret, and the 1880 *Spalding Guide* explained:

> The League has no desire to cut down salaries, but would be glad to offer still stronger inducements to young men of intelligence and fine physical development, of brain and brawn, of mind and muscle, to engage in ball playing as an avocation that the compensation to players shall be sufficient to remove all temptation to dishonesty....The highest interests of the game will be served rather by an increase than a reduction of salary expenses.[11]

That same *Guide* also said that:

No club shall be prevented from contracting with a player for the reason that he is already under contract with another club: Provided the services to be rendered under the second contract is not to begin until the expiration of the first contract.[12]

Although most players suspected the existence of the reserve rule soon after it was implemented, it became public in 1881, and throughout the 1880s, the league owners staged a public relations campaign to convince the players and public that it was fair and in the best interests of fans, players, and owners alike. By 1884, National League owners admitted that the reserve rule was primarily a tool to regulate how much players were paid. The *Spalding Guide* explained (see Appendix 4 for the complete text):

The most difficult problem the League has had to solve, in legislating for the government of the professional fraternity, has been that of how to control and regulate the salaries of players. The club rivalry for the possession of the best players each season, has been, from the very onset, an obstacle to an equitable arrangement of the salary question, and this has led to an increase of club expenses of this kind until the subject became one involving the future existence of even the most wealthy of the League clubs....

From the basis of the rule that "a player's services are to be paid for according to their real value to a club," the question has resolved itself into one in which he is to be regarded as worth all he can get, either by coercion or by reckless competition for his services. All reasonable arguments involving an equitable estimate of a ball player's work on the basis of the relation it bears to that of any other occupation he may be competent to engage in as a means of livelihood, are disregarded....

Efforts were made to establish special rates governing the several positions of a club team, so as to regulate the pay according to the work done. But all such efforts failed until the rule reserving eleven men, at a stated minimum salary, was adopted.... By reserving eleven men at a salary of not less than $1,000 a season the clubs placed a barrier to the further progress of the fancy salary business, and besides this they placed themselves on a securer financial footing than it was possible for them to obtain under the old order of things.... The reserve rule does not lessen the salary of any player ... but it simply places a barrier to the reckless competition for the services of men who, outside of the ball field, could not earn a tenth part of the sum they demand for base ball services. It is a defensive law against an abuse which has grown out of an excessive rivalry between individual clubs for certain over-estimated material for their field business. Below we give the letter of the law for the information of our readers.[13]

The ideas of this passage were reiterated throughout the 1880s. National League owners argued that if left uncontrolled, the free market would bankrupt their industry. High salaries were said to be good because they would attract players to the game and keep them honest. But owners argued that a player's worth had nothing to do with the revenue he created or with market conditions, but was linked to what he would be able to earn if he were not a ball player. Owners argued that the $1,000 minimum salary was generous when compared to what a player would earn as a laborer. Owners contended that the reserve rule did not lessen the salary of any player, and then explained that owners needed legislation to prevent "excessive rivalry" and "unscrupulous" owners from driving up salaries.

The magnates blamed the players for their salary dilemma, and rationalized the reserve rule in the hope of making it appear fair and necessary. In reality, the rule was designed to save the owners from themselves at the expense of the players. They did this during a decade when the American economy was strong and baseball profits were growing. The rule did help to lower salaries. In 1877, the average player was paid more than $2,000, but by 1880, the first year the reserve rule was used, the average salary had clipped to below $1,400. After the 1883 season, owners bragged that the league had "financial success beyond precedence."[14] Doubtless, the rule was implemented to increase profits. But it is also likely that owners, reflecting capital's mentality during this era, felt compelled to control as much of their industry as possible, and this one rule enabled them to completely dominate the most significant aspect of it. Management believed that such control would guarantee order, harmony, and stability. It would also help to ensure good wages, steady employment, and the fair treatment of players. Consequently, the reserve rule, they argued, was not only financially necessary, but also just.

Owners generally saw themselves as above the players, and they often depicted them as greedy man-children incapable of comprehending the intricacies of their industry or of understanding what was best for them. Prior to the reserve rule, players were ridiculed for changing teams for the purpose of making more money. Owners had expected them to remain loyal to their teams while at the same time selling or trading them as they saw fit, or moving teams from one city to another to increase profits. The *Spalding Guide* reported in 1884:

> One of the weaknesses of professional players is their aptitude to "grasp at the shadow while losing the substance." This is a habit they are prone to indulge in the moment their season of service in the field ends each year, and they begin to seek for "better pasture," something which the majority seem to think is comprised solely in the fact of obtaining a larger salary. A player, we will say, is in receipt of a salary of two hundred dollars a month for six months' service, in a thoroughly responsible club, where he is well treated, and is sure of a permanent position so long as he does faithful service in his position. At

the end of the season, he is offered a salary considerably in excess of that he is receiving. Without due consideration of the relative positions of the two situations—the club he is with, and the one he is asked to join—and tempted by the fancy terms offered him, like the dog in the fable, he grasps at the shadow of the increased salary, and, in consequence, loses the substance of the surety he leaves behind him. Experienced players ought by this time to have practically realized the fact that it is far more to their advantage in every way for them to accept a moderate salary from a sound organization, which has an established reputation for fair dealing with its employees than to sign for a salary double in amount offered by a less responsible club....

This is especially important in the case of a player having a family. The sensible player will prefer the home position with a sure salary, even if it is not very large, to a mere stopping place for a temporary period at fancy figures. The permanency of a club's abiding place is also a matter for consideration.... Then, too, there is the reputation for considerate treatment of its professionals to be taken into consideration. A club may pay its salaries when due, and yet treat its men simply as hirelings. The club to engage with is the one which acts toward its players as if they were part and parcel of the organization, and to be considerately cared for as such.[15]

National League owners viewed the control of salaries by the reserve rule as essential to maintaining stability and profitability. However, other measures were needed to insure that the game remained popular with middle-class patrons. Like other progressive businessmen of this era, National League owners believed that alcohol was the root of many of society's problems. The owners viewed the players as undisciplined and child-like and in need of strict controls to insure their sobriety.[16] Under the leadership of Chicago owner Albert Spalding, the league initiated policies that were designed to keep all players temperate. Spalding argued that thousands of dollars in "public patronage" was lost each season because of drunken players. These players "disgusted the best class of patrons" and hurt attendance. He concluded that "the drunkard must go."[17]

This was not the first attempt by owners to control players' drinking habits. As far back as 1869, Harry Wright had attempted to keep his Red Stockings temperate. However, the new policies were far more inclusive and generally more effective.[18]

The 1881 *Spalding Guide* explained the League's alcohol policy:

... The effect of the new penalties and system of discipline, prescribed by the League, will be, primarily, to hold to a stricter accountability than heretofore that class of players who are in need of some powerful restraining influence to help them guard against a tendency toward intemperance and excess.... Hereafter it is not proposed to permit or tolerate drunkenness or bummerism in the playing members of League Clubs. It is not designed to interfere with the personal liberty of any player, by the imposition of foolish and impracticable restrictions upon his conduct while off the ball field, further than to require that he shall not disgrace his club and his avocation by scandalous and disreputable practices. A player's habits and deportment when not before the public in his professional capacity are matters which he alone can regulate by the light of his interests and his conscience ... Who does not know that the ball players in America receiving the highest compensation for their services are they who are scrupulously temperate and well-governed in their habits? There are players of the other class of a higher degree of skill, but who are handicapped in the matter of compensation and standing by reputation for objectionable habits.... A player's reputation is not confined to any one city; it is well known and correctly gauged all over the country, and sobriety and gentlemanly conduct make firm friends who will, some day, be of value and benefit to a player after he has, voluntarily, or by reason of some disabling injury, retired permanently from base ball.[19]

While the *Spalding Guide* was urging players to regulate themselves when "not before the public," National League owners were trying to regulate players' drinking and personal habits year-round. Policies were passed that lowered the pay of players who drank, regardless of what they did on the field. The 1882 *Spalding Guide* went so far as to say that a temperate player should receive twice as much pay as an intemperate one, even if their performances were identical.[20] Pinkerton detectives were hired by teams to follow players to make sure they remained sober. In 1888, the league passed a short-lived rule that forbade players from investing in saloons or breweries. This outraged many players. Saloons were viewed as a good source of off-season income, since many patrons were attracted to an establishment owned or operated by a professional baseball player. Many players hoped to support themselves with these businesses when their playing days were over.[21]

Spalding was against even modest alcohol consumption by players. He demanded total abstinence from April to October, explaining that players were obligated to keep themselves in "perfect physical condition."[22] Those who drank were referred to as the "drinking class of players" and were often fined, blacklisted, or suspended. Sobriety, according to Spalding, was "more essential to success than any special skill they may possess in playing." He expanded on this by claiming that "having a choice between an ordinary fielder and batsman who is a strictly temperate man and a drunk who is skilled ... the manager always takes the temperate man." Drunkenness was often blamed by National League owners for a team's failure, and some squads required players to make temperance pledges.[23]

In spite of the league's policy on alcohol, some teams did not try to regulate its consumption. When these teams did poorly, rival owners often blamed their failures on alcohol. Some star players like Mike "King" Kelly were notorious drunks but were still paid huge sums of money because of their talents and crowd-drawing ability. Despite his popularity, Kelly was still followed by detectives and periodically threatened with suspension, but none of his employers ever followed up on these threats.[24]

During the 1880s, the National League also implemented a number of other policies designed to control players. One of these involved giving umpires increased authority. They could fine players who used abusive or threatening language five to 25 dollars and have fans who made "loud, insolent or insulting remarks to players" removed from the park.[25] However, umpires themselves were not immune to the league's excessive regulation. At least one umpire was expelled after the 1882 season simply for being connected with a pool room. In addition to a 30-dollar annual uniform expense, players were required to pay 50 cents per day when their team was on the road to offset expenses.[26] Players could be fined for wearing dirty uniforms, not being in dress code, missing practice, talking back to managers, consorting with gamblers, gambling, keeping unreasonable hours, missing bed checks, or even having bad table manners. Even managers or players who were released were not completely free of their former team's control. They still had to wait 20 days before they could sign with another team.[27]

To paternalistic that league and team rules were adhered to, teams often hired detectives to follow players and even perform bed checks.[28] In 1886, every Chicago player was followed at least once during the season. Detectives submitted reports to Spalding, who said he saw nothing wrong with the policy and could see no reason why players should object to it.[29] Team captains were also involved in the regulation of players. Cap Anson fined Fred Pfeffer $100 in 1887 for juggling a ball at first base, and on another occasion he had his entire team fined $150 to $250 each when he caught them setting out to "do the town."[30]

This controlling attitude of the National League toward its employees mirrored the posture of capital toward labor in the United States during this period. Not only did owners want to control their workforce and wages, but they wanted to reduce employees to the status of dependent children who felt subordinate to employers and therefore would likely be passive and malleable.

In addition to fining players who broke rules, owners could also suspend players without pay, for almost any offense. The 1880 National League Constitution stated:

> A club is not only empowered to punish or discipline a player for so much as remains of the season during which the offense was committed, but can go beyond that, beyond the life of its contract with that player, and suspend or disqualify him for the whole of the ensuing season during which he is as absolutely shelved, disabled, annihilated, so far as playing in or against any League club is concerned, as though he had lost an arm or a leg.[31]

National League owners claimed that "the power to suspend is additionally conferred upon each club for any act or deed of omission or commission by which a player's services to his club are impaired in their efficiency and value." Owners said that this authority protected them against "intemperance ... unsound physical condition, moral recklessness, loose play, general demoralization, and dishonorable or disreputable conduct." Owners explained to players that this control over them insured discipline, "by reaching into the pocket and pride of a player."[32]

Teams in financial trouble often suspended highly paid players to save money or unpaid players who demanded the money owed to them. Even star players, like Charles "Old Hoss" Radbourn, who won 60 games during the 1884 season, were suspended. Players could even be suspended by an opposing team. Opponents' managers could lodge a complaint against a player and force the player's team to discipline him.[33]

Suspended players could appeal their punishment to the League Board of Directors. However, the player had to pay $200 to do so, and he only got his money back if he won his appeal. The board of directors would only hear appeals at its annual meeting, which took place after the season was over. This made it difficult for players to afford the appeal, because they did not get paid in the off season, and travel to the annual meeting and the $200 dollar fee could be prohibitively expensive. The player needed two-thirds of the vote to overturn the suspension, and since the board of directors was made up entirely of league owners, the overturning of a suspension was rare.[34]

Owners also had the power to expel and blacklist players and managers.[35] The blacklist was to be used as a cure for "gross acts of intemperance or insubordination" or to "punish men who subverted discipline and order within the League ranks." The league policy on when a player could be blacklisted was intentionally vague, to give owners leeway in deciding who would be added to the list. Many owners were quick to blacklist players. League president Hulbert expelled ten "chronic drunks" after the 1881 season, and in 1885 an entire team of players called the "Blacklisted" barnstormed the nation, drawing large crowds.[36]

League magnates claimed that the power to expel and blacklist players was essential to their success. The *Spalding Guide* explained in 1882, "No piece of legislative work has been accomplished by the League ... is so well calculated to lead to good results than the establishment of the blacklist." It went on to say that suspension and expulsion were the only way to rid the league of "drinkers, gamblers, insubordinate players and knaves."[37]

Blacklisted players could not play for any other National League team, and any franchise that employed a blacklisted player was subject to expulsion from the league, as were any teams that competed against a team that had a blacklisted player on it. Blacklisting also helped the league to enforce the reserve rule. Section 36 of the league's constitution stated:

> Any player while under contract with a League club, who shall, without the consent of such club, agree to enter the service of any other club after the expiration of such contract, shall be liable to expulsion by said League club.[38]

Once blacklisted, it was difficult for a player to be reinstated. The constitution stated that "no blacklisted or expelled player shall be reinstated in the League by the League except by the unanimous vote of the eight league clubs."[39]

In spite of the numerous measures implemented to control salaries, league capitalists still believed that wages were too high and plotted to put a tighter cap on them. They did this even though the American economy and the popularity of the professional game were both growing during the 1880s. At the National League's annual meeting after the 1888 season, John T. Brush, owner of the Indianapolis club, proposed that the league set up a salary scale, rather than allow individual owners to determine how much they would pay players. The idea was especially popular with the owners of teams in smaller markets like Detroit and Pittsburgh, who sometimes found it difficult to pay the prevailing wage.[40]

The Brush Plan called for players to be divided into five different categories: A, B, C, D, and E. "A" players would receive a seasonal salary of $2,500, "B" $2,250, "C" $2,000, "D" $1,750 and "E" $1,500. Each player would be classified based on his batting, fielding, base running, teamwork, conduct, and "earnestness and special qualifications." This last category enabled owners to lower a player's classification if he stayed out too late or behaved in a way that was deemed undesirable by management. In addition, slumps or errors could result in a player's classification being lowered, because they would be blamed on the player's bad habits. A provision of the plan that was rarely enforced stipulated that teams that were found in violation would be fined $2,000 and the players involved were to be given their unconditional release. The league would determine how a player was to be classified, and the league secretary would execute the contract on behalf of the club. The owners also agreed that players classified C, D, or E should be given additional tasks such as collecting tickets and sweeping the bleachers and that no player should be given advance money to tide him over in the off-season. The plan was adopted by a vote of six to two with the New York Giants' John B. Day and Boston Beaneaters' Arthur Soden casting the only dissenting votes.[41]

These men opposed the plan because they believed that it was unnecessary and immoral. They also owned teams in large markets and did not need any more salary control measures to make a profit. A.G. Mills, a league consultant, believed the plan was illegal. He also thought that the reserve rule already gave the owners tremendous control over salaries. He commented that a manager who "can't handle salary with the powerful reserve rule at his command ought to have a wetnurse."[42]

Owners argued that there were several advantages to the plan. Because it would decrease salaries, team profitability, especially in smaller markets, would increase. This would ensure the stability of the industry and ultimately would increase the number of jobs available to players. Owners contended that the plan would also act as an inducement to improve player behavior on and off the field, since both of these were taken into account when classifying a player. League president Nick Young explained that the plan "places a premium on honest and efficient work on the ballfield, and requires good, general deportment off the diamond. It will prevent players from drawing large salaries because of their previous records."[43]

Owners also claimed that the plan would keep down the salaries of young players and prevent jealousy between players on rich and poor clubs who would otherwise have had substantially different salaries. The emphasis on personal habits would also improve the quality of play, since owners always equated temperance with performance, and no player, no matter how skilled, would be classified high if he was a drinker.[44]

Some players were not opposed to the plan, because they believed that the owners would not abide by it and would pay players extra money under the table.[45] To prevent this, the league required players to sign an affidavit, issued by the secretary of the league, which said that "the consideration prescribed in said contract includes salaries, bonuses, rewards, gifts, and emoluments and every other form of compensation expressedly or impliedly promised him for his services as player during the term of such contract...." The affidavit went on to say that if proof was brought to the league that a player had received money not listed on the contract, then the player could be blacklisted and the team fined $2,000. President Young, determined to enforce the new policy, told the press, "I will establish something like a secret service department ... to get reliable reports."[46]

In spite of all these efforts, the plan was not a success. Many owners, especially those of rich teams, never fully believed in it, and some saw it as illegal. As many as two-thirds of the teams ignored it, and the plan was officially dead by 1890. During its short life, the plan created much animosity and mistrust between players and owners. It showed how far the owners would go to impose controls on players' wages, and it became one of the main reasons for the players' revolt of 1890.[47]

By the late 1880s, there were hundreds of teams and scores of leagues scattered across the United States. These leagues were often after the same

players that the National League sought, and competition for players between leagues drove up wages and reduced profits. When the International Association was created in 1877, National League salaries increased by as much as 15 percent. When the new league proved to be too financially weak to compete for the best players, salaries quickly declined. The emergence of the American Association in 1882 and Union Association of 1884 caused salaries to jump again. Most National League owners believed that such market-induced salary increases were not acceptable and that measures had to be taken to prevent them.

National League owners realized that they controlled only a small part of the American baseball industry. The reserve rule, classification, suspension, or expulsion would do them no good if a player were free to go outside the National League to seek employment. As often happened in American industry during this era, National League magnates set out to organize a system of alliances and agreements with their competition to create a more orderly and controlled industry.

John T. Brush became the president of the National League's Indianapolis team in 1887. A year later he convinced the league to implement the infamous Brush Player Classification Plan that was one of the reasons for the 1890 players' revolt. In 1891, he became the owner of the National League's Cincinnati team. He sold his interest in the Reds in 1902 and became the owner of the New York Giants (National Baseball Hall of Fame Library, Cooperstown, N.Y.).

The first attempt by the National League to extend control over their players beyond the league was the League Alliance of 1877. The Alliance was a loose association of teams from across the United States. Members agreed to honor each other's contracts and expel any player who did not honor his contract or was guilty of "disreputable" conduct.[48] Teams also agreed not to play any club that employed an "ineligible" player. All Alliance teams would use National League rules, and the National League Board of Directors would be the final arbitrator in any dispute. The League Alliance would allow only one member team in each city, an obvious effort to limit competition.[49] Members agreed to refrain from playing games on Sunday, not to use umpires who had worked on a Sunday, and not to let other teams use Alliance teams' parks on Sunday. Members were also expected to forbid the sale of alcohol and gambling in their parks, and teams were not to play each other until their seasons officially began.[50]

Spalding and other owners bragged of this "paternal policy," but membership was limited, and the Alliance was abolished in 1883. Many member and non-member clubs believed that it was nothing more than an attempt to create a National League-dominated monopoly. Future attempts by the National League to reduce competition and bring professional baseball teams under its control would be far more successful.[51]

The League Alliance did not regulate the baseball industry enough for most National League owners, especially when the American Association was formed in 1882 and did not join. For one year the two leagues were involved in a trade war, competing for their industry's most valuable raw material: players.[52] While the two leagues competed, suspended and expelled players could still find employment, and dissatisfied National League players could revolve to the new league.

From its inception, the American Association was a financial success. Some of its teams drew more fans than any in the National League.[53] Its owners publicly berated many of the National League's player-control policies. They even claimed that their league was dedicated to the proposition of "liberty for all."[54]

In reality, the American Association was structured much like its rival and exerted a great deal of control over its players. As the 1880s progressed, the American Association's constitution became more and more like the National League's. Players who were guilty of fighting, drunkenness, carelessness, indifference, insubordination, "disreputable conduct" or conduct regarded by a club as prejudicial to its interests or dishonorable could be suspended indefinitely. The league also reserved the right to "inflict any penalty that it deems proper to any player at any time."[55] Clubs were required to notify the league of all player contracts. If a player did not sign a contract, the team was obligated to notify the league so the player could be put on the ineligible list. Released players were expected to sign with the Association team that the league chose. If the player refused to sign with this club, he was then placed on the league's ineligible list.[56]

Publicly, the National League extolled its rival, claiming that the American Association fostered "honest play and temperate habits in the rank and file." The National League complimented the way the American Association mimicked many of its policies and stated that owners in both leagues hoped to one day "join hands."

In reality, National League owners had little affection for any rival. They probably increased the number of players that each National League team could reserve for the 1883 season in response to the American Association's signing of National League players midway through the 1882 campaign for the following season. League magnates believed that these reserved players could not jump to any team and thus would be unable to join the American Association.[57] Years later the *Spalding Guide* would report:

> The American Association ... increased the minor abuses of the professional system, "revolving" and contract breaking were developed; and it was out of these evils that the adoption of the much-reviled but useful "reserve" rule became a necessity as a matter of club defense against the rascalities of the rougher element of the professional fraternity; and it is a fact which cannot be gainsaid that without the reserve rule at the period of its adoption, neither of the clubs of the National League or American Association could have escaped bankruptcy.[58]

The author of this statement had a poor grasp of his league's history, forgetting that the reserve rule was implemented more than two years before the American Association existed. There is no doubt that real competition made expanding the rule imperative in the eyes of the National League's owners.

Owners in both leagues realized that players and wages could only be regulated if an agreement was reached between them. This resulted in the National or Tripartite Agreement of 1883. First proposed by National League president A.G. Mills, the agreement defined both the National League and the American Association as major leagues and the Northwestern League as a minor league. The National Agreement eliminated uncontrolled player movement between the American Association, National, and Northwestern Leagues. Teams in all three leagues could reserve all of their players, and member teams would honor each other's reserve list. Member teams also agreed not to sign any player who had previously refused to sign a contract with the team that controlled him. National League and American Association players would receive a minimum of $1000 and Northwestern League players $750 per season. When new leagues came under the jurisdiction of the agreement, the minimum salary was adjusted for that league depending on its wealth and level of play. Eventually, the agreement was altered so that players in leagues classified as minor could move up to a higher league. However, to do so, the player would have to give the team he played for a prescribed sum of money that would be determined by the league's status under the agreement.[59]

All contracts were to be seven months long, beginning April 1 and ending October 31. No team could negotiate a player contract until October 10, although this rule was occasionally ignored, and some players did sign three-year contracts. All teams agreed to honor each other's blacklists, suspensions and expulsions. Any team that employed an expelled or suspended player or any team that played a team that employed such a player was itself subject to expulsion from its league. Players were expelled if they played on a team within four miles of a team under the National Agreement unless they first got permission from their team. Clubs would have to wait twenty days before they could bargain for any released player, and disputes between teams or players and teams would be submitted to a six- man board of arbitration made up of three representatives from the National League and three from the American Association.[60] The agreement did not include rules on Sunday games and alcohol, and league policies toward these issues differed widely throughout the 1880s.[61]

The National Agreement of 1883 and the subsequent amended agreements were landmarks in the history of efforts to control players, and they were key reasons for the increased profits that major league owners reaped during the remainder of the 1880s. In addition, they also marked a new regime of efforts to regulate owners as well. Prior to this, only league constitutions regulated teams. These agreements did restrict owners, but not to the degree that the National Agreement did.[62] The new agreement restricted the independence of baseball owners and forced them to adhere to its dictates. The power of the individual club owner was limited by League and Association authority, and this was seen by many as a positive change for the baseball industry. Henry Chadwick wrote in 1885:

> At that period (1882) of League and American Association history, there existed constant revolving and mutual contract breaking in the ranks of the clubs of both organizations; and a few wise legislators inaugurated the arbitration system, out of which was evolved the mutually protective National Agreement, which for the past two years has proved to be the very foundation of the organization of the existing professional stock companies of the entire country.[63]

The National Agreement did leave clubs with some important powers. Owners still negotiated player contracts, disciplined players, and hired and fired managers. However, all club actions were now made subordinate to the League Constitution and the National Agreement, and no club regulation could conflict with these.[64] The agreement practically eliminated bidding wars for players, and it dramatically increased the value of clubs since teams under the agreement's authority were prohibited from going into another club's territory. Prosperous organizations no longer had to fear profit-reducing competition moving into their territory.[65]

The National Agreement remained the foundation of the baseball industry until 1890; however, it was modified periodically. In August, 1885, a $2,000 salary limit was established for the National League, and all clubs were forbidden to give salary advances. Although many teams did not adhere to the limit, it still angered many players.[66]

In 1886, a clause was added to the agreement stating that for a ten-day period after a player had been released, only teams from the league the player had been in could sign him to a contract. If more than one club wanted the player, then lots would be drawn to determine who had his rights. If the player failed to report to the team that picked him, he was then blacklisted. After ten days, if no team in the league the player came from wanted him, he could sign with a team in another league.[67]

At least partially as a result of this agreement, minor league baseball grew during the 1880s. Spalding argued that the extended reserve rule protection:

> ... has produced a good effect both in clubs and players, but in order to still further encourage the organization of these sectorial leagues, I think this protection should be extended ... acknowledged as it is by both players and clubs that the reserve rule is absolutely necessary for the perpetuity of the game on a professional basis.[68]

By 1890 ten leagues and more than one hundred teams were controlled by the National Agreement, and eight more leagues had been granted temporary protection under it. These clubs employed over 1400 players who made an average annual salary of about $1,000. Member teams played games that attracted almost eight million fans and grossed over $2,750,000 per season. Total profits frequently reached $250,000 annually. Owners claimed that these profits were low considering how much they had invested, and they continually argued that low profit margins made the controls that they had implemented essential to their industry's survival.[69] Many owners wanted to increase the power of the leagues, and Spalding hoped one day to merge the major leagues into "one great stock company." Reflecting the business attitude of the period, the baseball magnate explained that "in the natural order of things the two leading organizations should eventually consolidate."[70]

Owners also argued that players benefited from these controls. They claimed that the National League had ended gambling, attracted the best class of patrons, and gained the public's faith. All of these had helped to stabilize the industry and create jobs. Most owners agreed with *Sporting Life* when it wrote, "There is probably no other business in which the interest of the employers and employees are so nearly identical."[71] Owners argued that because their interests were identical, it was up to the league to regulate the players in order to insure prosperity for all. Spalding contended, "The only possible system which will yield financial success, alike to players and capitalists in the professional club business, is that of having employees in the entire control of the clubs, leaving the players in the position of paid employees only."[72] Spalding also said that discipline was needed to "protect and promote the mutual interests of professional baseball clubs and professional baseball players," and that it was the club's responsibility to regulate "that class of players who are in need of some powerful restraining influence."[73]

Baseball's owners believed that management and labor had to be kept separate. Players were viewed as uneducated and unable to understand the intricacies of the baseball industry. Management claimed that without rigid controls, players would throw games, drink excessively, and drive up salaries to the point where teams and leagues would fail. Sixty percent of all team expenses were salaries, and owners claimed that profits would be inadequate if market conditions determined wages.[74]

Capital wanted combative players on the field but passive employees off. Owners often corresponded with each other, explaining how to ensure this combination. Owners recommended that "quick-tempered, passionate men" not be hired, and former team captains often found it hard to find employment because "the player who has once tasted the fruit of authority is rarely amenable to control when occupying a subordinate position." Longevity with a team was also admired, because it was viewed as synonymous with loyalty and passivity. When they argued against free agency, owners often claimed that any man who would change teams for money did not have the "proper heart" for the game.[75]

In spite of these claims, the owners realized that the reserve rule worked to their advantage; however, most believed that the players lacked the will and capital to challenge the status quo, and for most of the 1880s players did not fight the controls placed on them. Most were young, uneducated, and happy to be playing baseball for a living.[76]

Prior to 1887, contracts were vague and stated that the players had to abide by the League Constitution. Many players opposed this, because they realized the owners could change the constitution at will. Thus, players were agreeing to abide by a set of rules that continually changed. This was the primary reason that the players lobbied to have the reserve rule written into their contracts instead of leaving it an unofficial and unwritten league policy.[77]

League magnates overestimated the passivity of the players. Eventually, the combination of the reserve rule, classification plan, player sales, increasing owner harassment, and control over players' personal lives caused the players to break out and form a league of their own, the Players' League, in the hope of forming a new baseball order.

# 4

# Business and Labor in the 19th Century: The Changing Relationship in the Baseball Industry

American society underwent fundamental changes in the last decades of the 19th century. Prior to the Civil War, U.S. businesses tended to be small, family-controlled, local enterprises. The nation was largely rural, and the primary mode of production was agriculture. Craftsmen were often self-employed, and if they did work for a large concern, they usually had much control over the production process. The Civil War and the boom that followed it changed America forever. A large standardized rail network, the transcontinental telegraph system, and improved postal system brought the nation together and made the quick movement of people, raw materials, manufactured goods, and information possible. The country's population grew, and increased production, improved productivity and technological innovation helped to increase per capita income.[1]

During this so-called Gilded Age, the modern corporation was invented. Factories became much larger, and with the improvement of steam power and the invention of the electrically powered machine, they no longer had to be located near water. Mass production and part standardization became common, and the salaried manager replaced the owner/boss.[2] Often, as the power of these managers and as capital expenditures on machinery increased, the role of the skilled worker in the decision-making process decreased. In addition, the role of the skilled worker in the production process was diminished because, whenever possible, management reduced the skills required to perform specific tasks.

This intentional "de-skilling" of the work force reduced the power of labor and made workers more susceptible to the whims of capital.[3]

New technology, expanding markets, and increased corporate size created a need for improved administration, coordination, and multi-unit business enterprises.[4] Often corporations were organized into trusts to reduce the role of market forces in determining costs and profits. The corporation took on an identity of its own, and armed with modern accounting methods, lawyers, politicians, and large amounts of capital, these huge concerns exerted influence far beyond their boardrooms and factories.[5]

Big, in the eyes of the corporation, was beautiful. Small farmers were bought out by agricultural corporations. The butcher was replaced by the meat processing factory, and the local flour milling operation was replaced by Pillsbury's large factories that processed the grains and then produced pre-packaged products. During the boom decades that followed the Civil War, class divisions in America were more sharply drawn. Stockholders, managers, and workers fought to determine which forces would control prices, profits, and wages and who would have a voice in how the production process would be implemented.[6]

The baseball industry, although not nearly as large as the dominant corporations of this period, was still out to achieve the same goals, and in most respects it was more successful. It is doubtful if any businessmen in America were as successful in regulating their industry and controlling labor and prices as baseball owners were under the National Agreement.

Baseball owners did have to overcome some problems unique to their industry. In most American businesses, capital allowed market forces to determine wage rates, because unorganized workers would battle each other for jobs and keep wages low. This attitude was not prevalent in professional baseball because there was a tremendous demand for the limited supply of professional-caliber players. If any team in any league attained the services of even half a dozen players who were substantially better than the other players in the league, then that team could dominate. This would cause financial stress on all of the teams in the league, since runaway winners reduced fan interest. Baseball players were mobile, and they could not be replaced by machines. Consequently, baseball capital did not advocate allowing the market to determine the value of its labor.

Baseball labor was slow to organize. Players were young, poorly educated, transient, and generally well paid compared to workers in other industries. Competition on the field was fierce, and many were reluctant to associate with their adversaries off the diamond. Players were also aware of the growing power and control of management and were reluctant to confront it by organizing. These attitudes helped management to completely dominate the industry by the end of the 1880s.

In order to increase productivity and decrease the importance of any one worker, many firms implemented the *Principles of Scientific Management* espoused by Frederick W. Taylor. Although Taylor's ideas were not fully crystallized until his book was published in 1911, many of his ideas were being implemented in American factories long before this. Taylor believed that all aspects of the production process had to be simplified to the point where they took little skill to perform. "Rule of thumb" production methods had to be replaced by "scientific" production procedures. Taylor argued that managers should manage a firm, foremen supervise the daily, rudimentary activities, and workers perform these activities.[7]

Taylor preached that only managers could understand the whole production process. In that process workers were to be just another replaceable part. With management less dependent on their skills and with a surplus of unskilled labor available, management could lower wages paid to skilled workers while productivity and profits increased. Taylor wanted a homogenized, unskilled, and non-unionized work force that was closely watched and evaluated by the foreman and taken care of by a paternalistic corporation.

Taylor argued that productive workers would be happy and that his management techniques would increase material wealth and wages for unskilled workers so dramatically that workers would not view unions as necessary.[8] He wanted to remove the group consciousness that had been necessary in so many production processes and remake the factory worker into an isolated, self-serving individual.

Industrialists throughout the nation fought to implement Taylor's ideas. Workers were told that scientific management was more efficient. Foremen were given much power over the work force, and stopwatch-controlled pieceworkers replaced skilled craftsmen.[9] Order, efficiency, productivity, standardization, repetition, and cost-effectiveness were the goals of management, and if an alienated work force was the result, then this was an acceptable and necessary price to be paid.

The values that Taylor epitomized were embraced by the baseball industry. By the mid-1880s, players had virtually no say in any aspect of their industry. Team captains took on the role of foremen. Their dictates were to be carried out without question. They determined how a team would execute its offense and defense, who would play, and often how players were to behave off the field. All aspects of a player's production were carefully measured, and if an individual failed to meet his "production quota," he might be released. Skilled players could not be replaced by unskilled performers, but as the league and teams became more of a fixture in their communities, fans began to identify more with the team and less with the players. This helped to make players interchangeable. Although organizations were relatively small, they still became very specialized. League and team functions were carried out by professionals whose primary goal was efficiency. All of these developments helped profits to grow.

American civic and business leaders were obsessed with order and control in the late 19th century. Progressive thinkers believed that all aspects of society could be organized and regulated so that institutions would maximize efficiency and individuals would be productive and free of vice.[10] Workers were not deemed capable of understanding the new social order, so management believed that they had to be reduced to nothing more than clock-regulated components of the industrial process. Control of the corporation was turned over to a new "subspecies of economic man," the salaried manager. Management argued that all would benefit from the increased productivity and wealth that this new order would create. Consequently, they argued that workers should embrace and not fight these changes.[11]

Pools, trusts, and holding companies were all used by American industry during this period to regulate markets and insure profits. Pools set prices and allocated different shares of the available market to participating corporations. They were designed to give a corporation a monopoly over a particular product in a given region and thus keep prices artificially high. Firms involved in pools often cheated by giving rebates or special rates to expand their markets. However, despite this, pool members were usually more profitable than companies at the mercy of the free market and always better prepared to survive economic downturns.[12]

Market instabilities that began with the panic of 1873 convinced capitalists that without broad control over all aspects of a particular industry and without a collective strategy, they would constantly be subject to the whims of the marketplace.[13] This led to the formation of trusts. By trading stock for trust certificates, vertical and horizontal combinations were created that gave corporations almost complete monopolies and enabled them to "concentrate and rationalize" the sales process. A board of trustees could act as a board of managers and make operational and investment decisions for all of the companies in the trust.[14]

Trusts were formed in the petroleum, cottonseed oil, linseed oil, sugar, whiskey, and lead processing industries. David Duke's American Tobacco Company, Eastman Kodak, Diamond Match, and Campbell's Soup all destroyed their competition and created virtual monopolies. All of these trusts successfully built their own manufacturing and distribution networks and thus integrated mass production with mass distribution.[15]

Organized labor, farmers, and small businessmen opposed the new business order. All three clung to the republican ideals of individuality and independence. These groups often turned to the courts and sometimes met with success. In 1893, the Ohio Supreme Court ruled that trusts were illegal, but this did not stop companies from merging, and it often left preexisting trusts intact. It did force some trusts like Standard Oil to restructure into holding companies which had been made legal in New Jersey in 1888, but this did nothing to reduce their dominance of the marketplace or increase competition. Even the Sherman Anti-Trust Act of 1890 did little to stop horizontal combinations. Although it gave the courts some power to attack these monopolies, most were reluctant to act.[16]

Although the baseball business was minute compared with the nation's largest corporations, it, too, adopted many of the measures employed by big business to reduce competition. The National League was formed during the same decade that the railroads and other huge corporations were merging and forming monopolies. Baseball magnates loathed and feared the free market as much as any industrialists, and they employed equally creative measures to regulate markets and prices and insure control of labor.

Just as railroad pools gave particular lines monopolies and thus guaranteed profitable rates, the National Agreement insured that most American teams were unopposed in their cities. It also enabled ticket prices to be set by the league just as pool members set rates. However, the National League could regulate its prices more successfully than most other businesses that were in pools. In most pools, important customers often worked out secret deals that gave them products or services at reduced prices or arranged to receive rebates. Because of the league's tough stand early on, control of ticket prices was assured, and teams rarely gave anyone special rates.[17]

Even the attitude of the owners of the industrial and baseball monopolies toward workers was similar. Both believed that the worker had to be controlled, although only baseball needed a wage-restricting method like the reserve rule. Other industries could rely on the millions of immigrants, scab workers, union busting, and the market to keep wages low. Like other industrialists, baseball owners argued that their monopolies would benefit workers because they would ensure industry survival, expansion, and an increase in the number of jobs.

Generally, baseball players did not resist the controls placed on them, and many players spoke out in favor of the reserve rule. They were still highly paid, their industry was relatively healthy, and some clubs treated them very well. As long as regulation was viewed as necessary to the industry's health and not abusive, they were willing to live with it. When they perceived it as oppressive, excessive, and an affront to their dignity, they resisted.

Corporate leaders in the decades following the Civil War saw control of markets and prices as essential to success. However, if labor was not also regulated, and if organized workers were allowed to dictate wages, hours and output levels, then all of the other controls would be meaningless. This insistence on the increased regulation of labor made it inevitable that capital's relationship with its workers would be tenuous in the new corporate order.

Prior to the Civil War, skilled workers had formed craft associations and unions, but these were generally small and cooperated with ownership.[18] They usually regulated their members, insured product quality, and expelled drunks and other workers who did not meet association standards. Union members often divided jobs at the manufacturing facility and supported each other when disabled or unemployed. Their most important bread and butter issue was the ten-hour workday.[19]

Often craftsmen would become petty capitalists, so there was rarely a significant division between owners and workers.[20] Class mobility was more possible in America than anywhere else, so a strong class consciousness was rare. Even wage operatives who may have felt alienated were always able to vote and thus had a vested interest in the system. (In the 1840s about eighty percent of eligible voters voted.)[21]

Craftsmen viewed industrial capitalism as a threat to their independence. From 1860 to 1890, factories became more prevalent, and thousands of farmers and immigrants eagerly flocked to them in search of employment. Wage labor became more common, and the traditional craftsman/boss partnership became an antagonistic relationship in which the operative often battled with the foreman and clock for independence and autonomy.[22]

Baseball played an important role in the new social order that was emerging. After a day of toil, workers often found themselves in one of the thousands of saloons that sprung up all over America during this period, and too often their meager earnings were spent on whiskey and gambling. Although most workers were working during game times or were too poor to afford a ticket, they still followed and often bet on the local team. Workers realized that many players came from the same social and economic background as they did and enjoyed the way they often resisted authority and argued or "kicked" umpires. During the 1880s, the slogan of the New York Giants was "We are the People," and although the players earned princely sums compared to workers, many were only an injury away from joining their adoring fans on the lower echelon of America's new social order.

The new working class was unskilled, unorganized, immigrant and often at odds with skilled, native-born workers. Capitalists fought hard to gain control over the labor force. Numerous periods of economic decline caused prices and profits to drop, and foreign competition, especially from the British, often cut into profits. Labor had to be controlled so that new machines could be introduced and production rates and productivity could be increased.[23]

To resist the growing power of the corporation, many workers organized. Craft unions were the first to be formed, and although their influence declined with the emergence of the factory system, they still remained important throughout the 19th century. Skilled workers organized themselves by trade, and work rules and production procedures were usually set by workers for an entire industry and not for the company that employed the worker. Workers who were loyal to their craft organization would be reluctant to change production rates or methods, as this would be seen as an affront to the sovereignty of the union.[24]

In many industries, workers were responsible for production standards, methods, and rates. They were expected to adhere to these regardless of what the employer said, and to deviate would cause a worker's manliness and loyalty to be questioned.[25] Capital tried to combat worker unity and power by increasing the use of machines, reducing the skills needed to perform most industrial tasks, and de-personalizing the boss/worker relationship. To a large extent, these conflicts between skilled workers and management over wages and sovereignty dominated the labor/capital relationship until the turn of the century.[26]

The great hope of skilled workers was the American Federation of Labor. Formed in 1886, the A.F.L. was a confederation of local, national, and international unions. It did not advocate the destruction of the capitalist system, but instead urged members to fight for their just share of the system's benefits.[27]

During its early years the A.F.L. was led by the former cigar maker, Samuel Gompers. Gompers was an immigrant whose passions included history, whiskey, and bull sessions with fellow workers. He wanted skilled workers to define themselves as a class and together fight for higher wages, shorter hours, and better working conditions and against incentive pay. His unionism was "pure and simple" and elitist.[28] He did not identify with the growing unskilled masses, and he urged his members to segregate themselves and their struggle from these workers and the mass actions that they advocated.

Although Gompers was not a revolutionary, his perception of rigid division of society by class is evidence of the influence of Marx on his thinking.[29] He wanted workers to be strong, independent, and self-reliant. He believed that labor could hold its own in the struggle with capital as long as its resolve was steadfast. Gompers never wanted his members to become dependent on the benevolence of government for their needs, because government was controlled by the owning class and was therefore an unreliable benefactor. Instead, workers should rely on their union and its ability to extract fair rewards from their employers. This would help to keep workers independent, proud, and unified.[30]

By 1890, the A.F.L. had 200,000 members; however, affiliated unions met with mixed success.[31] From 1889 to 1892 there was a record number of strikes, but often A.F.L. unions met with defeat. Some craftsmen, like iron molders, bricklayers, and stonemasons, were able to retain high wages and relative autonomy in the workplace. However, in most industries, as skilled workers were replaced by salaried managers, the power of the union decreased, and members had to accept a loss of wages and control. Even when workers in other industries struck in sympathy, capital was usually victorious, and by 1894 the number of sympathy strikes had declined dramatically.[32]

The second great labor organization of the period was the Knights of Labor. The Knights originated as a small brotherhood of garment cutters in Philadelphia in 1869.[33] By 1885, the union had 600,000 members and a year later 700,000. This success was short lived, and by the end of the century the union was almost dead. There were fundamental differences between the Knights and the A.F.L. The Knights were led by Terence Powderly, a thin-skinned man who had little in common with the men he represented. Powderly was opposed to the trade unionism of the A.F.L. because it accepted the wage system and neglected the vast and growing number of unskilled workers. Powderly called Gompers and his fellow craft unionists "gin-guzzling, pot-bellied, red-nosed, scab-faced, dirty-shirted, unwashed, leather-assed, empty-headed, two-faced, itchy-palmed scavengers."[34]

Originally the Knights wanted to restrict their membership to manual laborers.[35] However, Powderly eventually defined a worker as anyone involved in the production process, and this led the union to include people like draftsmen, timekeepers, and teachers. Regardless of what trade an individual performed, he was expected to be loyal to the union over his craft.[36]

The Knights supported the eight-hour day, income tax, land reform, and the voluntary abstinence from alcohol consumption. They also advocated the public ownership of railroads, telegraphs, and public utilities, and they wanted other industries to be run on a cooperative basis.[37] The union was opposed to strikes, because its leaders believed that they generally hurt workers. Instead, they advocated negotiation and arbitration to settle labor/capital disputes. They also did not believe in signing contracts since these gave validity to the wage system, and they feared and opposed the growing power of industrial monopolies much the way baseball's most important 19th-century labor leader, John Montgomery Ward, and his constituency feared the baseball monopoly.[38]

Samuel Gompers was the cofounder and first president of the American Federation of Labor. Within the A.F.L., there were a number of separate craft organizations, and most of the union's members were skilled, white, male workers. Gompers appealed to Ward and the Brotherhood to join the A.F.L., but the players' union turned down their offer (Library of Congress).

Socialism played an important role in the American labor movement of the late 19th century. Although ruthlessly attacked by capital and government and harangued for being "un-American," the nation's socialists viewed themselves as traditionalists out to fulfill the promise of the American Revolution.

Eugene Debs was the leader of America's socialist movement. He began his career as a labor leader with the Brotherhood of Locomotive Firemen. Like most lodge leaders of this period, Debs believed that labor should work with capital to improve the quality of the products produced. In 1878 he explained that "the only advantage the Brotherhoods have over corporations was to give them a class of honest and intelligent laborers, men on whom they can depend, men who are equal in every way to the responsibilities under which they are placed."

The young Debs believed that workers should be grateful to the corporation for providing them with jobs. He viewed the union as an instrument that would protect owners as well as workers and prevent unchecked

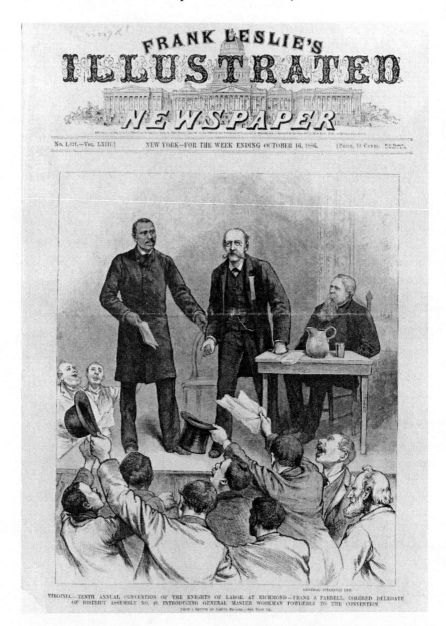

Terence Powderly (center) was the Grand Master Workman of the Knights of Labor. He took control of the union in 1879, and by 1886 the Knights had 700,000 members. Unlike its rival, the A.F.L., the Knights accepted both skilled and unskilled workers, women, and African Americans. The Knights attempted to get Ward and the Brotherhood to affiliate with them, but the union turned down their offer (Library of Congress).

individualism, which he believed would lead to anarchy. This support for capital was evident in his lodge's motto: "Benevolence, Sobriety, and Industry." He advocated a harmonious relationship with capital, because he thought that serving its interests would also benefit labor. He believed that his union should be primarily concerned with bread-and-butter issues like death benefits for widows and insurance. He also favored a free economic system, individual mobility, and a politically active workforce.[39]

As the size and power of the American corporation grew, the power of the worker decreased. This caused Debs to reevaluate his conception of what a union should be. Early in his career, Debs believed that each trade in the railroad industry should be independent and primarily concerned with the "moral conduct" of its members. However, by the mid-1880s, Debs's perception of the corporation had changed. Instead of respecting workers and deferring to their expertise, the modern corporation was determined to control all aspects of production, eliminate labor from the decision-making process, and lower wages. The modern corporation, in the eyes of Debs, was a threat to the industrial citizen and a destructive social and economic force. Debs believed that these changes were bad for workers and the nation and that opposing them was his patriotic duty.

During the great railroad strike of 1888, the conductors of the Burlington railroad remained loyal to the corporation. This weakened the worker's position and helped to convince Debs that federated workers could be divided and defeated. After the strike, he began to advocate the union of all workers regardless of skill. The omnipotent corporation could only be successfully opposed by a unified and well-organized labor force.[40]

In 1895 Debs was imprisoned in Woodstock, New York, for his role in the Pullman strike of 1894. He emerged from prison a socialist. Debs had seen the corporation use the blacklist, divisions among organized labor, scab labor, the reduction of worker control of the production process, and the centralization of the decision-making process to weaken workers.[41]

To combat this, he advocated the collectivization of industry, a reduction of competition, and an increase in the political influence of workers. He claimed that the natural course of the American ideal was to go beyond giving each citizen an equal say in the political process to giving him control of the production process. With collective control of industry, the police, military, and legislative powers would also be harnessed so that they would be advocates of the citizenry and not the new corporate elite. Debs viewed these changes as natural and as fundamentally American.[42]

One of the key elements of the worker/owner and worker/worker relationship in the late 19th century was the worker's evolving concept of "manliness." Debs wrote and spoke extensively on this topic. He believed that the employee had to view himself as the moral equal of his employer. He believed that an individual's manliness was defined in a public fashion. A man's actions as a citizen, his relationship with fellow members of the community and workforce, and his ability to support his family were all essential to maintaining a "manly stature."

Although Debs feared that unchecked individualism could lead to anarchy, he also believed that a man's loss of control over his position in the workplace would lead to his loss of self-worth and sense of manliness. A man had to be responsible for his deeds, and to give up this responsibility was to relinquish his masculinity. The corporation hoped to take away individual responsibility and, consequently, in the eyes of Debs and others, the worker's manliness.[43]

Most unions expected workers to adhere to a code. The honorable craftsman would not tolerate a man who was not honorable. Although a union existed for the good of all of its members, it still had to regulate the

drunk or slacker who could blemish the work and reputation of all of the organization's members. The union had to ensure the honor of its members by regulating their behavior. This was especially true in a democratic society that valued the individual and gave him tremendous freedom.[44]

By the late 19th century, many workers believed that they had to confront the boss because he frequently wanted to take away the worker's control and individuality. At the same time, the worker had to support his fellow laborers because they would help to ensure the collective good and maintain standards by which all workers would be proud to live. Workers were expected to make their pay rates public and to fight piecework and specialization which could cost jobs and dehumanize the production process. The manly worker was also expected to stand up to the boss and disobey objectionable orders even if it meant being fired. He was also expected to work at a rate that was satisfactory to the group.[45] Individuals were expected to have a manly bearing toward the boss or foreman, but

Eugene Debs was the leader of the American Socialist Party and its presidential candidate in five elections. An early supporter of craft unions, Debs grew to believe that these could not compete with the growing power of the modern corporation, and he turned to socialism (Library of Congress).

they were ostracized if they exerted too much individualism, operated more than one machine, worked too many hours or at a rate that was not satisfactory to the group.[46]

The modern market economy was interpreted as a direct assault on the worker's manhood. Market forces could eliminate jobs and give employers a rationale for reducing wages. The individual became a small part in a large institution, lost much of his control, and consequently his manliness.[47] At its root, the labor/capital conflict of this period was a fight to determine if this traditional concept of manhood could be preserved.

Employers wanted workers to change their definition of manliness so that they would be better equipped to function in the modern corporation. Advocates of scientific management claimed that it would ultimately benefit the workers by conserving their strength and making them more efficient.[48] Capital continually told workers that the new production methods would ultimately help everyone, because everyone would benefit from the increased wealth. Such arguments missed the point. Even if trusts and monopolies did use their increased profits and power to benefit society, they would still have been opposed by workers. The corporation's brand of paternalism was in conflict with the worker's definition of self, and the two could not happily coexist. Consequently, workers fought to preserve the old order, which they believed allowed them to be autonomous and kept the production process harmonious even while they remained loyal to each other. Employers worked to destroy the concept of the autonomous worker and wanted employees to define themselves by their relationship with the corporation and not by their class or trade. This would have required workers to redefine manliness. They were loath to do this because they believed that the monopolists were unconcerned with community needs and determined to destroy the workers' individuality. Such goals made them unworthy of a "manly" worker's respect.[49]

Baseball players of the late 19th century cannot easily be placed on the American labor spectrum. Many of the great labor issues of the period such as the ten-hour day, immigrant labor, and the introduction of part standardization and mass production procedures were irrelevant to them. However, in other areas, players, despite their high salaries, could easily relate to other workers.

Prior to 1876 players, like other workers, had a great deal of control in their industry. Many were player/owners, and those who were not could freely move from team to team in an attempt to earn higher wages. The creation of the National League and consequent development of the National Agreement reduced the players' power. The reserve rule enabled owners to regulate salaries and was unique to the baseball business. However, management also employed many of the tools used in other industries to ensure player cooperation. The blacklist, suspension, confrontational rhetoric when job actions were threatened or employed, and the use of Pinkerton detectives to spy on labor were all used by management to control its work force and defeat it when it finally acted.

The Brotherhood of Professional Base Ball Players was formed in 1885, enacted its most radical job action in 1890, and ceased to exist one year later. (See Chapters 6, 8, and 9.) The rapid fall of this labor movement is not surprising. This was an era of struggle between labor and capital in most industries, and until the early 1890s, it was not clear which side would win. The complete defeat of the players in 1890 was reflective of the general defeat suffered by labor at about the same time.

Baseball players were labor elitists. They prided themselves in being men of means, capable of behaving like gentlemen. Like Gompers, they felt little kinship with the unskilled masses, and they never tried to join a larger labor movement, or become involved in any labor issue that did not affect them. On the contrary, they never even attempted to unify as a trade. When the Brotherhood formed in 1885, it did not invite players from the American Association or the minor leagues to join. Such a union might have been able to counterbalance the power of the National Agreement, which attempted to regulate most players and teams.

Although the Brotherhood did not join a larger labor organization, it is still likely that its leaders were influenced by some of the era's prevailing attitudes toward capitalism and the role of labor in the new economic order. Many 19th-century workers still believed in the free labor ideology that saw property ownership as the key to individual liberty. Consequently, worker/owner cooperation and profit sharing were seen as key elements in ensuring the well-being of workers. Although never fully incorporated into the American economic mainstream, some companies in Pennsylvania and Massachusetts, the home states of Brotherhood leaders John Montgomery Ward and Tim Keefe, did implement such programs, and a similar program of profit sharing was advocated by Ward when the Players' League was being organized. Keefe had been exposed to much labor militancy as a young man, and this clearly made him more radical than his fellow Brotherhood leaders.

The Haymarket bombing on May 4, 1886, shocked much of America and increased the opposition to organized labor. Ward had a keen sense of public opinion, and it is likely that this was one of the reasons why the Brotherhood never aligned itself with the Knights of Labor or the American Federation of Labor despite the desire of both organizations to get the Brotherhood to join them.

In addition, baseball players were faced with an unusual dichotomy that their counterparts in other crafts did not have to confront. Like other artisans, baseball players worked side by side and often developed close bonds with each other. At the same time, players had to compete with their fellow workers on the field. In essence, one man's success resulted from another's failure. Other craft workers could advocate competition-reducing craft-wide procedures and production quotas to which all workers would be obligated to adhere. Such uniformity was an impossibility in professional baseball.

Like the unions of the nation's labor elite, the players never accepted the concept of mutualism or an attitude that "an injury to one worker was an injury to all." The minor leagues continued to treat players poorly, and their pay remained low. The Brotherhood never spoke out against this. Even players in the National League, especially pitchers, were overworked to a point where their careers were often ruined. Most teams only employed one or two pitchers, and these men pitched a tremendous number of innings. It is not surprising that Spalding claimed that pitchers wore out in about five years and that their arms were "not good for much else when their careers ended." There were even some deaths blamed on sore arms and overwork.[50] Players never raised a strong voice against such career-threatening overwork and abuse.

There were other problems inherent to the baseball labor movement. Players changed teams often and competed against each other, so solidarity and mutualism were difficult to achieve. Most were young and perceived themselves to be immortal, when in fact their careers were almost always short. They only worked for six months a year. Thus any strike would take a huge percentage of not only their yearly but also, potentially, their career earnings. Youth and affluence tended to make the players a carefree lot. While they played, most major league players could live the good life. And although adored by the public, any season-interrupting job action would have almost certainly resulted in a public outcry against them. Small businessmen, farmers, and laborers might support factory operatives in their attempts to gain higher wages, but not a 24-year-old baseball player who made $2,000 to play baseball for six months.

The basic structure of baseball may have also worked to discourage mutualism. More than any other team sport, baseball isolates the individual participant. The fielder acts alone when the ball is hit to him, the hitter is isolated at the plate, and the pitcher alone is responsible for each pitch. However, the game also requires intricate teamwork on the bases and when playing defense. On the one hand, baseball encourages a player to be a "petty entrepreneur" and on the other to develop a sense of mutualism with his fellow players. Such a dichotomy within the game's structure may well have worked to erode solidarity and a sense of mutualism.

When the Brotherhood was formed, it advocated many of the same things that Debs's Brotherhood of Locomotive Firemen did, such as "benevolence, sobriety and industry," discipline and improved quality of work.[51] Even during the height of the Baseball War, Ward reiterated these sentiments when he explained, "insubordination, intoxication and like breaches of discipline are punishable now as much as ever."[52]

The union's leaders believed that such qualities and goals would help the worker to retain his manly stature. Players also maintained their manly bearing by standing up to umpires or opposing players. However, when it came to confronting management, most players showed less resolve than workers in other industries. (See Chapter 5.) They gave up all of their power without a fight when the National League was formed, and as the league magnates increased their authority, most players went along passively. They might have feared the growing monopoly, but they did little to stop it.

Historian Ruth Allen said of the famous Gould strike of 1885 that the workers wanted to be recognized by management as "men equally powerful in and responsible for the conduct of the Gould Railroad Southwest System."[53] When the Brotherhood revolted, its leaders pronounced similar goals; however, their resolve never equaled that of their counterparts in the railroad industry. Industrial workers had to fight state and federal governments, the corporation, Pinkerton detectives and the courts to achieve their goals. It is no wonder that they usually failed.[54] Players were opposed by the owners, but other instruments of control were rarely employed.

The courts were generally sympathetic to the players. They repeatedly ruled against the reserve rule. Had the players been more aggressive and unified, they may have eliminated the rule, thus allowing market forces to increase player mobility and wages.

By the 1890s, even the labor elite was threatened by the growing power of the corporation and mechanization. Trade unions fought this trend, often by going on strike. But even if wages were not reduced, workers almost always relinquished some control over the decision-making and production processes and ultimately ended up serving the employer's needs rather than their own when the strike was settled. This was certainly true in the baseball industry. Even with the reserve rule, players were able to prevent a drastic erosion of wages until the early 1890s; however, by 1890, they had no say in how their industry was to be run, a condition that would continue to exist long after the Brotherhood rebellion ended.[55]

The players had limited tools with which to fight management. Although the "producers" in their industry, it is doubtful if strikes would have worked. First, many players would not have honored the picket lines. If the players did show solidarity, management could have brought in scab labor. Conventional industries could rely on unskilled immigrants and poor blacks to cross picket lines. Baseball was dominated by second-generation Irish and Germans who usually came from urban regions, and it is from their ranks that the industry would have drawn its scab labor as well. The hundreds of minor league players scattered throughout the nation were all desperate for a chance to play in the major leagues and would gladly have crossed strike lines. Although most were not as skilled as players at the major league level, there would have been only a relative decline in play that the public might not have noticed. Since the fans would most likely have been opposed to any strike, they may have shown equal support for the replacement teams. Even if fan support did decline, wages also would have gone down, so owners might have continued to make money. It would not have taken long for some strikers, especially marginal players fearful of losing their jobs, to break ranks and return to the fold.

When the players did finally react in 1890, their goals were to create a league that was cooperatively owned and controlled and in which profits were divided between players and owners. This was similar to the cooperative enterprises that Powderly and the Knights hoped to conduct. However, the players' resolve proved to be weak, and their league folded before they could become partners in the decision-making process. Their unwillingness to fight for a say in their enterprise's management is proof that many never believed they deserved the power that was initially given to them in the new league. Ultimately, the players proved to be a passive labor force willing to give up power and even their manliness in exchange for the high wages that their industry offered.

By 1900, Debs's American Socialist Party had little in common with Ward's Brotherhood. Debs believed that only by developing a national working-class consciousness could workers combat the power of the modern corporation. The mature Debs was opposed to the idea of a labor elite, claiming that it divided and weakened American labor.[56] Ward and the Brotherhood had little sympathy with such thinking. They had no concern for the national labor movement and were too young and preoccupied to worry about class consciousness.

Ward and Debs did have some common ground. Debs, although opposed to the increased use of management specialists in industry, advocated the use of labor specialists in his union. Ward also believed that the rank and file should follow the dictates of its leadership. Debs believed that strikes were generally harmful to workers and rarely supported them.[57] He instead encouraged workers to implement change at the ballot box. Ward also opposed strikes, although his reasons might have been different. However, his solution to the abuses of management was a new economic order in the industry, and his movement was never affiliated with any political movement.

The American economic system underwent fundamental changes in the last decades of the 19th century. The power of the corporation grew dramatically, and this reduced worker autonomy, threatened wages, and affronted workers' manliness. Workers attempted to combat this growing corporate power by joining craft or industrial unions or advocating socialism, but these attempts at resistance were generally unsuccessful in staving off the new corporate order. Owners in the baseball industry also worked to reduce competition, regulate markets, and control player behavior and wages, and generally they were at least as successful as their industrial counterparts. Players attempted to resist the growing power of owners, but a variety of factors, including their own lack of resolve, led to their defeat.

# 5

# The Baseball Player
# as Worker

From 1855 to 1870 almost 90 percent of all baseball players came from the middle strata of America's economic structure. Most of these men were small proprietors or skilled craftsmen, but about 20 percent of them had achieved white-collar status. Almost no unskilled workers played the amateur or professional game during its formative years.[1]

The social composition of the Cincinnati Red Stockings was typical of teams of this era. It consisted of two insurance men, a bookkeeper, two hatters, a marble cutter, a piano maker, a jeweler, and an engraver. As skilled craftsmen and small businessmen, they would have earned about $525 to $750 per year. Thus the $600 to $1,400 they received for less than six months' work as baseball players was a substantial pay increase for most team members.[2]

The professionalization of baseball in the 1870s caused conflict in many of the old baseball clubs. Many of the clubs that fielded amateur nines found that their members were contemptuous of the professional players that joined their teams or whom they played against. They disliked the fact that their clubs were now represented by non-members who often came from the working class. Many upper-class club members had disdain for tradesmen, even those who brought the club fame and money with their success on the diamond.[3]

Amateur teams had always valued the postgame parties as much as the games, and players took great pride in playing with men who were their social equals. Gentlemen participants "played" at the game, and many claimed that paying players destroyed "that subordination and good feeling necessary to the success of a nine."[4]

As professional teams became more prevalent, the public's and players' perception of the game changed. The game ceased to be a form of recreation and became an occupation. Professional players worked at baseball. They were expected to be disciplined and follow the rules set down by clubs and captains. Players were also expected to develop their skills and specialize in a position, just as other craftsmen specialized in a trade.[5] Newspaper accounts reflected this change in attitude and regularly wrote of players "going to work" or "working" at a particular part of their game.[6]

Many people opposed the professional game because it was seen as a threat to the pure "American" game that had developed in the pre-professional era. Even players in the National Association of Base Ball Players were generally held in low regard by members of the upper class despite their high wages.[7]

As the professional game developed, more players came from America's urban masses. Such men often had poor manners, were foul-mouthed and enjoyed alcohol and the company of prostitutes. *The New York Times* wrote in 1872, "In every point of view the professional baseball player is an eminently undesirable person and he ought to be completely suppressed."[8]

As the social status of players declined, the desire to control them increased. And just as craftsmen in other industries fought for "functional autonomy," the professional player fought to maintain a degree of control in his industry. Ultimately, as in most industries, players at all levels of the professional game became nothing more than employees, who, although well paid, had no control over the management of their industry. The baseball craftsmen became the baseball proletariat.[9]

Compared to workers in other industries, baseball players earned a fortune. In 1880, common laborers received $1.15 to $1.50 per day, and skilled workers rarely earned a daily rate of over $2.73.[10] By 1891, laborers still only earned about $1.39 per day and factory operatives only received about $.18 more than this. As late as 1893, workers at the relatively high-paying Pullman factory still only earned an average of $2.63 per day.[11] In spite of the tremendous growth in the gross national product in the post-Civil War era, wages did not dramatically improve, and the work day declined only slightly, from 10.5 hours in 1870 to 10 hours in 1890.[12]

Player salaries varied widely from 1869 to 1890, depending on skill level, fan drawing power, position, wealth of the owner, existence of the reserve rule, and other salary control policies and the existence of competing leagues. Most National League regulars received salaries of at least $1,500, and by 1890, the best players could expect to earn more than $4,000 for a season's work.[13] In spite of these wages, which were often higher than those of salaried managers in other industries, players were still defined by themselves, owners, and the public as workers and therefore had little social status.

There were several reasons why men who received such high wages were still regarded as workers. The road to the major leagues was arduous. Throughout the nation, thousands of young men honed their playing skills by the hour in the hope of playing professional baseball. In the 1880s, there were approximately 2,100 professional players in the United States, but of these only about 240 were employed by the American Association or the National League.[14] The rest played on minor league teams dispersed throughout the nation. These teams were often poorly capitalized and paid players as little as ten dollars per month. Travel was difficult and food and lodging spartan. Teams regularly folded by midseason, leaving players unemployed, far from home, and broke.[15] To get to the major leagues, almost all players had to play in the minor leagues. This experience was instrumental in molding the players' image of themselves as laborers, and it helped to create a bond between them.

Most players accepted their status as workers because most came from working-class backgrounds, and many worked in the off season as laborers. In the 1870s and 1880s, the majority of players were of Irish or German descent and were poorly educated. Illiteracy was common, and few players had skills other than baseball with which they could earn a living. Irish parents were different from those of more established nationalities because they did not look down on the profession of baseball. On the contrary, the game was viewed as one way an Irish lad could step up the social ladder.[16]

Surveying players in 1887, the *New York Clipper* found that most defined themselves as workers and believed that they would always be members of the proletariat. Many lamented the fact that they might one day have to support themselves by working as lowly umpires.[17] Some players had skills, but few were trained to do white-collar jobs. Buck Ewing worked as a carpenter and teamster for ten dollars per week before he became a professional catcher, and he continued to work at these during the off season after his career began.[18] John Kerins, the Louisville catcher, was employed as a boilermaker, John Glasscock, the great shortstop, worked as a shipwright when the season ended[19], and John Clarkson of the White Sox learned the cigar business and practiced this during the off season and when he retired.[20]

As the game's popularity grew in the 1880s, some players were able to capitalize on their celebrity when they retired. This status helped to enable about two percent of the players to open successful businesses. However, 40 percent of the players during this period worked as laborers when their careers ended. An even larger portion got low-paying white-collar jobs or opened small unprofitable businesses. Saloons were their most common place of employment, but many worked as store detectives or in pool rooms, gambling establishments, and bowling alleys. Even great players were still not respected by the middle class, and few saved much money; consequently, most worked in saloons that catered to the working class and often were not very profitable.[21]

Owners tried to prevent players from getting involved in alcohol-related industries. It was not uncommon for players who worked as bartenders or who owned an interest in a drinking establishment to be told by management to quit, sell their interest, or risk losing their jobs in the National League.[22]

About five percent of the players got jobs in the baseball industry after their careers. Former players worked as coaches, managers, umpires, and groundskeepers, but few of these positions paid well or had much status.[23]

There were a handful of players who used their income and off-season time to become educated and enter the middle class. John Montgomery Ward, Hal McClure, and "Orator" Jim O'Rourke all became successful lawyers. Albert Bushong became a dentist, and Tim Keefe and John Morrill opened successful real estate and brokerage firms.[24] An even smaller group of former players became team owners or well paid managers. This group included Albert Spalding, Charles Comiskey, Connie Mack, Ned Hanlon, and John McGraw.[25] Interestingly, none of these men ever acquired a reputation for being benevolent toward players, and most were despised by their employees.

Baseball players often referred to themselves as workers. Jim Mutrie, manager of the New York Giants and his players, frequently used the slogan "We are the People," and John Ward often referred to the players as "working men."[26] Like workers in other industries, baseball players wanted the public's respect. Many fought management's controls because they were viewed as an attack on the players' manliness, but many supported management's ban on gambling and Sunday games because they believed that these policies would increase their status.[27]

Injuries were common during baseball's formative years. The game in the 1880s was extremely fast and dangerous, and many players played with a reckless abandon. Fields were poorly kept, equipment crude and sports medicine nonexistent. As in other industries, the principle of payment for services applied, and so players would not get paid if they did not play due to sickness or injury. This meant that many injured players would stay in the lineup, which often resulted in the development of small ailments into career-ending injuries.

The average National League or American Association career was about six years, and few players played for the same organization for their entire career. Players made high salaries, but had less security than men employed in most other trades. Unlike craftsmen who might better their lot over time, players almost invariably had to accept a reduced standard of living when their careers ended, which was usually by their 30th birthday.[28]

Sadly, many players fell victim to the same social ills to which other workers succumbed. Alcohol was a serious problem, especially when young, unmarried, illiterate players had to pass the time on road trips. This often led to other problems for players. In August of 1888, *The Sporting News* reported that the arrest of players was "common."[29] In 1890 the *Players' League Guide* reported that the previous year one professional player committed suicide, three were killed by accident, three died in mishaps that occurred during games, and one was shot in a street brawl.[30]

Typically the public also defined the players as workers. Working men tended to respect ballplayers, and there is little evidence that they resented their high salaries. Gompers compared them to merchant seamen who he claimed were "in a state of slavery."[31] After the Union Association folded following the 1884 season, their players were blacklisted by the National League and American Association. Trade unions pleaded with these leagues to employ the players, claiming they were "working men kept out of employment by a body of capitalists."[32] Many workers in the growing industrial towns of the West and Midwest loved baseball and felt an affinity toward players. Often these workers would combine labor rallies with an afternoon at the ballpark, thus linking community spirit, labor solidarity, and support for the home nine.[33]

It was the middle class and its press that looked down on the players. As the baseball industry matured in the 1880s and the division between management and players became more rigid, the status of players, in the eyes of the middle class, declined. *The New York Times* wrote that a baseball player was "...a shiftless member of the laboring class, prone to drink, having a loose moral code, and preferring to avoid an honest day's work by playing ball."[34] Papers regularly ridiculed players who sought more money, often cynically referring to "the hard lot of men who toss the ball for a living."[35]

The sporting press, which often catered to middle-class readers and advertisers, ridiculed players and their working-class status. Harry Palmer, a well known sportswriter of the era, called players "devil-may-care types who took poor care of themselves and worried little about the future."[36]

*The Sporting News* wrote of King Kelly in July of 1888:

Here is an ignorant boor who has a salary that compares with the prime ministers. To earn it all that is asked of him is that he give the Boston club two hours of his best services daily. Instead of filling his part of the contract, however, Kelly for some imaginary grievance ... gets drunk and demoralizes the team.... The League should organize a drum corps whose duty it should be to drum such fellows out of the profession.[37]

Kelly's drinking was legendary, and for this he deserved criticism. However, sportswriters, like the middle class, missed an important point. Kelly was paid a huge salary because he generated huge revenues for his team. The fact that he may have been ignorant was irrelevant. Like the owners, writers were critical of what players made because they compared these sums to what players would earn if they could not play ball. The fact was, Kelly was a great player, drew thousands of fans to the park, made his team owners a large amount of money, and earned all of the salary that he was paid.

Even some businesses were leery of baseball players. A Cincinnati hotel reported in 1890:

This hotel, which has for years catered to the base ball trade, has suddenly discovered that the professional ball player is an eyesore to the better paying class of patrons and does not want any of the Knights of Knickerbockers to again darken its threshold. It is argued that professional players are the most disorderly people that travel and have little idea of decency and manners.[38]

Generally, first-class hotels and rail lines did accept the patronage of baseball teams, but only because it brought them much revenue. Among themselves, proprietors often talked disdainfully of "rowdy" players, and certain establishments did ban them.[39]

More than any other class of people, it was baseball owners who viewed players as workers. As in other industries, as owners' control of the workforce increased, its respect for its employees decreased. Players were not viewed as individuals but as part of the production process. Just as Taylor advocated measuring the performance of each individual and determining what maximum worker output should be, baseball owners became more reliant on statistics to establish the worth of a player. As in other industries, numbers could be used to measure the productivity and value of an employee.

When extolling the virtues of a player, owners would often use terms like quiet and businesslike, steady, well behaved, cool or obedient.[40] The self-disciplined, independent craft worker of the 1860s and early 1870s had been transformed to a controlled player whose greatest personal attribute was doing what he was told. Taylor himself could have asked for little more.

The worker/player had to be supervised. In other industries, workers were fined, fired, and blacklisted for challenging the authority of the firm or the foreman or not meeting production quotas.[41] Baseball was no different. Players were required to report to spring training one month before the season began. From then until the season ended, they were expected to do as they were told.[42] Players had to abide by a labyrinth of team and league rules that regulated when they went to bed, how much alcohol they drank, on-the-field behavior, and how they behaved at the dining table. Players who did not abide by management's rules were tailed by Pinkertons, blacklisted, and released.[43] The owners' logic was simple. Controlling players would lead to exemplary behavior on and off the field. This would attract middle-class patrons and thus help profits grow.

By its nature, baseball is the most individually oriented team sport, and yet early management downplayed individual achievement. They constantly extolled the virtues of place hitting, bunting, finesse pitching, defense, teamwork, and intelligent play, and downplayed the importance of aspects of the game that brought individual glory and fan adulation like home runs and strikeouts. Balls were kept dead to prevent them from being hit out of the park and to keep run production low.[44] This was done in spite of the fact that fans have always liked offense more than defense and that historically the more runs scored, the more people have come to the parks.[45] Management wanted a homogenized work force in which the team, and not individual stars, was credited with success. This would reduce the influence of players and enable owners to restructure their teams without the loss of fan support. In addition, less scoring would be reflected in the players' offensive statistics and management could use these numbers to justify lower pay. [46]

Owners claimed that players benefited from being controlled. Reflecting the paternalistic views of the period, Spalding argued that players needed strict rules to prevent them from developing "debasing habits." These controls "purified" the players and helped them to achieve a special status in America that athletes in other nations did not enjoy. Spalding once explained that after the season ended, his players could return to college, their law office or workshop without feeling embarrassed about their summer profession. He attributed the respect that players were given by the public to the fact that they were controlled and thus well behaved.[47]

In private, the owners were contemptuous of players, and their public rhetoric would reflect this when the players broke ranks in 1890. Prior to that time, owners had an interest in improving the status of its players because this would make it easier to attract middle-class patrons. This was especially true in the post-Haymarket era, when all labor was looked at as dangerous, and the middle class often lumped workers, socialists, anarchists, and strikers together and believed that all were a threat.[48] Consequently, the *Spalding Guide* frequently extolled the virtues, education, and variety of interests that players possessed. The baseball industry feared its workforce, and its attempt to publicly define it as educated, unorganized, and middle class was necessary to gain public favor. Owners also hoped that by defining their employees as middle-class, the players would not view themselves as workers and this would reduce labor solidarity.

In spite of the owners' efforts, baseball players were held in low regard by much of the public. Sometimes teams had to stay in third-rate hotels because better establishments did not want them. Mothers rarely wanted their daughters to date players.[49] When Robert Todd Lincoln's daughter married Chicago pitcher Warren Beckwith, Lincoln called his new son-in-law a "baseball buffoon."[50]

Even umpires were not respected. The *Chicago Tribune* said of them, "The average League umpire is a worthless loafer easily tempted and swayed by improper considerations and a very unsafe and eminently unworthy person in whose hands to place the arbitration of a game of ball played in the presence of great crowds of ladies and gentlemen."[51]

Owners extolled the virtues of players like Cap Anson, who saved over fifty thousand dollars during his career and invested much of it in Chicago Club stock.[52] But Anson was the exception. Fighting, crime, and alcohol continued to be problems, and they continued to give management a pretext to increase control over players.[53]

Baseball management's relationship with its workforce was similar to the capital/labor relationship in other American industries. Although most teams were owner-managed and much smaller than corporations of the period, they were still rigidly structured and led by a president, secretary, treasurer, and board of directors.[54] Owners feared the masses from which most of their players came and believed that only through discipline and regulation could order be maintained. They believed that the basic flaw in the great democratic experiment was that it allowed the individual too much freedom, and that only by the strong hand of capital could worker/players be forced to toe the line and enable the industry to thrive.[55]

The industrial corporation that emerged in the post-Civil War era organized management and labor in an entirely new way. Since control was gospel, failure was often blamed on a lack of it. Spalding argued in 1884 that alcohol "undoubtedly bankrupted a third of the clubs."[56] No proof was ever offered to substantiate this point, but to Spalding this was not necessary. He viewed his industry as an organism that would flourish if guided by certain principles. Failure could only result from a deviation from these principles, and this deviation was almost always the result of players or some other facet of the industry not being properly disciplined. This belief in the necessity of absolute managerial domination caused owners to discourage players from becoming leaders or forming cliques that might inspire players to question management. In spite of his own origins, Spalding viewed class barriers as impassable, and thus mobility within the industry had to be prevented. Spalding explained:

> The trouble in this respect is, that in nearly every professional team there will be found one or more players who are not contented with doing faithful service in the one position in the team which they are competent to fill, but are continually striving either to become captains or aiming higher to ultimately work themselves into the manager's place.[57]

As American society changed in the late 19th century, so did its definition of manliness. This alteration of the ideal of male identity had a profound impact on the game and business of baseball. Rural America had long viewed harmony between the individual, community, and business interests as essential to survival. In most small towns in the pre-industrial and newly industrialized nation, an individual's fulfillment of personal obligations toward family, business, and community and his willingness to cooperate were viewed as essential to survival. Consequently, all of them were essential aspects of manliness.[58] Economic or social status might separate men in a given community, but adherence to the manly code made it possible for any man to be the equal of another in the most basic sense. Pre-industrial workers generally cooperated with each other and employers. Citizens in rural towns were raised to respect the needs of the community and to subordinate individual goals when they conflicted with these needs.[59]

Industrial capitalism dramatically changed society. Modern capitalists deemed conflict necessary, and owners, hell-bent on increasing profits and their control over the marketplace, quickly ushered out the cooperative ideals of the earlier decades and confronted labor in an attempt to regulate and control it. Laborers, faced with a loss of their identity and a decline of living standards, redefined manliness and fought back.

But workers did not forget their cooperative, small-town, rural past. It was essential for them to stick together and support the well-being of the group over the aspirations of any individual.

The shop owner or foreman was no longer seen as a partner but as an adversary who had to be confronted. The code of manliness now required that workers stick together and confront the shop foreman when-ever he tried to push them beyond what they believed was acceptable. Workers were expected to have a "manly bearing" toward the boss and to disobey objectionable orders even if it cost the worker his job.[60] The older, rural norms that emphasized cooperation were not dead, but instead they were altered to fit the new urban, industrial world.

During baseball's formative years, when it was an amateur game played by urban artisans, clerks, and proprietors, its participants were expected to adhere to the middle-class code of manliness that advocated the Victorian virtues of self-control, sobriety, and finesse more than win-ning, fun, and profit. Swearing, talking back to an umpire or disputing his call, offering an opinion before an umpire ruled, talking on the field, or disobeying a captain could all be punished with a fine because all were believed to be the result of a player losing control of his emotions and act-ing in an unmanly fashion. Maintaining this "manly demeanor" was expected of all players despite the fact that most were under 25 years old, and some were only teenagers.[61]

As the professional game developed, many players no longer came from the middle class and thus were not proponents of the middle-class value system.[62] These changes were reflected in the behavior of players on and off the field. This often alarmed owners, who hoped their working-class employees living in an industrial age would maintain a pre-indus-trial willingness to cooperate with management no matter what its demands and continue to adhere to a middle-class code of behavior.

This was an unrealistic expectation. The professional game drew increasingly from the urban and rural poor. These individuals had often adopted an industrial working class code of manliness that advocated con-fronting authority and did not frown on rowdy, emotional behavior. These were the traits that middle-class owners viewed as boyish. Clearly the cul-ture of the game's owners was in conflict with the culture of the men they employed to play it.[63]

Increasingly the amateur and professional games were played differently. Amateurs who played on middle-class clubs participated to have fun and yet were expected to have "manly restraint." Professionals played to win, and yet displayed boyish excitement. Their game became labor and a player's survival depended on his ability to maintain a certain skill level.[64] It was no longer manly from the players' working-class view-point to hold in one's emotions. Instead, players struck out at those who opposed them: umpires, captains, and fellow players. Bench jockeying, fighting, sign stealing, umpire baiting, and cleat sharpening were all com-mon, and all were viewed as a manly way to confront your opponent.[65]

This was similar to the way factory operatives refused to be passively controlled by their foreman. An unwillingness to fight back was an unwillingness to exert your manhood.

A conflict developed between middle-class amateur players and working-class professionals over how the game should be played. Amateurs wanted to keep the game less physically demanding so that they could continue to play it at a respectful level. Thus they resisted changing the playing rules. Professional owners and players wanted to thrill patrons with the players' skills and generally were more supportive of rule changes, although owners did not always have players' best interests in mind when they considered how to alter the game.

In the professional game, rule changes were generally initiated for three different reasons: to make the game more difficult and thus more exciting for fans to watch, to increase the number of runs scored and thus fan support, or to decrease the number of runs scored and thus lower individual hitting statistics and player costs. In the professional game, the flat bat that encouraged bunting was outlawed early on so that players would hit the ball hard, thus speeding both the offensive and defensive components of the game. Despite the outcry from the less skilled gentlemen clubs, the fly rule was changed in the mid-1860s so that balls caught on one bounce were no longer outs. This rule change may seem insignificant, but in the era before fielding gloves were used, it took a large amount of grit for a fielder to catch a pop fly or line drive. The sporting press debated the fly issue for months, arguing the merits of the more gentlemanly game versus the more difficult professional contest. Ultimately, the professional rule won out.[66]

Owners often discussed what rule changes should be implemented, and they frequently found it difficult to reach a consensus. Generally, during periods when owners believed they had eliminated competition and thus could be less fearful of increased driving up salaries, rule changes would be made that increased offense. In 1889, the number of balls needed for a walk was reduced to four, and this, coupled with the shoulder-to-knee strike zone, forced pitchers to throw more accurately. This meant they often threw slower and led to a corresponding increase in offense during the celebrated 1889 season. In 1893, in another attempt to increase fan support, the pitcher's mound was moved back to its current sixty feet, six inches, initiating another offensive upswing. This was done during a decade when the National League had established a complete monopoly, and thus they did not have to fear the improved offensive statistics driving up salaries.

Rules were also adjusted to reduce offense. In 1883 the National

League broke ranks with the American Association and allowed pitchers to throw overhand. At the same time, roster sizes were increased so the teams could carry more pitchers. In 1888, the number of strikes needed for a strikeout was reduced to three. These changes generally improved pitching, increased the number of strikeouts, and reduced offense.[67]

Publicly, owners extolled the virtues of their game and the middle-class manliness of their players. However, once the National League was formed and players lost their management role, they were treated like children. Gambling had long been popular with middle- and working-class men, and during the game's formative years, gambling halls were often located in or near the parks. This was not viewed as a problem when players were from the middle class. However, owners did not trust the working-class players who dominated the mature professional game and therefore vehemently attacked gambling.

Rules that regulated players' lives off the field were ubiquitous, and players who had what Spalding called "excellent habits" were often favored over more free-spirited athletes. Chicago's Paul Hines was even told by the team's owner that if his play did not improve, his father would be notified.[68]

Owners publicly praised the umpires. Chadwick wrote "upon his manly, fearless and impartial conduct in a match mainly depends the pleasure that all, more or less, will derive from it." The umpire was always right, and he was expected to maintain control on the field and in the stands. Players were expected to show a gentlemanly respect to him and his rulings. However, like the players, the umpires were not respected by the owners; they were poorly paid and often ridiculed behind closed doors.[69]

There were instances in which the owners benefited from the players' working-class code of manliness and thus encouraged it. Owners expected their players to play hurt and argued that to do so was manly. Working-class players had long associated manliness with physical toughness and a willingness to ignore pain and injuries and thus expected themselves and their peers to play when hurt.

Pitchers often pitched with sore arms, and position players regularly played with broken bones. When Chicago pitcher Larry Corcoran asked for time off to rest his sore arm, the team's owner, Albert Spalding, called him a "little sniveler." There is no evidence that any of his teammates was outraged by this remark.[70]

The great paradox of the capital/player relationship in the late 19th century was that owners believed that players could be manipulated by management into adhering to three different codes of manliness. On the field players were expected to be tough competitors who were impervious to pain and willing to do whatever it took to win: values associated with the working-class code of manliness. At the same time players were expected to be cooperative and place team goals ahead of those of the individual: values associated with an earlier era in which workers, owners, and the community worked together for a common good. Finally, players were expected to be under control, subordinate to authority, temperate, and act as "gentlemen": values associated with a middle-class code of manliness. Not surprisingly, over time, this insistence that players adopt new codes of manliness as management saw fit was resisted by players. This resulted in an increasingly adversarial relationship between capital and labor on and off the field.

Baseball underwent fundamental changes as it evolved from an amateur game played by middle-class gentlemen for fun to a professional contest played by members of the working class for pay. Adopting the progressive belief that all aspects of their industry had to be controlled and with an inherent mistrust of their workforce, baseball owners stripped their players of any autonomy and made them well-paid members of the proletariat.

Generally, players accepted this. Most were young and well paid, and the nature of their profession made solidarity difficult. However, while management was removing players from the decision-making process, a new code of manliness was being adopted by the American working class. Management failed to respect this new code and often attacked their players' sense of manliness and treated them like children. They expected players to display the new, more confrontational, working-class manliness on the diamond. However, when the contest ended, they expected players to resume a more cooperative, pre-industrial attitude toward owners and to adhere to a middle-class behavioral code.

It was foolish for owners to believe that this dual personality could be maintained in its workforce indefinitely. In 1885, players organized. Five years later their confrontational game personality overwhelmed their more passive off-the-field disposition. This caused them to strike back at the rigid controls implemented by management in its attempt to keep them in a childlike state off the field. Interestingly, baseball, a game always associated with boyhood, would have its foundation rocked by a revolution because the industry's owners did not understand the importance of respecting its workforce and treating its members as men.

# 6

# The Formation and Development of the Brotherhood of Professional Base Ball Players

By the mid-1880s, professional baseball had evolved from an amateur game played by shopkeepers, artisans, and white-collar workers, to a poorly organized and undercapitalized business, to a profitable and popular monopoly. It had begun to attain the special status in the psyche of the nation that it still holds today, and future growth seemed assured. In the late 19th century, Mark Twain explained this when he called the game, "the very symbol, the outward and visible expression of the drive and push and rush and struggle of the raging, tearing, booming 19th century."[1]

Not only did the game become a symbol of the century, but it was also the beneficiary of many of its inventions. The bicycle, telegraph, trolley car, camera, typewriter, phonograph, and railroad all helped to increase baseball's popularity.[2] The nation was becoming more urban, and the inhabitants of burgeoning cities found the game entertaining and a good outlet for the pressures of urban life.[3]

All of these helped to make the period 1885 to 1889 the first "Golden Age of Baseball."[4] Spurred by its growing popularity, team owners built new, larger ballparks, such as Philadelphia's 20,000 seat Palace Park, which opened in 1887.[5] Crowds of 5,000 people were not uncommon, and revenues increased. The season was expanded to more than 100 games, and often this did not satisfy the public's growing demand for baseball.[6] The surge in attendance caused profits to soar. Spalding's Chicago Club, which had made a $20,000 profit in 1883, increased this to as much as $100,000 in 1887.[7] Although some clubs remained in the red, more began to make money, and most baseball magnates believed that their industry was well positioned to increase its popularity and profitability for years to come.[8]

The previously installed controls kept player salaries below what the free market would have dictated, but still owners lamented what they had to pay players. Star players were enormously popular with the fans and often commanded salaries of more than $4,000. Team payrolls were sometimes as high as $40,000 to $60,000, and owners frequently complained that such costs would ruin the game.[9]

Generally, by the end of the decade, most National League teams were stable and profitable. Those that failed did so because poor management allowed an uncompetitive product to be offered on the field. However, reflecting the monopolist sentiments of the period, owners used these failures as proof that players needed to be controlled more and paid less. A free market that allowed poorly run teams to fold was unacceptable. Only a system that guaranteed a profit for all investors would satisfy the owners.[10]

In the fall of 1885, William Voltz, a Philadelphia sportswriter and minor league manager at Chattanooga, attempted to organize the National League players into a players' lodge.[11] Although Voltz was opposed to some owner policies such as the reserve rule, he did not intend for the union to be radical or a catalyst for major change in the baseball industry. Instead, he envisioned a players' benevolent association that would work at securing health insurance and loans for active players and a general care fund for needy ex-players.[12]

Voltz's efforts to organize the players failed primarily because they were reluctant to follow an outsider. However, when the talented, bright, and respected shortstop of the New York Giants, John Montgomery Ward, proposed a similar union to Giants teammates Tim Keefe, Jim O'Rourke, Danny Richardson, Mike Dorgan, Buck Ewing, Joe Gerhardt, Roger Connor, and Mickey Welch in October of 1885, the players quickly responded, and the Brotherhood of Professional Base Ball Players was created. The organizers agreed to keep the union secret for the first year so they could attract enough members to reduce the likelihood of reprisals from National League owners.

Despite this secrecy, the union grew quickly. The founders organized the remainder of their Giants teammates soon after the organization was created. By early summer of 1886, a majority of players on seven of the eight National League teams had joined the association, and by the fall of that year all eight teams had chapters and the Brotherhood had more than 100 members.[13] The union never tried to organize players outside of the National League. Beyond this, little is known of the union's formation

*Left:* Tim Keefe was a star pitcher in the National League who amassed a total of 342 career wins. Keefe was close to John Montgomery Ward and became his brother-in-law and the secretary of the Brotherhood of Professional Base Ball Players. Keefe jumped to the Players' League in 1890 and finished his career in 1893 with Philadelphia. He was inducted into the Hall of Fame in 1964 (Library of Congress).

*Right:* Danny Richardson was a competent infielder and outfielder who played on five different teams from 1884 to 1894. Richardson was a founding member of the Brotherhood of Professional Base Ball Players in 1885, and he also jumped to the New York Players' League team in 1890. Controversy followed when some claimed he colluded with Buck Ewing and A.G. Spalding to undermine the new league during the 1890 season and discussed plans to return to the National League in 1891. Although many players continued to suspect Ewing, most of Richardson's fellow Brotherhood members exonerated him when the Players' League folded (Library of Congress).

because Ward and the Brotherhood's other leaders did not leave a detailed account of their organizing efforts.

Each Brotherhood chapter had a president, secretary, and a representative to the executive council of the Brotherhood, which "exercised executive and judicial functions." The union also established a relief committee of three chapter representatives who were appointed annually by the association's president. This committee could authorize payments of up to ten dollars per week to sick or injured players. In addition to Ward, the union's leaders included Tim Keefe, Jim "Orator" O'Rourke, and Daniel Richardson, all of whom were players. Although these leaders would play an important role in the union and the Players' League, none ever threatened Ward's authority, or differed from him significantly in their view of what the union's goals should be or how the union should be run.[14]

The Brotherhood was a traditional, conservative craft union, and this was evident in its goals, which explained that the union hoped to:

OLD JUDGE CIGARETTES Goodwin & Co., New York.

James "Orator" O'Rourke starred in the major leagues from 1876 to 1893, primarily as an outfielder, and then returned to play one game for the New York Giants in 1904 at the age of 52. O'Rourke was a member of the Brotherhood of Professional Base Ball Players' eight-man central committee and a key figure in the players' revolt. The opinionated, clean-living O'Rourke graduated from Yale Law School and had a successful career as a lawyer when his baseball career ended (Library of Congress).

> Protect and benefit ourselves collectively and individually. To promote a high standard of professional conduct. To foster and encourage the interests of the game of baseball.[15]

Brotherhood members were required to take the following oath:

> I (candidate) do solemnly swear:
>     To strive to promote the objects and aims of this Brotherhood, in accordance with its Constitution and By-laws;
>     Never to take undue advantage of a brother in good standing;

Never to permit an unjust injury to be done to, or continued
against, a brother in good standing, while it is in my power to prevent
the same;
To assist a brother in distress;
To render faithful obedience to the will of the Brotherhood, as
expressed by the decrees of the council, or by a vote on my chapter.
To all this I make my solemn oath to Almighty God, and in the
presence of these witnesses.[16]

Soon after the union was formed, Ward explained its conservative
philosophy. He claimed that people "would perhaps be surprised if they
were to know that the players generally were possessed of good judgment
and sound discretion and are as a class intelligent and fairly well educated."[17] Ward's assessment of his players' education was not completely
accurate, but this public description clearly shows that he wanted his players to be viewed as conservative members of the labor elite and not as rad-
icals determined to change the established order. He claimed his movement
was "no utopian scheme for the disorganization of the existing order" and
that baseball had "nothing to fear."[18]

Such assurances were typical of craft union leaders of this era. On
numerous occasions, leaders of the American Federation of Labor made
similar claims, and even Eugene Debs echoed these sentiments while working for the Brotherhood of Locomotive Firemen.

Ward assured the public that the players did not wish to abolish the
reserve rule, explaining that it was "necessary to the prosperity and continued existence of the games." He also said that the union had no intention of protecting players who "misbehaved," explaining that "any member
of this organization who misbehaves and subjects himself to discipline by
his club, that is not a matter with which the Brotherhood will have anything to do with."[19]

Ward showed great respect for the owners. He explained that "under
the guidance of the League and American Association the game of base
ball in all its departments has unquestionably advanced." He credited ownership with making the game popular and claimed that most players were
well paid and treated.

Ward did advocate creating a new standard players' contract that
would specifically define what powers the owners had over their players.
However, he argued that such a contract and the labor stability that the
union would provide would ultimately help the baseball industry. The
labor leader called his union "another and last step in the establishment
of base ball as a permanent occupation and business. The game has been
thoroughly organized from the standpoint of manager, and now it is just

as thoroughly organized from the standpoint of player."[20] Ward claimed no "spirit of antagonism to capitalists except insofar as the latter might at any time attempt to disregard the rights of any member."

Ward did believe that some team owners ill-treated their players and these abuses had to be addressed. He argued that because owners had such "diverse interests," the concerns of the players had not always received sufficient consideration. Ward also argued that some clubs violated contract obligations, abused the reserve rule, blacklist, and expulsion rules, and forced injured players to work the gate without pay. He also questioned how clubs could expect injured players to abide by team rules when they did not receive any pay and why some players were suspended when they demanded that the teams pay them their salaries or because club officials disliked them. Ward also opposed the league policy of charging players $5.20 for using profanity, fining players for being late, often when they were on time, and even fining players for poor play by blaming it on dissatisfactory off the field habits. In addition he wanted to change the policy of requiring players to have physicals with team doctors because many players claimed that these physicians would deem a healthy player too injured to play so that owners could avoid paying a player who was performing poorly. [21]

Ward claimed that some captains and managers overworked players, and he believed that this exploitation often wore out players who were them discarded. In spite of these misgivings, Ward was not opposed to the basic structure of professional baseball, and he gave no indication during the union's formative years that any of his goals were radical.[22]

By 1887 the Brotherhood had over 125 members, each of whom paid five dollars per month in dues. Despite the fact that most National League players were members and few advocated dramatic changes in the status quo, management did not want to recognize the organization. They viewed it as unjustifiable and an "impertinent interference" with their business.[23] National League owners mistrusted and in some cases hated the organization, not because it advocated any significant changes in their industry or was a real threat to their authority, but because it was a union and thus created the potential for labor solidarity. They feared that it could eventually evolve into a threat to capital's absolute authority. Most magnates were not willing to tolerate this.

The Brotherhood was similar to other traditional craft unions of the era. It had been established primarily so that members could collectively help themselves and their families. However, by 1887, the union had become increasingly willing to confront management in an attempt to initiate significant changes in the industry. Many union members wanted to reduce player sales, trades, the use of blacklists, suspensions, and stop the employment of Pinkerton spies. Players were also angered by the $2,000 salary limit that was introduced in 1887 and the unwillingness of the league to recognize their union. These grievances prompted Ward to initiate a series of meetings with Spalding and National League president Nick Young.[24]

During the late summer and early fall of 1887, Ward and his management counterparts ran campaigns to sway the public to their points of view. Ward was firm but conciliatory, and he offered numerous compromises to the key player/owner disputes. His efforts were frustrated by management's refusal to even acknowledge the union's right to bargain for its members.

By 1887 Ward's primary goal beyond union recognition was a new standard players' contract. He wanted it to state specifically what controls the owners had over the players. He believed that the "implied restraints" of the National Agreement gave the owners too much power over his constituency. He was not opposed to the reserve rule, claiming that the majority of the players were still in favor of it, but he did believe that it should be modified so that it gave a team control of a player for three to five years rather than for the player's entire career. He was opposed to player sales without the player's consent, and he claimed that no sale should take place unless the player was under contract.[25] Ward also wanted all of a player's earnings reported on the contract. If this was done, the $2,000 salary cap would have been a thing of the past, since many clubs gave secret money to their stars. If these payments were made public in the contracts, then management could not tell any player that teams were limited by league policy as to how much they could pay.[26] In spite of the changes that Ward hoped to initiate, he frequently claimed that he did not want a confrontation with management, and at this point, never hinted that any sort of job action would be taken.[27]

Ward believed that the Brotherhood was good for baseball and deserved the right to represent the players in collective bargaining with management. He wrote that the union had "put the game on a high standard, fostered interest in it, promoted professional conduct and purged the game of disagreeable features." The industry was now stable enough to loosen controls on players, and he requested a good-faith effort by management to initiate this process.[28]

Ward's sentiments were similar to those of Gompers and the American Federation of Labor. Both men viewed organized labor as a tool that could be used in conjunction with management to improve an industry. This cooperation between labor and management would help to make an industry more stable and profitable, and ultimately this increased stability and profitability would benefit workers. However, there were rising tensions between capital and labor during the 1880s. The Haymarket disaster of 1886, and the corresponding fear of all organized labor that resulted, made capital suspicious of any union regardless of how reasonable its demands were.

National League owners often had business interests outside of baseball, and like most magnates of the period, they feared and mistrusted all labor organizations. They also realized that any alteration of the player/owner relationship in the baseball industry would probably result in reduced owner control, something they believed would reduce profits and potentially lead to chaos.

The disagreements over recognition and the new contract were publicly aired for almost a year. The union was sometimes allowed to send members to league meetings, but they were never acknowledged as Brotherhood representatives. Management believed that it was necessary for them to maintain complete control, and any changes, even in something as basic as the player contract, had to be initiated by them. Owners proclaimed that they had to "protect themselves against the eccentricities and whims of the average ball player" but that "faithful and reliable players had certain rights which had to be recognized and respected."[29] It is interesting that management would use words like "faithful" in an industry where players were bought and sold like cattle and released when injured. The message was clear. Good employees were deemed to be passive and uninterested in having any authority over the policies that regulated their industry.

On September 22, 1887, Ward wrote National League president Nick Young and outlined his union's concerns. Young agreed to meet with Ward to discuss rule changes and the contract, but he continued to insist that Ward would come as a player and not the head of a players' union. Young called the union a "secret organization" and claimed that its goal was to guarantee its members immunity "against the enforcement and provisions of the contract."[30] This was said despite Ward's continued assurances that the Brotherhood, like most traditional craft unions, had no intent to protect any members involved in wrongdoing. Ward also told Young that the union had no intention of demanding anything from the league, but it did want the opportunity to voice its opinions at league meetings.[31] Ward did tell the league that since they were unwilling to recognize the union, then it might "be obliged to go it alone." Ward did not explain what he meant by this, and there is no indication that the magnates took his threat seriously.[32]

The league's continued refusal to recognize the union and create a new players' contract caused the baseball public to speculate on what the union would do. Ward was still conservative and conciliatory, but he did propose some untraditional alternatives that the players could pursue if the owners continued not to recognize them. In the fall of 1887, he said in an interview, "Let me say, however, that there is plenty of money at our disposal to organize any association or League. We know of a number of capitalists who want to invest their money in baseball." He went on to say that new parks could be built and that "it is not the league the public goes to see but the players." He also told the press that unless the Brotherhood was recognized by the owners, its members would refuse to sign contracts for the 1888 season.[33]

Some viewed such rhetoric as nothing more than a ploy to get concessions from management. These observers believed that the players were too well off to threaten the status quo. It is interesting to note that Ward never talked of creating a league that was not to a large degree controlled by capital. Ward simply wanted the players to have a say in their profession, not to control their industry. In light of the owners' abuses, these goals seem modest.

National League president Young and his fellow owners proved to be worthy adversaries for Ward and the union. They realized the fear that their middle-class clientele had of organized labor. Consequently, they continually explained that since the Brotherhood was formed for the "mutual benefit" of all players, it would use its power to guarantee players immunity from punishment for any wrongdoings that they committed. Young claimed that it was "absolutely necessary" for a club to have the "better hand" of the player. If not, the game would be destroyed by its old enemies: drunkenness, gambling, and revolving. The owners made these claims in spite of the union's continued assurances that they had no intention of protecting undesirable members.[34]

On November 18, 1887, Ward met with a committee of National League owners headed by Spalding. Both sides sparred extensively to find out the goals of the other, and to determine what concessions were possible. Ward publicly told management that he would not explain the union's goals without formal recognition. However, he secretly assured them that the Brotherhood's goals were modest and would not threaten the basic structure of the baseball industry.[35]

Although he frequently attacked Ward publicly, Spalding, the most influential owner, respected him and believed his claim that the union was not out to abolish the reserve rule or threaten management's control. Spalding also believed that union recognition would improve management's relationship with the players and help the owners to stabilize the industry. He became convinced that even if the union was recognized, it would not prevent additional player control measures from being implemented. Consequently, Spalding and the other National League owners recognized the union in November, 1887. [36]

Once recognized, the Brotherhood and management created a new standard contract that explained all of the obligations that clubs and players had to each other. This was a modest gain for players, but in no way threatened management's sovereignty. The reserve rule remained intact, but now it was written into each contract instead of the contract just referring to the National Agreement, which could be altered by the owners at will.[37] Clubs agreed that they would never reserve a player for less than $1,000, and that they would also write the entire sum to be paid to a player on his contract. This would officially end the $2,000 salary limit, since many teams had long ignored it and paid players secret money. Now these sums had to be written into the contract. The owners promised Ward that the salary limit would be stricken from league rules. Players would no longer have to pay the 50 cents per day traveling expenses or the 30-dollar annual uniform fee. If a club folded, the team that replaced it would be required to pay players at least as much salary as the old team did.

The players, reflecting the conservative nature of the union and its leader, agreed to the prohibition of the consumption of alcohol during the season. However, management would no longer have the power to arbitrarily punish offenders. First-time offenders would be fined 25 dollars; second, 50 dollars; and third, 100 dollars. Additional offenses would result in a player's suspension.[38] Ward proclaimed his satisfaction with the plan and even said that its anti-alcohol provisions would "help keep players away from saloons where they didn't belong."[39] Satisfied that his union had exerted its manliness and been treated fairly by the owners, Ward encouraged his constituency to sign contracts for the 1888 season.[40]

Ward's satisfaction with the new contract is proof of just how conservative his union was. Even with management's concessions, they still had enormous control over the players. From April 1 through October 31, players were subject to "the entire control of the club." In most circumstances, teams could discipline players as they saw fit. Players accused of dishonesty, insubordination, playing for a club with which they were not under contract, betting, or excessive drinking could be suspended or expelled. Players could be fined up to 50 dollars for almost any infraction, and injured players were not to be paid until they resumed playing. Players were also expected "cheerfully and promptly" to obey the field captain, and despite previous promises, they continued to be charged 30 dollars each season for their uniforms.[41]

In the winter following the 1888 season, after the league had acknowledged the Brotherhood and revised the standard player's contract, Spalding organized a world baseball tour with the express purpose of promoting baseball. Spalding took two teams with him: the Chicago Club, captained by Cap Anson and a group of All-Stars called the All American Team, led by Ward. Most of the other Brotherhood leaders were also on Ward's squad.[42]

While on the tour, the owners implemented Indianapolis president John T. Brush's classification plan. The plan classified a player as A, B, C, D, or E depending on his playing ability and living habits. All players classified at a given level were to receive the same pay, and this amount was set by the league. (See Chapter 3.) Ward and his colleagues learned about the plan when they were in Cairo, Egypt, and felt betrayed. They confronted Spalding, but he claimed to have had nothing to do with it. Ward was outraged and called the Plan the "last straw."[43] League officials had promised to rescind the $2,000 salary limit and instead had implemented a policy that would further reduce player salaries.[44]

Players reacted to the plan in different ways. Many did not oppose it as strongly as Ward did. In their view, management would not adhere to it, just as they had often ignored the $2,000 cap. Other players were not opposed to the salary limits of the new plan because even with them they would be well paid.[45]

Most players were opposed to the grading system, however, because they viewed it as demeaning. Like workers in other industries, they did not like the idea of management publicly evaluating their playing skills and personal habits, and they believed that forcing the lower classified players to perform tasks such as cleaning up the park was degrading to them. Such a reaction was similar to the response of other craft workers if forced to perform tasks that were not worthy of their skills.[46]

Ward never fully trusted capital, so he was not surprised by the classification scheme. However, he did feel betrayed. He had agreed not to try to abolish or alter the reserve rule, but only with the stipulation that no player be reserved at a lower salary. The new plan now made it mandatory that most players receive salary reductions for the 1889 season.[47] Ward believed that the time had come for players to stand up to their bosses.

Early in the 1889 season, Ward made continued attempts to meet with management to discuss the classification plan. Management refused to meet with Ward or any of the union's executive committee. When they finally relented, they told the union that they would not meet with them

The World Base Ball Tour was organized by Albert Spalding to promote baseball abroad. The tour did not make money, and it did little to spread baseball's popularity. During the tour, the Brush Classification Plan was introduced, and many players believed that Spalding invited some of the Brotherhood leaders to go on the tour so they would not be in the United States when the plan was introduced (National Baseball Hall of Fame Library, Cooperstown, N.Y.).

until after the season. This was not satisfactory to Ward because his constituency would have scattered, and the owners would already have received their income for the year.[48]

Many players were angered by management's unwillingness to meet with them and advocated striking on July 4. Ward counseled against this, claiming that such an action would not bring about all the needed reforms and would not be supported by the public.[49] By now Ward realized that power in the baseball industry was so centralized and capital's control over the players so complete that only a fundamental change in the player/owner relationship would bring about the needed reforms. The captain lashed out at management, claiming they were "worse than Rockefeller" and "stronger than the strongest trust."[50] He went on to say that the "classification law, with its attendant evils and breach of faith, was the last straw."[51]

Ward was not the only labor leader of the era who became more militant as traditional methods of dealing with capital failed. Even Eugene Debs, a man generally associated with the more radical elements of the American labor movement, began as a traditional craft union leader. It was only after capital's control had grown to the point where traditional unions were often powerless to confront it that Debs turned to socialism. A similar transformation occurred with Ward. Frustrated with capital's unwillingness to deal honestly with his union, he changed course in an attempt to rectify what he believed were fundamental flaws in the player/owner relationship. Like Debs, he probably would not have chosen this course had the traditional labor/capital relationship resulted in his constituency being treated in a fair and manly fashion and provided it with a voice to which capital would listen.

The 1889 season was one of the most unusual, exciting and successful in baseball history. On July 4 the game's growing popularity was made clear when more than 100,000 patrons flocked to the eight games played at National League and American Association parks. In the National League, the New York Giants and Boston Beaneaters were involved in a close pennant race, which the Giants ultimately won by only one game. The battle for the championship excited fans of both teams and 283,257 and 201,989 "cranks" paid their way into Beaneater and Giant Games. Most other National League teams drew well, and total league attendance exceeded 1,355,000, an enormous total in an era without the automobile or night games.

The American Association also had an exciting pennant race and even more fan support. The Brooklyn Bridegrooms finished the season two games ahead of St. Louis. In their 69 home games at Washington Park, they drew an astonishing 353,690 fans, an average of more than 5,000 spectators per game. Second-place St. Louis drew 236,278 patrons, and the league attracted more than 1,576,000 people to the 547 games it played.

After the regular season was completed, the National League's Giants and the American Association's Bridegrooms met in a postseason championship. Although the Giants lost three of the first four games, they went on to win the next five games to capture the series six games to three. More than 47,000 excited fans would watch the nine games, helping to make the postseason series a financial success and a fitting end to 19th-century baseball's most successful season.

The season was profitable for owners and lucrative for players. Boston earned a profit of $100,000, which was shared by owners Arthur Soden, William Conant, and James Billings. Despite minimal profits due to a high payroll and huge expenses to build a new ballpark, Giants owner John B.

Day believed so strongly in the future profitability of his franchise that he refused to sell his team for $200,000 at the season's end. Each Giants player received a "World Series" bonus of $570 and their cross-town rivals received a bonus of $389 per player.

Ironically, most leaders of the Brotherhood were paid extremely well in 1889, and some believed that management did this to reduce the likelihood of a radical action by players. Ward and Tim Keefe each received $1,000 raises in 1889, and Ned Hanlon and Fred Dunlap also received substantial pay increases for the season. In all, despite the classification plan and other measures to control salaries, eighteen American Association and National League players earned salaries of $3,000-$4,000, eight earned between $4,000-$5000, and four earned $5,000 in 1889.

These high salaries and the success of the 1889 season did little to reduce the tensions between players and owners. Talk of a general strike was common, but most owners ignored it. New York Giants owner John B. Day, who had a reputation for treating his players well, called the idea "nonsense, a little Bluebeard story," and Spalding said it was "absurd."[52] Owners realized the extent of their monopoly and believed that players would never risk even a few weeks' pay by striking. Capital believed that players had to accept whatever was given to them, because there was no other place for them to ply their trade.[53] When a strike vote was taken on July 2, 1889, the players voted against it. Most claimed it would not be successful or supported by the public.[54]

The players did initiate several job actions during the season. One of better-publicized occurred in the American Association. When St. Louis Browns utility man Yank Robinson showed up for a game in dirty pants, he was told by team owner Chris Von der Ahe to get them cleaned. Robinson instructed a young boy to take them across the street to be laundered. When the boy returned, the gateman would not let him into the park, which caused Robinson to yell out, demanding that the boy be let in immediately. Von der Ahe saw Robinson yell at the gateman, berated him from the stands, and fined him 25 dollars.

Robinson's teammates threatened to boycott the upcoming series with Kansas City unless the fine was lifted, but Von der Ahe refused to give in and instead threatened to fine or blacklist the entire team. The players did go to Kansas City, where they lost all three games. Many people, including their manager, Charles Comiskey, believed the losses were intentional. *The Saint Louis Globe* called the incident "the most serious revolt ever known in a ball club and the time has come when players will, if pressed too far, assert their independence."[55] There were several other similar incidents during the 1889 season, but none of them expanded into a league-wide job action.

At the end of the 1888 season, Deacon White and Jack Rowe were sold by Detroit to Pittsburgh. Both of these players had originally played in Buffalo and had moved to Detroit when the franchise moved there after the 1885 season. The players decided that they wanted to return to Buffalo and play on the International League team that now played there and in which both players held stock. White explained that "no man is going to sell my carcass unless I get half." The National League steadfastly refused to let either player perform in Buffalo, and William Nimick, the owner of the Pittsburgh team, exclaimed, "If they do not want to play in Pittsburgh, they'll play nowhere." Nimick was willing to fight the players in court in order to keep them.[56]

The baseball lords blacklisted the two players and announced that any man who played against White or Rowe would be expelled from the National League. Ward advised White and Rowe to report to Pittsburgh for the 1889 season, explaining that it was better to play there than not at all. He may also have induced them to make the move by promising that they could be player/owners on the Buffalo team when the Players' League was created in 1890. Ward did not want to fight the reserve rule in court because he believed that even if the players won, the victory would only bring chaos to the baseball industry. At this point Ward had already begun to formulate his plan for the Players' League, and he saw no reason to disrupt the 1889 season or do anything that would turn the public on the players. Both White and Rowe reported after receiving large contracts, but the issue had galvanized the players and forced them to realize that only drastic action could change the status quo. Ward and his union were prepared to act.[57]

After the 1888 season, Ward was sold by the New York Giants to the Washington franchise for $12,000. He refused to go, and the Giants' ownership acquiesced to his demands, but this also helped to make Ward a more radical leader. He wrote an article in *Lippincott's* magazine entitled "Is the Base Ball Player a Chattel?" In it he claimed that being sold made him feel like a "piece of livestock."[58]

During the 1889 season, Spalding admitted that the world tour was organized partially to get the Brotherhood leaders out of the country so that the classification plan could be implemented without incident. He claimed that salary controls were necessary for the industry's survival and that the fans should be happy that the problem of spiraling salaries had been rectified. However, most teams ignored the classification plan's salary limitations and continued to pay star players enormous sums of money under the table. The best estimate is that despite the implementation of the plan, average player salaries increased $165 in 1889 over their 1888 levels.[59]

Management may have ignored the classification rule, but it continued to exert enormous control over the players. The number of player sales increased, arbitrary fines and suspensions were common, and the blacklist continued to be an ever-present threat. Players were angered when owners justified these controls over them by claiming that the game needed stability to prosper and yet frequently sold and traded players and moved franchises from one city to another.[60] As the 1889 season progressed, fans and newspapers speculated as to what Ward and his union would do to combat the owners' ongoing abuses and assert their manliness. It is doubtful if many imagined the revolutionary step that Ward and his colleagues were planning for the 1890 season.

# 7

# The Adversaries:
# John Montgomery Ward and
# Albert Goodwill Spalding

To a large degree, the two sides in the Great Baseball Rebellion mirrored the personalities of their respective leaders. During the 1880s, Albert Goodwill Spalding emerged as the dominant National League owner, and he would lead the league against the players in 1890. John Montgomery Ward, the man who founded the Brotherhood of Professional Base Ball Players in 1885, would lead the players in their struggle with the owners in 1890.

Spalding was born in Bryon, Illinois, on September 9, 1850. His mother, Harriet, had inherited a substantial sum of money, allowing the young Spalding to be raised in modest comfort. At eight, Spalding's father died, and four years later he and his mother moved to Rockford. Spalding was a shy young man, but early in his life he grew to love baseball and proved to have a natural talent for the game. This helped him to develop confidence. As a teenager he played on some of the best teams in the region, and earned a reputation for being one of the area's best players.[1]

Spalding came of age when professional baseball was in its infancy. His mother discouraged him from becoming a ballplayer, claiming the profession did not have enough status. Instead, she encouraged him to pursue a career in business. Spalding ignored his mother's wishes and signed a contract for forty dollars per week with the Excelsior team of Chicago in September of 1867. This was two years before the open professionalism of the Red Stockings, and National Association teams were not supposed to pay players. Consequently, Spalding was officially hired as a store clerk at the Excelsior store. This mattered little when the team folded after one game. Spalding then signed on with the Forest City team, and he played with them through the 1870 season.[2]

In 1871, Spalding joined Harry Wright's Boston Red Stockings for $1,500 per year. By 1874 he was the team's highest-paid player, earning the princely annual sum of $2,000.[3] Pitching in the National Association of Professional Base Ball Players, Spalding established himself as one of the premier pitchers in the game. He led the league in wins from 1871 to 1875, winning 56 games in 1875 alone. Just as important, the shrewd and calculating young man was able to work side by side with Harry Wright, one of the fledgling industry's young business stars.[4]

In July of 1875, while under contract with Boston, Spalding signed a contract to be the captain and play for William Hulbert's Chicago White Stockings for the 1876 season. Spalding also convinced his Boston teammates Ross Barnes, Cal McVey, and Jim White to jump to what was to become the National League. The great Adrian "Cap" Anson would also join the White Sox from the National Association's Philadelphia franchise, and he would prove to be the new league's best player over the next 22 years. Although Spalding would finish the 1876 season with a record of 47 wins and 13 losses while managing the team, it would be his last full season as a player, and he would retire after the 1877 campaign with 252 career victories and only 65 losses. Although still only 27 years old, Spalding was more interested in the sporting goods and baseball business than in playing the game.[5]

Spalding is an important transitional figure in major league baseball. He began his career during the game's gentlemanly infancy, and he never did adopt the more profane traits that became common in the mature professional game. While playing in the N.A.P.B.B.P., he saw the chaos of that league firsthand. He blamed its shortcomings on the lack of management control of players, and he lost respect for the men in uniform, believing that they were incapable of adequate self-discipline. He believed that the industry had to be organized on sound business principles, and this meant keeping players subordinate to management. He also had contempt for the gamblers who frequented games. He worked hard to keep them out of National League parks to prevent their influences from corrupting the game.[6]

In 1882, William Hulbert, the Chicago owner, died, and Spalding emerged as the team's president and principal owner. His team would dominate baseball for the rest of the decade, and Spalding would quickly become the most powerful owner in the National League. Like many progressives of the period, Spalding had a desire for harmony and rationalized procedures in business, and like Teddy Roosevelt, he often talked of the "good trust."[7] He believed that efficiency was the key to any organization's success, and only by controlling markets and competition could this be attained.

Experts were needed to run the baseball industry, and that meant that players could not own clubs or have any input in off-the-field decisions. In 1877 he wrote:

> The power must be placed in the hands of the club, which is a responsible organization. It is much safer when in such keeping than if it were in the hands of roving players with no special responsibility....[8]

Spalding claimed that organized labor was socialistic and had no place in the baseball industry. Years after the Brotherhood revolt, he remarked:

> The idea was as old as the hills; but its application to Baseball had not yet been made. It was, in fact, the irrepressible conflict between labor and capital asserting itself under a new guise....[9]

Spalding developed a special disdain for the Players' Union. He claimed that its leaders had tricked players into joining it by telling them that it was a mutual benefit society. Players, he claimed, were made to sign an "iron-clad oath" by leaders who "correctly estimated the weakness of character and lack of moral courage of the average Brotherhood member." Spalding called the union's members "evasive, contradictory and mendacious." He argued that their movement had no moral foundation and would eventually perish under its own weight. He called the player's movement a "revolutionary scheme" to make players "club magnates," and players who joined the union were ungrateful for all that capital had done for them.[10] Like owners in other industries, Spalding viewed his workers as childlike, easily led, and undisciplined. To counter this, management had to be strong, and willing to confront them, even if it meant stripping the players of their manliness.

Spalding believed that only he had a true vision of what professional baseball should be. He called himself the "guardian of the nation's sport," and viewed anyone who disagreed with him as an enemy of the game. Ballplayers did not understand the industry, and if left to their own devices, they would frighten away the essential middle-class patrons and destroy the industry.[11]

Baseball was not the only industry in which Spalding was involved. In 1876 he and his brother started Spalding Brothers Sporting Goods company with $800 borrowed from his brother-in-law William Brown.[12] Soon his company was supplying the National League with equipment and using the league to promote its products.[13]

By 1887, Spalding Sporting Goods had offices in 23 American cities and stores in 65. The company employed 3,500 people and manufactured more than 1,000,000 bats annually. That same year, the company signed a contract with its chief rival, Reach Sporting Goods, to make baseballs for

Spalding. Reach borrowed from its rival to expand production capacity and found itself unable to repay the loan. Desperate, they sold out to Spalding for $100,000.[14]

To control competition, Spalding cut deals with his retailers. He agreed to sell his products to all of them at the same price. In return, retailers had to agree to sell the products at prices set by the Spalding Corporation. The magnate called this his "square deal," and in fact it probably did help small retailers. It also ensured an orderly market and most likely increased sales over the long run and ensured that profits would remain high.[15]

Spalding's corporate power spread beyond baseball and sporting goods. Anticipating the increased use of urban rail travel, he purchased a large turnstile manufacturing company in 1884. Soon after this, he dominated this industry in the Northeast.[16] Spalding also entered the bicycle business, and by 1898 his company was one of the largest in the country. Realizing that profits were reduced by competition from small companies, he organized the American Bicycle Company in May of 1899. In reality, A.B.C. was a trust. It sold bonds and purchased stocks in small bicycle companies. Spalding claimed that this stabilized the bicycle business and benefited everyone involved. It also caused prices to soar.[17] The scheme eventually failed when the demand for bikes declined during the first decade of the new century, but not before it had earned Spalding a fortune.

By 1892, Spalding's empire included the hugely profitable Chicago baseball team, real estate, and his sporting goods empire. That year his holdings were reorganized as a New Jersey corporation with capital stock of over $4,000,000.[18] Although he gave up the presidency of the team in 1891, he continued to hold most of the company's stock, and he continued to be one of the dominant figures in National League affairs. He helped to guide the league through the troubled 1890s, and he continued to support policies that restricted labor and encouraged monopoly. Until his death in 1915, Spalding constantly reaffirmed his belief that markets had to be controlled to maintain stability, and that organized labor was a threat to the American way of life. The baseball rebellion of 1890 would be the greatest threat to the new order that the National League had forged. Ultimately, he would emerge triumphant, and his stamp would remain on the national pastime for more than 60 years after his passing.

John Montgomery Ward, the founder of the Brotherhood of Professional Base Ball Players and the leader of the players' revolt of 1890, was one of the most interesting and dynamic men ever to play major league baseball. Ward was a distant cousin of Aaron Ward, the founder of the famous mail-order company. Born in the working-class community of Bellefonte, Pennsylvania, on March 3, 1860, John was one of three sons of Ruth and James Ward. His mother was a schoolteacher and his father a tobacconist until he died in 1871. Ward's mother passed away three years later, and Ward was then raised by his uncle Philo Ward and his wife Hannah. It is likely that, growing up in a working-class community, and having a tradesman as a father, Ward learned about the ideology of class struggle early in life.[19]

Ward's parents owned properties in Bellefonte and nearby townships. The sale of some of these helped them and his grandparents to raise him in modest comfort and enabled him to enroll in Pennsylvania State College in 1873 at the age of thirteen.[20] Ward did not complete his first year at Penn State. Prior to matriculating he had only had several years of elementary education, and he was not emotionally or academically prepared for college. He went home without earning any college credits, but he returned in 1874 determined to succeed, and this time he was able to handle the academics of the university.

Although only an adolescent when he entered Penn State, Ward soon developed into one of the school's best baseball players, and he may have been one of the people responsible for organizing its first baseball team in 1875. His talents as a pitcher, hitter, and fielder became well known, and the young Ward played on many of the region's amateur and semiprofessional nines. While playing for Lock Haven in either 1875 or 1876, James Kelly, the team's catcher, told Ward that it was possible to curve a pitched ball. Although not an accomplished practitioner of the pitch, Kelly proved to be an adept teacher, and soon Ward was one of the best curve ball pitchers in the country.[21]

Ward left Penn State without a diploma in 1877. Although it was not a noted institution of higher learning in the 1870s, Penn State did expect its students to adhere to a strict code of conduct, and the young John Montgomery Ward was not able to live up to this code. Ward was popular on campus, and he spent much of his time with members of the baseball team, who often were reluctant to live by the school's rules. Ward was suspended from school in October of 1876 because he had missed school to play a baseball game against Lock Haven.[22] After he was reinstated, he was involved in several incidents that some would classify as college pranks or minor transgressions. Unfortunately for Ward, the officials at Penn State saw them as offenses that could not be tolerated. In January of 1877, Ward and a friend, William Calvin McCormick, were brought before a disciplinary panel and accused of being off campus without permission and stealing chickens from a nearby farm. Ward denied the charges to no avail, and he was dismissed from Penn State in early 1877. He was still only sixteen years old.[23]

After he left school, Ward sold fruit trees. He soon grew bored of this and hopped a freight train to Renovo, Pennsylvania, where he joined a semiprofessional team called the Resolutes. He was supposed to be paid 15 dollars per month, but after two weeks the team had played no games and had not paid him, so he jumped to another team in Williamsport. He stayed there about a month and then joined the Philadelphia Athletics after receiving a $75-bonus and a $100-per-month contract.[24]

From Philadelphia Ward went to teams in Milwaukee and Jamesville, Wisconsin, Buffalo and Binghamton, New York, and finally, at the age of 18, the National League's Providence Grays in 1878, where he quickly developed

Capt. JOHN WARD, S. S. N. Y's.

GOODWIN & CO. New York

*Top:* John Montgomery Ward was a star pitcher, infielder, and outfielder for four different teams from 1878 to 1894. Ward was one of the most interesting and dynamic men ever to play major league baseball. He founded the Brotherhood of Professional Base Ball Players in 1885, was a key figure in the formation of the Players' League, earned a law degree from Columbia University while still playing, and married Helen Dauvray, an early star of the American stage. After he retired, he had a successful career as a lawyer and became one of the best amateur golfers in the United States. He was elected to the Hall of Fame in 1964 (Library of Congress).

*Bottom:* John Montgomery Ward. Although a fierce competitor on the field, Ward was also comfortable among New York's elite, and this would serve him well after he retired as a player and became a successful New York lawyer (National Baseball Hall of Fame Library, Cooperstown, N.Y.).

into one of the game's best players.[25] Ward stayed at Providence through the 1882 season. During his five-year tenure, he was used primarily as a pitcher and won 146 games while losing only 84. His worst earned run average over this span was 2.59, and on June 17, 1880, he pitched the second perfect game in National League history. He accomplished an even more impressive one-game feat when he pitched a 1–0 shutout against Detroit on August 17, 1882. The game did not end until Ward's teammate, Charles "Old Hoss" Radbourn, hit a home run in the 18th inning, and this remains the longest one-man shutout in baseball history. In 1879 he won 47 games and helped Providence to win its first pennant.[26] Ward gained a reputation as a tough competitor who played within the rules but who would not back down from an opponent or an umpire if he believed that he or a teammate was being unjustly treated.

Ward's years at Providence were not without problems. On October 10, 1880, with all of the team's games completed, but with the club obligated to pay players for another twenty days, it released them in order to avoid paying the remainder of their salaries. Ward had signed a two-year contract prior to the season, but was still not paid for the twenty days.[27] Ward also witnessed injustices done to others. He was particularly upset when Charley Jones of Boston, the game's first home run king, was blacklisted by the team's owner, Arthur Soden, for the entire 1881 season. Although still only 21 years old, Ward was already aware of capital's power and the inability of players to resist it.[28]

Albert Goodwill Spalding was a star pitcher during baseball's early professional era. He became the owner of the Chicago White Stockings, started an extremely successful sporting goods business, and successfully led the National League owners in their 1890 battle against the Players' League (National Baseball Hall of Fame Library, Cooperstown, N.Y.).

During the 1881 season, Ward was challenged for the number one pitching spot on the Providence team by Old Hoss Radbourne. During this era, most teams relied on one hurler to pitch most of their games, so Ward found himself on the mound less and less. By 1882, Radbourne was the team's number one pitcher. Ward played more and more in the outfield, and he improved his defensive and offensive skills. However, he still wanted to pitch and was often moody, temperamental, and even more combat-ive.

After the 1882 season, Ward was sold to New York (the team was yet to be called the Giants). John Day, the team's owner, generally treated his players well, and he raised Ward's salary from $1700 to $3100. The hand-some, articulate, and sometimes flashy young man was well suited to New York. He enjoyed talking to the press, was a star player on a very good team, and actively participated in the social life that the big city offered. He, the city, and its baseball "cranks" immediately took to each other, and Ward would live in or near New York for the rest of his life.[29]

Ward pitched his last game in 1884. Years of pitching and a shoulder injury suffered when he slid into a base in Cleveland made it impossible for him to pitch, and he won only three games that season. However, Ward was too good an athlete and too much of a competitor to allow his inabil-ity to take the mound to end his days on the diamond. Instead, he went to the outfield and learned to throw left-handed. When the shoulder had healed enough, he returned to the infield, where he became the team's shortstop and field leader.[30]

By 1887, he was considered the league's best shortstop and was nation-ally famous. One writer extolled his skills by explaining that he "raised the standard of playing shortstop beyond anything it has attained in his time," while another wrote "as a field general, Ward has no superior."[31]

Ward was also a great innovator. While at Penn State he made the area where the pitcher stood into a mound, and many believe that he was the first to do this. He was also the first to employ the intentional walk against superior hitters, and he developed a sophisticated cutoff system to ensure that balls hit to the outfield got relayed to the desired base as quickly as possible. Ward was given credit for helping to perfect the double play, and he was one of the first players to signal for a pitchout when he predicted that a base runner was about to steal.

Ward was a natural right-handed hitter. However, he was hit by many pitches over the years, and he became tentative at the plate. Unwilling to give in to this fear, he practiced endless hours, learned to bat left-handed, and continued to be one of the league's most successful hitters.[32]

Ward studied baseball as if it were a science. He had an intimate understanding of all of the game's rules, and he was one of the first play-ers to scrutinize the "angles, curves and centrifugal force" involved in hit-ting and fielding. He also studied the psychology of opposing players and often exploited their weaknesses and fears, especially when running the bases.[33] Finally, 60 years before Jackie Robinson played for the Dodgers,

Ward tried to convince the Giants to sign George Stovey and Moses Fleet-wood Walker, both of whom were black, to play for the Giants. Although the team refused, this incident illustrates Ward's open-mindedness in an era when many people involved in the sport were openly racist.[34]

Ward's interests and talents were not confined to the baseball dia-mond. In 1882 he published *Base-Ball: How to Become a Player*, one of the first books on baseball. In the early chapters, he displayed knowledge of ancient, modern European, and baseball history. He wrote poetically of the game, explaining that it required "all the manly qualities of activity, endurance, pluck and skill" and also gave in-depth explanations about the structure of professional baseball, playing strategies, and the best tech-niques to employ to improve as a player.[35]

In 1883, a more mature Ward returned to college. He enrolled in Columbia College and graduated *cum laude* with a degree in law in the summer of 1885, and a year later he earned a Bachelor of Philosophy degree.[36] Although he would not practice law until his playing career ended, his legal training gave him a different outlook on the owners' treatment of players and helped to make him a worthy opponent of management.

Although the leader of the most revolutionary movement in base-ball history, Ward was an elitist, much like Gompers. While playing in New York, he lived in a fashionable downtown apartment instead of in the Harlem House on 115th and Third Avenue, which was nearer to the Polo Grounds and where most of the players lived. Unlike many players of this era, he drank only in moderation, and he trained in the off season to keep fit. He was generally reserved, and some viewed him as arrogant. While some players saw Ward as too controlling and a dandy, he had a combative streak that at times could be vicious. Early in his professional career he was involved in an ongoing battle with pitcher Lee Richmond. Both pitchers threw at each other often, and neither ever backed down. In 1884, he was so angry at umpire John Gaffney that he attacked the official and cut him so badly that he had to be taken to a surgeon. This resulted in a fine and suspension for Ward. These incidents illustrate an important aspect of Ward's personality. He prided himself in being a gen-tleman who adhered to a middle-class behavioral code. However, he had a fierce pride and working-class willingness to confront those who did not show him respect. These traits would play a key role in the players' revolt of 1890.

Ward also understood the business of baseball better than most play-ers of his era. He encouraged management's efforts to attract "ladies" and "middle-class patrons" to games, explaining that they made baseball a "fashionable" and "manly" sport.[37] Ward viewed himself as the social and intellectual equal of capital. He also believed that the special skills of his constituency set them apart from other workers; consequently, he never wanted the Brotherhood to join a larger labor movement.[38]

On October 12, 1887, Ward married divorcée Helen Dauvray (baptized Helen Gibson), who had begun her career at age five and become one of New York's most popular stars of the stage. (Different accounts report that Dauvray was either 26 or 30 at the time of the wedding.) Ward's new wife was also a successful businesswoman and had become modestly wealthy investing her stage earnings in Comstock mining stock. She was an avid baseball fan and had long been a regular at Giants home games. Dauvray was a short, attractive but not beautiful woman who had a full figure, dark eyes, small hands, and an expressive face. The wedding was the talk of New York.[39]

The marriage went well at first. The traditional Ward had

Helen Dauvray was the first wife of John Montgomery Ward, star player and leader of the Brotherhood of Professional Base Ball Players. Dauvray was an actress of some renown, and her insistence on returning to the stage and her husband's unfaithfulness caused them to separate in 1890 and divorce in 1893 (Hampden-Booth Theatre Library, N.Y.).

forbade his wife from returning to the stage, and initially she did not seem to mind. Her life revolved around Ward, his game, and New York society. However, by early 1889, Ward and Dauvray had become estranged; they were legally separated in April of 1890 and divorced in 1893. A number of factors led to the demise of the marriage. Prior to meeting Dauvray, Ward was having a relationship with a young married beauty named Jessie McDermott. Ward continued to see her after his marriage, and on at least one occasion he had a fight with her husband, George. Helen learned of the affair, and this was one reason she refused to accompany Ward on the 1888 World Baseball Tour. By January, 1889, she had returned to the stage, and the celebrated marriage was all but over. One of the provisions of the divorce ruling was that Ward could not remarry while Helen was alive.[40]

Ward was a natural leader. He was serious, believed in strict discipline, and looked down on players who drank too much or did not stay in shape. Although he had an aristocratic manner that may have alienated some players, he was charismatic and approached most tasks with a sense of mission. Today he would be described as a winning ballplayer. One scribe wrote of him:

> He combined rare executive ability, commanding power and thorough knowledge of the game from both the players' and magnates' standpoints. Ward had the absolute confidence of his fellow players and the fear and respect of the club owners.[41]

Ward's leadership skills were often given as a reason for his team's success on the field. Throughout his career, the teams that he played for often won more games than the sporting press and public expected.

Ward was also impeccably honest. Early in the 1890 season, the National League owners tried to buy him off so that he would abandon the Players' League movement and found that he had no price. In 1890 when most teams were inflating their turnstile counts, he instructed his Brooklyn Players' League employees not to because he did not want them to lie.[42]

Ward was a tough taskmaster. He believed that while the game was on, players had to be subordinate to their captain. He explained that the captain should have "exclusive control of players on and off the field and should have certain other powers and a more extended jurisdiction over the players and playing department."[43]

The controls that Ward exerted over the players did not mean that he was a lackey for management or that he shared capital's paternalistic attitude toward them. Instead, he was a classic craft union leader who was obsessed with improving the quality of his industry's product. To do this it was necessary to make the whims of his workforce subordinate to him. Only by making his goals their goals could his teams reach their potential. He got along well with his charges and always treated them with respect. He was "one of them" and explained that he was "for the player first, last and all the time." Their appreciation for him was shown in September, 1888, when he returned to the Giants after being injured and was given a big reception by his teammates.[44]

Ward took the business of leadership seriously, and it took a toll on him. In the middle of the 1887 season, the baseball world was shocked when he lost his position as the Giants' captain and was replaced by Buck Ewing. Some reports said that Ward had resigned, and others explained that teammates had grown tired of his strict leadership style and forced management to take the captaincy away from him. What is undisputed is that Ward believed that as the players' leader he was responsible for their behavior both on and off the field, and there is no doubt that this angered some of his teammates. This responsibility for off-the-field behavior was usually given to the team manager, who was almost never a player. Ward's message was clear. It was necessary to regulate players, but it should be done by one of them and not management. Gompers, Debs, and Powderly would all have agreed.

Management continually described Ward as a radical, socialist, or anarchist in 1890, but there were no foundations to these claims. Instead, he was a traditional, pre-corporate capitalist, out to insure a fair share for his constituency, preserve its honor and manliness, and help his industry grow so that capital could realize a fair profit.

Like most mainstream labor leaders of his era, Ward was not anti-business. He believed that it was the players' responsibility to help their industry to grow and prosper. This would help the owners to increase their profits and would insure jobs and high wages for the industry's workforce which he represented. However, he also believed in players owning stocks in their clubs so they could profit from the industry's prosperity. He owned stock in both the New York and Brooklyn Players' League clubs in 1890, and he hoped that one result of the Players' League would be increased player ownership in baseball.[45]

If Ward had such a traditional attitude toward capitalism, why did he lead a labor movement that was perceived to be so radical? To answer this question, one must examine Ward's relationship with management and his evolving attitudes about honor and labor control during the period 1882 to 1889.

In 1882, when there was still limited player movement, Ward criticized managers who abused the free market, explaining:

> The greatest evil with which the business has of recent years had to contend is the unscrupulous methods of some of its managers. Knowing no such thing as professional honor, these men are ever ready to benefit themselves, regardless of the cost to an associate club. The reserve rule itself is perhaps made necessary by the peculiar nature of the base ball business, and the player is indirectly compensated by the improved standing of the game.[46]

At this point Ward believed that the baseball industry needed to control player movement to prevent such abuses by capital. He called revolving an "evil," gambling a "baneful influence," and believed that a strong organization was necessary to deal with these.[47] He supported the reserve rule, explaining:

To this rule, more than any other thing, does baseball as a business owe its present substantial standing. By preserving intact the strength of a team from year to year, it places the business of baseball on a permanent basis, and thus offers security to the investment of capital.[48]

Ward believed that the reserve rule gave capital incentive to invest in the baseball industry, and that without it owners would be "invested in baseball stock with the possibility of seeing it rendered valueless at the end of six months by the defection of a number of their best players." In 1886 he claimed the rule made the game more "popular and solid."[49] Finally he explained, "The reserve rule, on the whole, is a bad one, but it cannot be rectified save by injuring the interests of men who invest their money, and that is not the object of the Brotherhood."[50]

When he organized the Brotherhood in 1885, Ward did not intend to use it to initiate dramatic changes in his industry. He believed that the National League had done a good job of stabilizing the baseball industry and that players had benefited from this. He was not opposed to most of the controls placed on players by management, because he believed they were necessary to create stability, which benefited everyone involved in the industry.

Ward's union had worked hard to get the reserve rule written into players' contracts so it would not be an "ex post facto" law, and until the late 1880s, most of its constituency was no more opposed to the rule than Ward was.[51]

A number of factors contributed to Ward's decision to turn on the National League, its rules, and its monopoly. By the mid-1880s, he no longer credited management with being responsible for baseball's popularity. He argued that "the club owners have had absolutely nothing to do with the uplift of the game. About 25 percent of the credit belongs to the players and 75 to the newspapers." He believed that the game prospered in spite of the owners and that extensive daily newspaper coverage helped the public to realize how great the game was and prevented management's regular abuses from destroying it.[52] Ward also argued that baseball brought out a "partisan spirit" in a team's community and stated that the fans did not go out primarily to witness the game, but rather to watch the home team uphold the "honor" of the town.[53]

Although there was increasing labor unrest during the mid-1880s, there is little evidence that labor's rhetoric or actions had much direct influence on Ward and his union. It is impossible to know how much Ward knew of the changing labor/capital relationship in America, but it is evident that he never viewed his movement as a part of the wider actions that were sweeping the nation. Ward saw his constituency as too specialized to be a part of a more general labor movement, and although he often used the rhetoric of class struggle to discuss the players' relationship with capital, he would eventually turn his back on organized labor when it offered help for his cause. This elitism cost his constituency needed labor support during the 1890 season. However, other events caused him to become more antagonistic toward capital.

In 1885 Ward earned his law degree. Although he never said that this changed his outlook on the game, it is clear that he became less tolerant of management after he received his diploma. He was appalled when Mike "King" Kelly was sold by Chicago to Boston in 1887 for $10,000 and did not get even a portion of the sale money. This anger at increasing player sales was intensified when the Giants made at least two attempts to sell him. He believed that before a team sold a player it should release him and then allow the player to make his own deal with the team of his choice.[54]

Ward began to see the reserve rule not as a tool to stabilize the industry, or to control undisciplined owners, but as a means of making tremendous profits for capital at the players' expense. He believed that it helped to keep the strong teams winners, but hurt the weaker clubs because they were denied access to most of the best players. The rule, which had once been necessary as an "institution of good," had become an "institution of evil."[55]

Owners blamed players for the problems caused by revolving. Ward scoffed at this, explaining that it was the owners who were responsible for these problems and they had taken away some of the players' basic rights because they lacked the honor, discipline, and self-control to solve them. He wanted to "open baseball up to the market" to encourage growth in the industry, but he wanted teams to have a relatively equal revenue base so that the richest teams would not go on wild spending sprees for the best players and thus destabilize the industry. He believed that more enlightened capitalists would have devised such a system.[56]

At first Ward talked of modifying the reserve rule so that a player would only be a team's property for a prescribed number of years. He argued that such a modification would not only help the players but would also improve the game because it would prevent players from "overstaying their time" on one team.[57]

From 1887 to 1889, player sales became more common, the classification plan was introduced, the blacklist and suspension were used more regularly, and there was a general increase in the control exerted over players. Ward viewed all of these as an affront to the players' manliness. He explained, "no body of men, however well paid, will long submit to being deprived of any part of their individual honor."[58] He was incensed by the classification scheme and called it an "exhibition of venality, lying, and despicable subterfuge." He went on to say that "no such combination of corruptionists and their tools can live…. The days of the National League are numbered."[59] Ward also argued that the National Agreement created a monopoly that stifled competition, prevented new leagues from developing, and thus cost his constituency jobs.[60]

Like most labor leaders throughout the nation, Ward had grown disenchanted with capital and no longer believed that the interests of his constituency paralleled those of the owners. In August of 1887, Ward wrote an article in *Lippencott's* magazine entitled: "Is the Base Ball Player a Chattel?" In it he explained the players' grievances. It also marked the emergence of a more radical Ward who was convinced that the industry had to be changed not only for the sake of the players, but also for the game and business of baseball. It read:

> … like a fugitive-slave law, the reserve law denies him a harbor or a livelihood, and carries him back, bound and shackled, to the club from which he attempted to escape. We have then, the curious result of a contract which on its face is for seven months being binding for life, and when the player's name is once attached there to his professional liberty is gone forever….
>
> Instead of an institution for good, it has become one for evil; instead of a measure of protection, it has been used as a handle for the manipulation of a traffic in players, a sort of speculation in livestock, in which they are bought, sold, and transferred like so many sheep….
>
> Clubs have seemed to think that players had no rights, and the black list was waiting for the man who dared assert the contrary…. Encouraged by the apparent inactivity of the players, the clubs have gone on from one usurpation to another until in the eye of the base-ball "magnate" the player has become a mere chattel. He goes where he is sent, takes what is given him, and thanks the Lord for life….
>
> The tangled web of legislation which now hampers the game must be cut away, and the business of base-ball made to rest on the ordinary business basis. There will be little need, then, of extra-judicial rules to regulate themselves, like those of the dramatic and other professions, by the law of supply and demand; "base ball law" … will be laid away … contracts may be for periods of more than one season, the leagues will be composed of cities of nearly equal drawing strength, and the percentage system will be re-enacted, thus reducing to a minimum the temptation to compete for players….
>
> When the game is governed by the law of the land, when its financial conduct is placed in the hands of thorough businessmen … these changes will come.[61]

Ward opposed the National League owners not because they were capitalists, but because they were bad businessmen. Although accused of being a socialist and an anarchist, Ward was instead, like many craft union leaders of his era, a free-market capitalist who believed that fair-minded, honorable ownership and a hardworking and well-disciplined workforce could benefit everyone involved in the baseball industry and help the game to grow and prosper.

Although there were various factions among baseball owners and players, Albert Goodwill Spalding and John Montgomery Ward emerged as the leaders of their respective groups and generally represented the views of their constituencies. Spalding was a typical 19th-century capitalist concerned with order and control of markets and labor and mistrustful of unions. Ward held views common to labor's elite. He expected his constituency to behave in a professional manner on and off the field, and he was respectful of management's place in the emerging modern capitalist system. However, he also had a combative streak that made him willing to stand up to management when necessary. Eventually their differences would be magnified, and each would play a decisive role in baseball's greatest confrontation of the 19th century.

# 8

# The Players' National
# League of Base-Ball Clubs

The players' revolt of 1890 was the culmination of tensions that had been building between National League owners and players for several years. Throughout the 1880s, most players had supported the reserve rule and other provisions of the National Agreement. However, by the end of the decade, most player-control measures were viewed as immoral.[1] Many players believed that the owners were abusing the reserve rule. They no longer believed that it was necessary to insure stability and profitability in the industry. Instead, the rule was now perceived to be solely an instrument to reduce salaries and drive up player value.[2] It was an attack on the players' rights, and players with a strong sense of manliness were obligated to stand up to it.[3]

The reserve rule was not the only affront to the players' manliness. Arbitrary suspensions, expulsions, and blacklisting continued, as did the continued sale of players.[4] The sale of Mike "King" Kelly from Chicago to Boston for $10,000 was especially shocking to the players and helped them to realize just how much they were worth. The popular Kelly claimed the sale made him feel like a "dog" and a "slave."[5] These sentiments intensified when St. Louis Browns owner Christian Von der Ahe, angry at his team's loss to Detroit in the 1887 World Series, sold Bob Caruthers, Dave "Scissors" Foutz, and Albert "Doc" Bushong to the Brooklyn Bridegrooms for $18,000. These lucrative sales made players angry, and many began to demand a percentage of the money teams received when they were sold.

Players also believed that many owners abused their power. Players were outraged when Buffalo suspended an injured Charlie Foley, without pay, for an entire season, and then reserved him for two years when he returned to health. Buffalo would not play him, pay him, or trade him, thus ending his career. When outfielder Charles Wesley Jones refused to play until Boston owner Arthur Soden paid him $378 in back pay, he was given a two-year suspension.[6] Even more offensive to the players was what was done to popular Chicago shortstop Ned Williamson. After Williamson was injured during the 1888 world tour, he had to pay for his own hospital expenses in England. Williamson's play was limited in 1889, and as a result, he received only slightly more than one-third of his pay from team owner Albert Spalding. His career was over a year later.

Perhaps the most egregious assault on player rights occurred in mid-June of 1889. Mordecai H. Davidson, who owned the American Association's Louisville franchise, was angry at his team's 8–40 record, and as a result he fined his second baseman, Dan Shannon, for making errors and his catcher, Paul Cook, for bad base running. The teammates of the two men came to their defense, and they threatened not to play in the June 14th game unless the fines were rescinded. Davidson, unwilling to back down, threatened each of these players with a $100 fine if they refused to play and $25 if they lost. Six players did refuse to play on the 14th and 15th and Davidson levied $1200 in fines for missing the two games and an additional $500 for bad language and refusing to slide. This money was withheld from the players' checks. Fellow American Association owners became concerned when the players threatened to form their own Brotherhood chapters. Fortunately for both the players and the owners, Davidson sold the team in July. All of the non-strike fines were reimbursed as were the June 14 strike fines. The six players did have to pay $100 per man for the missed June 15 game. Although the players were placated somewhat by this compromise, anger lingered. Despite all of the controls over player behavior and salaries, teams still folded, and when they did, players were sold off to the highest bidder. If a player refused to report to his new team, he was automatically reserved for the $1,000 salary minimum.[7]

Baseball players were competitive by nature, and most of them had a difficult time justifying the monopoly that the National League had created. All players were asked to battle for victory on the playing field, while their owners forged a system that made them immune to the competitive forces of the marketplace. Ward was angered at this hypocrisy and explained, "The owners are monopolists who deny to others the right to engage in the same business as themselves." The classification plan outraged him because owners claimed that it was necessary to protect poorer franchises like Indianapolis and Louisville. Ward responded that these organizations should either leave the National League or the richer clubs should share their profits with them or split gate receipts fifty-fifty. He coldly announced that "Indianapolis has about as much right in the National League as Oshkosh." His message was simple. If baseball owners wanted to make their teams immune to market forces, then the owners, and not the players, should bear the cost of this immunity. [8]

Months later, Brotherhood leader Fred Pfeffer echoed these sentiments when he said, "Money and the love of freedom outbalance money alone.... Now I imagine that when there is open competition, the players in the long run are sure to reap the benefit. The Brotherhood has knocked out the greatest monopoly that ever existed."[9]

Although it was never fully enforced, the Brush Classification Plan was also a factor in the players' decision to revolt. Some players believed the plan was designed to do more than regulate salaries. Many veteran players had multi-year contracts and would not be immediately affected by it. Newer or less skilled players were bound by one-year contracts and thus would be regulated by the plan. Although there is no proof that this was the owners' intention, some players believed that a goal of the plan was to divide the veteran stars from their fellow players and thus make unified action more difficult. Even when the owners removed the plan from the League Constitution, the players were still angry and mistrustful of the owners. They also realized the extent to which the owners would go to increase their controls over them.[10] Players were particularly incensed when Fred Pfeffer, who was a stockholder and player for the White Stockings in 1889, claimed that not only did Spalding know of the plan when the world tour was under way, but that he organized it at least partially to get the Brotherhood's leadership out of the country when the plan was announced.[11]

Players were insulted that league magnates would not meet with the Brotherhood executive committee during the 1889 season. When Ward met privately and unofficially with Spalding in Chicago on June 24, 1889, he expressed the concerns he had with the classification plan to the magnate. Ward explained that contrary to what the owners claimed, some players had been reserved for less than their 1888 salaries in 1889. This was done despite the owners' assurances that it would not happen. He was also upset at the growing practice of player sales. Spalding, who by this point was growing more concerned with what the players might do, privately offered to modify the plan so that National League and American Association players with three years of service and "exemplary" habits would be exempt from classification. In addition, he proposed that when players were sold, the selling team would keep 50 percent of the money and the remaining fifty percent would be divided between the league and the player. None of these proposals was official, and even if they were, they were probably too late to placate Ward. Shortly after the meeting, he went to the press to chastise classification, and Spalding began to discuss expanding classification to the minor leagues with his fellow owners.

Many players believed that they were more concerned with "elevating the game" than the owners, who were concerned only with profits.[12] Management did agree to officially meet with the players in September of 1889, but Ward claimed that it would be impossible for him to assemble the union's negotiating committee. More likely, he realized the reconciliation was impossible, and he wanted to keep his union as distant from management as possible.[13]

From June 21 to July 8, 1889, Ward's Giants were on a road trip to the National League's western cities. On the trip's first stop, Cleveland, Ward complained of a sore arm and insisted that he could not play. The ailment persisted as the team journeyed from Cleveland to Indianapolis and then Pittsburgh. Ward traveled with the team, but he neither played in nor attended any of the games. This was unusual, since players rarely missed such a large number of contests because of a sore arm. When the team returned to New York on July 8, Ward was once again in the lineup and showed no effects from the ailment.[14]

Although it is impossible to know the condition of Ward's arm on this trip, it is doubtful that his absence from the lineup had anything to do with the alleged ailment. More likely, he was spending his time trying to round up backers and players for a new league that he hoped would begin play in 1890.

Ward had formulated his scheme early in the 1889 season. He believed that only a new order in the baseball industry would end the abuses of management and allow the players to regain their dignity. In the belief that the industry needed to be totally restructured, he had counseled against a strike during the 1889 season. This is also why he had asked Jack Rowe and Deacon White not to challenge the reserve rule in court after they had been sold.[15]

On July 14, 1889, Ward and representatives from the different Brotherhood chapters met at the Fifth Avenue Hotel in New York. The delegates were given the task of securing backers for a new league that would begin play in 1890. When they reported back later in the month, most had received positive feedback on the plan, and even some players had showed an interest in investing in the enterprise.[16] The Brotherhood worked hard to keep these plans secret and went so far as to hire police to guard meetings to prevent information from leaking.[17] Players were also assigned the task of checking the National League's turnstile count during the 1889 season. The game's popularity was soaring, and Ward wanted to accumulate as much financial data as possible to help convince investors that money could be made in professional baseball.[18]

Shortly after the July, 1889, New York meeting, Pittsburgh Brotherhood representative Ned Hanlon contacted Cleveland businessman Albert Johnson. Johnson was in the streetcar business, and Hanlon wanted to know if he had a suitable site for a ballpark near his streetcar line.[19] The magnate said that he did, and Hanlon explained the players' idea of forming a new major league. Johnson was very interested and became the players' first important backer.[20]

Johnson was an interesting mix of Gilded Age businessman, social reformer, and barroom card player and drinker. Although fond of baseball, he enjoyed the camaraderie of its players even more, often playing poker with them late into the evening. Johnson was opposed to the reserve rule because it interfered with the free market. He also opposed other player control measures on the grounds that they treated players in an "unmanly" fashion.[21]

Although his fondness for the game and its players and opposition to the established order were factors in Johnson's decision to get involved in the baseball industry, his primary motive for investing in the Players' League was profit. He believed that a baseball team playing along his streetcar line would increase ridership and make a profit at the gate. The magnate explained:

> I have seen streetcars on the opposite street loaded down with people going to games, and it occurred to me there was a chance for a good investment if I could get grounds on a streetcar line owned by my brother and myself.[22]

Without Johnson, there probably would not have been a Players' League. He gave the movement instant credibility. When players played in Cleveland during the 1889 season, many talked to Johnson about the planned league, and their interest increased. Johnson also worked hard at getting backers for teams. He often stressed the unfairness of the National League's treatment of its players, and he usually sought out sportsmen who he believed would be drawn to the national game for aesthetic as well as business reasons. However, most of the capitalists who eventually signed on did so because they saw the game's popularity growing and believed that money could be made in the baseball business.[23]

Johnson's Cleveland team was the first to be formed, but he, Ward, and their associates soon attracted other backers who created additional teams. The New York franchise was owned by stockbroker Edward Talcott, the postmaster and former state senator Cornelius Van Cott, tobacconist and real estate executive Colonel Edwin McAlpin, and Buck Ewing.[24] The Brooklyn team was owned by E.F. Linton, the Brownsville banker, and Wendell Goodwin, a Brownsville politician and streetcar line executive. Both men hoped that the Brooklyn team would bring more people into the borough and enhance their businesses. Boston was owned by Julian Hart and pitcher Dan Brouthers; Chicago by John Addison and second baseman Fred Pfeffer; Cleveland by Johnson and Cub Stricker; Philadelphia by J. Earl Wagner and F.S. Eliot; Pittsburgh by M.B. Lemon, John K. Tenor, and outfielder Ned Hanlon. Other investors included New York mayor Hugh Grant and businessmen Jim White, John Brown, and George Myer.[25]

James "Deacon" White and Jack Rowe owned at least 40 percent of Buffalo's stock. Many owners did not want a team there because it was viewed as a poor market. However, Ward had promised the two players this franchise when he convinced them to go to Pittsburgh the year before, and he did not want to go back on his word. From a business standpoint this was a mistake, because this was an unpopular team from the beginning.[26]

The Brotherhood claimed that the new league would "lift the stars out of the position of players and employees up to that of magnates and employers." National League magnates scoffed at their new rival and ridiculed players who had the "magnate bee in their bonnets." They claimed that allowing players a role in management was a recipe for disaster.[27]

All of the new league's owners were capitalists out to make a profit, and there is little evidence that any of them was especially progressive when it came to dealing with labor. Ward realized this, but did not believe that it would prevent him from forming his new order in the baseball industry. He hoped that the league's owners would respect the special skills of the players much like small capitalists had respected and worked with tradesmen prior to the emergence of corporate capitalism.[28]

If baseball's management would respect its elite labor force and realize that it was the reason people came to watch games, then, Ward believed, players would be justly rewarded and allowed to participate in the league's management. He also thought that all of the new owners were honorable enough to see the unfairness of baseball's previous labor policies, and he believed the new league's management would not try to initiate similar policies to control and humiliate players.

On November 5, 1889, John Ward and representatives of the league's owners announced the formation of the Players' National League of Base-Ball Clubs: The Players' League. The announcement defined the league as a "democratic alliance of workers and capitalists."[29] The league's manifesto read:

> There was a time when the League stood for integrity and fair dealing; today its eyes are upon the turnstile. Men have come into the business from no other motive than to exploit it for every dollar in sight. Once

it looked to the elevation of the game and an honest exhibition of the sport. Measures originally intended for the good of the sport have been perverted into instruments of wrong. The owners gave the managers unlimited power, and they have not hesitated to use this in the most arbitrary and incendiary way, and players have been bought, sold, and exchanged as though they were sheep instead of American citizens! Reservation became for them another name for property right in a player. By a combination among themselves, stronger than the strongest trust, they were able to enforce arbitrary measures, and the player had either to submit or get out of the profession in which he had spent years attaining a proficiency. Even the disbandment of a club did not free its players from the octopus clutch for they were then peddled round to the highest bidder. We believe that it is possible to conduct our national game upon lines which will not infringe upon individual and natural rights. We ask to be judged solely by our work, and believing that the game can be played more fairly and its business conducted more intelligently under a plan which excludes everything arbitrary and unAmerican we look forward with confidence to the support of the public and the future of the national game.[30]

The day after the league's formation was announced, control of the union and the league was given to the club's representatives. These men were also on the league's board of directors.[31] The league's charter stated that each team was to be governed by a board consisting of four players and four capitalists.[32] The league would be governed by a senate consisting of sixteen men. Each team owner and each team's players would choose one representative. The senate would select the league's president (Edward McAlpin), vice president (John Addison), and secretary (F.H. Brunnell). It would also serve as a board that players could appeal to when disciplined.[33] There would also be committees on finance, law, and rules, and players would sit with owners on all of these.[34]

The financial structure of the league was in many ways similar to the cooperative ventures that the Knights of Labor had hoped to form. One of the goals of owners and players was to create an economic balance between teams that would lead to a competitive balance on the field and higher attendance.[35] When the league was formed, each team was to share profits and losses. However, this cooperative plan was opposed by the teams in larger markets. For a time in early February, it appeared that the league would fold. F.H. Brunnell even remarked to the press, "It's all over; the whole thing has fallen to pieces." Brunnell, Johnson, and Ward then met privately, and after a night of discussion, Ward proposed a compromise. Capitalists in each club would control their own finances, but league profits would be pooled.[36] Gate receipts were to be divided evenly instead of the 25-percent share that the visiting club received in the National

League. This would help the franchises in smaller markets like Buffalo, Cleveland, and Pittsburgh, and create more stability. Team profits of up to $20,000 were to be divided evenly between that franchise's players and owners, and any amount over this would be divided among all eight clubs, with players and owners getting equal shares.[37]

Each of the eight teams provided $20,000 start-up money, and they also established a $40,000 league fund that would pay player salaries in the event that gate receipts proved inadequate.[38] There was also supposed to be a $20,000 bonus pool set up that would be divided by players at the end of the season based on how well their teams did in the standings.[39]

Each club's owners had to rent or build a ballpark. Most of these were relatively inexpensive wooden structures that were quickly constructed on city lots that the owners already owned. There were some, like Talcott's Brotherhood Park, that were the finest in the land and cost as much as $80,000 to construct. Generally, the Players' League parks were superior to those of the National League and American Association.[40]

The new league would not have a reserve rule, but all players were asked to sign three-year contracts for the same wage that they had received in 1889. However, if a player could prove that his salary had been lowered in 1889 due to the classification plan, then his Players' League contract would be based on his 1888 salary.[41] The owners agreed not to classify players or establish a blacklist. The players agreed that strict regulations against drinking and gambling had to be implemented, as both vices would hurt the league. Players were not to be released until after the season and then only when a majority of the board of directors agreed to do so. Players could not be traded or sold unless they consented, and the owners agreed to try to oblige players who requested to be sent to another team. Ward and some of the Players' League owners had tried to make an alliance with the American Association prior to the 1890 season that would have prevented the Players' League from signing their players. The American Association refused this offer and stayed allied with the National League, leaving the Players' League free to raid their players. [42]

Although the structure of the new league gave the players more control and potentially more money than they made in the National League, there were also potential benefits for the owners. Most of the best National League players belonged to the Brotherhood and jumped to the Players' League without a bidding war among the new owners. Of the 127 men who played for the league, 72 came from the National League, 22 from the American Association, and the rest from various minor leagues and amateur associations. Many of the game's stars, such as Ward, Cornelius McGillicuddy, Mike Kelly, and Fred Pfeffer, were early supporters.[43]

The National League retained the services of about thirty of its players, including stars such as Sam Thompson, John Glasscock, Tommie Bains, Charlie Bennett, Cap Anson, and Billy Sunday. The remainder of its rosters were filled with players from the American Association, minor leagues, and amateur ranks.[44]

The Players' League fielded teams in Boston, Brooklyn, Buffalo, Chicago, Cleveland, New York, Philadelphia, and Pittsburgh.[45] Prior to the 1890 season, the National League convinced Cincinnati and Brooklyn to jump from the American Association to the senior league. Washington and Indianapolis, the two weakest National League teams, were induced to leave the league. (Interestingly, the National League paid Indianapolis owner John Brush not to play in 1890. Although the amount he received has been disputed, some reports from the period claim that he was given as much as $60,000)[46] The remainder of the National League teams were New York, Boston, Philadelphia, Cleveland, Chicago, and Pittsburgh, which meant that the Players' League had teams in every National League city but Cincinnati.

Generally, players would jump from their National League team to the Players' League team in the same city. Teams hoped that this would increase fan interest, since many players believed that patrons were loyal to players and not teams. This devastated most National League teams. Pittsburgh, for example, was left with only one of its players from 1889 on its 1890 roster.[47] Cincinnati and Brooklyn, the two teams that jumped from the American Association, were better off than most, since none of their players had been members of the union. This meant that fewer of their players would leave and go to the new league. Players' League franchises that did not have National League teams with Brotherhood members to draw from filled their rosters with free agents or players from the American Association. That league's St. Louis and Baltimore franchises were devastated by the number of players who went to the new league. However, most teams lost some of their players, and when opening day finally arrived in 1890, 22 of the 24 major league teams had rosters that were largely new.[48]

Rule changes were implemented by the Players' League to help make the game more exciting. Buck Ewing, head of the playing rules committee, believed that fans liked offense more than the National League's "strike out and shut out" brand of baseball that emphasized pitching and defense.[49] To increase run production, a more lively ball was employed and the pitcher's mound was moved back eighteen inches to make hitting the ball easier. (Throughout the game's history, similar changes have been implemented by the major leagues, because it is still believed that offense is what draws fans to the parks.)[50] It is also possible that this greater emphasis placed on offense resulted from the working-class attitude toward manliness that players on the league's board of directors would have had. This would have attracted them to the slugging game more than the finesse game advocated by the middle-class National League magnates.

Keefe and Becannon Sporting Goods, which was partially owned by New York pitcher Tim Keefe, was given a three-year contract to supply the league with balls. It was hoped that all league equipment would eventually be purchased from player-owned businesses so that the playing and equipment industries could be integrated and players could be involved in all aspects of the industry. The league also printed and sold 75,000 copies of the *Players' National League Base Ball Guide*.[51]

The league introduced the two-umpire system, and officials were required to wear a white uniform. It was believed that the additional umpire would ensure better officiating and would help to keep players under control. The maintenance of order was deemed to be essential to the league's success. League officials wanted the same middle-class patrons as the National League; therefore, it was important that empowered players not be unruly. Teams were also able to use two substitutes per game instead of the one allowed in the National League.[52]

By the spring of 1890, the National League's owners realized that the Players' League was a well capitalized rival and that if it were not defeated, it could surpass the National League as the nation's preeminent league. It was a threat to the well ordered baseball industry that Spalding and his counterparts had worked since 1876 to create, and it represented something that National League owners and most industrialists feared: true competition and an increased role for labor in management. It had to be stopped.

From the baseball war's onset, both sides believed that only one league could survive. National and Players' League teams were competing for fans in seven of their eight cities, and it was doubtful if an adequate fan base existed to support two teams in most of these markets. The National League was well capitalized, was better organized, had more experienced management and a glorious past, but was handicapped by the obviously inferior teams that it was fielding. Its rival had the best players and adequate capital, but it also had high salaries and inexperienced management that had yet to prove that it was willing to make a long-term commitment to the baseball business.[53]

The National League selected a "war committee" to fight the Players' League and chose A.G. Spalding to lead it. Spalding hoped to battle the league in the courts, newspapers, at the gate, and finally by separating management from labor. He believed that the National League owners, because they had been involved in the industry longer and had invested more money in their teams, would be willing to lose more money over the short term than the Players' League capitalists, who Spalding believed were after a quick profit. He planned to fight his rival head on, explaining "I am for war without quarter.... I want to fight until one of us drops dead."[54]

In the early spring of 1890, the Players' League sent the National League a copy of its schedule, hoping that it would "avoid conflicting with our clubs."[55] Instead, the senior league made its schedule as close to its rival's as possible, hoping that this would cause the owners of the new league to lose large sums of money and give up. Since the new league was after the same middle-class patrons as its rival, it did not schedule Sunday games and insisted on a 50-cent admission fee. This meant that in each locality where both leagues had teams, they would almost always be competing for the same fans at the same time. It was inevitable that teams in both leagues would lose money.[56]

The National League believed that it could sustain the losses more easily than the Players' League. The success of the 1880s had enabled its owners to amass war chests that may have totaled $250,000. Most teams had already paid for their parks, while many Players' League magnates had gone into debt to secure facilities. Red ink would not only discourage Players' League owners, but would also make it difficult for them to secure more capital.[57]

Many Players' League owners wanted to change the league's schedule so that it did not conflict with the National League's. However, Ward and most of the players counseled against this, claiming that to back down would show unmanly weakness.[58] The problem with this plan was that the National League was out to break its rival and regain its monopoly, while the new league was out for profit. The duplication of schedules insured that the Players' League would lose money and thus fail in its primary mission.[59]

The National League did attempt to keep its players. To regain their favor, the league repealed the classification plan and the $2,500 salary cap. Since the classification plan had never been strictly enforced, getting rid of it was primarily a symbolic gesture. The share of the gate receipts given to visiting clubs was raised from 25 to 40 percent so that weaker clubs would have more revenue with which to attract and keep top players. The league allowed players to negotiate with other National League clubs if the parent club agreed, and it extended the contract-signing deadline to February in the hope that more players would return to the league.[60]

Some players who had signed Players' League contracts did break these agreements and "jumped" back to the National League. Ward made it known that these dozen or so "deserters" would not be allowed back into the Players' League.[61] The National League's Boston team signed first baseman Tommy Tucker to a three-year $13,500 contract, and Mickey Welch was given a three- year $12,000 deal by New York. The NL made huge offers to Danny Richardson, Buck Ewing, and Mark Baldwin, all of which were turned down, and Ward claimed that Cap Anson, one of the true superstars of the period, was active in trying to lure players back to the senior league.[62]

It was rumored that Spalding had offered Mike Kelly a $15,000 three-year contract to jump back to the National League. When asked about this, Spalding replied:

> You don't think for a moment that I would insult so prominent a player by a tender of such a paltry sum.... Mr. Kelly is worth $100,000 per year or nothing and he is painfully aware of this fact. Ball players come high, but we must have 'em. And they are worth all they get, too.[63]

This willingness to pay large salaries infuriated Ward and his colleagues. After years of saying baseball needed salary controls to survive, league owners suddenly became willing to sign players to huge, multi-year pacts. Ward explained, "And now these same men, who a year ago were claiming that baseball could not exist without these big reductions in salaries, are philanthropically offering double figures to their old players to retain their services."[64]

National League owners tried to create dissension among the players. Players' League owners and players were followed by detectives, and National

Adrian "Cap" Anson played 22 seasons with the Chicago White Stockings and is still considered one of the greatest players of all time. A strong-willed man, Anson remained loyal to Albert Spalding and the National League during the 1890 players' revolt. Though he would relent and play, Anson's initial loud refusal to take the field against Toledo and its black catcher — Moses Fleetwood Walker — is frequently cited as the moment that initiated more than 60 years of unabashed discrimination in major league baseball. He was elected to the Hall of Fame in 1939 (Library of Congress).

League owners worked hard to convince players in the rival league that their colleagues were not behind the movement. Generally, these tactics failed and the players remained solidly behind the Players' League.[65]

The National League hoped to retain its fan support by attacking the new league in the press and extolling its own accomplishments. During this period, many middle-class Americans had turned against organized labor, fearing it to be violent and revolutionary. Spalding hoped to fan these sentiments and turn the public against the league. He called the players "hot-headed anarchists out to overthrow the established business of baseball."[66] He extolled the virtues of his league explaining that the reserve rule "held the game together ... increased public interest and was great for players and everybody interested in baseball."[67]

The Giants' president, John B. Day, called the players "ungrateful" and claimed that their league was a "conspiracy of our well-treated players to ruin us."[68] Brotherhood leaders were called "subversive" and "red," and it was claimed in the 1890 Spalding Guide that only by employing "special pleadings, false statements, and a system of terrorism particular to revolutionary movements" was the union able to get players to jump leagues.[69]

Spalding continually extolled all that the National League and its monopoly had done for the game, and he acted as if the players had had little to do with the industry's success. Shortly after the 1890 season began, he wrote that the National League had "defeated crooked base ball, dirty work on the field, rough elements, want of discipline. Now we have to face the old problem again.... The slaughter is yet to come — the League is prepared for slaughter."[70]

Under the guidance of National League owners, Spalding claimed, the game had gained dignity and respect. The quality of play had increased, and even with the reserve rule, salaries had tripled, according to the League Guide.[71] Profits had not been extraordinary when compared to the huge amounts paid out in salaries. These arguments were constantly expressed in the press, and their intent was clear: convince the public that the players had been treated fairly and protected by the National League, destroy the public's support for the new league, and drive the players back into the fold.

Spalding predicted that his rival would resort to playing Sunday ball and selling beer at the parks and that these would help to destroy the business of baseball.[72] Sunday baseball and beer may be accepted today, but to Spalding they were synonymous with seedy mass entertainment and the working class. He believed that they would bring about disorder in the stands, a loss of middle-class support, and a reduction of revenue. These, coupled with the players' new-found freedom and management's loss of control, would lead to disaster.

Spalding believed that his side was fighting for more than profits and market share. He believed that the Players' League would bring "dishonor and disintegration to the most glorious and honorable sport on the green earth."[73] Viewing himself as a moralistic reformer and a concerned capitalist, he believed that his side had the righteous high ground and would ultimately triumph.

A well financed war chest and resolve among its owners were not the only cards in the National League's deck. The National Agreement was still intact, which meant that the league still had access to hundreds of minor league players that it could employ at relatively low wages.[74] It was no secret that most of these players were inferior to the departed stars, but the National League believed that it could minimize the impact of this. Since almost all franchises now fielded lower- quality teams, the owners believed that the games would be competitive and exciting. (This belief in the relative equal-

Mike "King" Kelly was one of baseball's first superstars. Kelly jumped to the Players' League in 1890 and remained loyal to the league despite being offered huge sums of money to return to the National League. Kelly was a legendary drunk, and he died of pneumonia in 1894 at age 36. He was elected to the Hall of Fame in 1945 (National Baseball Hall of Fame Library, Cooperstown, N.Y.).

ity of its teams did not prove to be true. The pennant was won by the Brooklyn team that had come from the American Association and thus lost fewer players than most other teams. The Pittsburgh franchise, which lost all but one player, finished the season with a 23–113 record and is still considered by many to be the worst major league team ever.)[75] The Players' League asked its rival to play its teams before or after the season, but the National League never seriously considered such competitions.[76] These contests would have shown the superiority of the Players' League teams and destroyed the fragile perception that the National League was still a major league.[77]

The National League and American Association did their best to give the illusion that little had changed. St. Louis owner Chris Von der Ahe told the press "My club is in good condition, although some people seem to be possessed of the idea that it has been wiped off the face of the earth."[78] All

National League owners claimed that chaos ruled in the new league. They reported that captains were ignored, umpires abused, and player stockholders, feeling infallible, were impossible to control. It was hoped that the middle-class public, fearful of its own labor, would avoid Players' League games.[79]

Ward's response to all of these claims was consistent and convincing. He was not opposed to the old league, only to the old order. The shortstop even offered to join the National Agreement, but only if the reserve rule and several other provisions were suspended. He claimed that granting exclusive territorial rights to a franchise was monopolistic and un-American. Just as players competed on the field, owners, Ward argued, should compete for fans. Not surprisingly, he was mocked by the owners and called naïve and not qualified to make sound business decisions.[80]

The owners also believed that the reserve rule could be used as a weapon against the Players' League. They claimed that any player who had signed a contract for the 1889 season was bound to the same team for the 1890 season. Since almost all of the players in the new league had played in the National League in 1889, all of them, in the owners' opinion, were still bound to their National League teams. Consequently, any player who signed with another team was in breach of contract.

In October of 1889, National League magnates were surprised when most of their players refused to sign contracts for the 1890 season. The deadline for contracts to be returned was October 21, but only Cap Anson had returned his by then.[81] Soon after this, all Players' League members received a letter similar to the following:

> Sir: You will please take notice that the New York Ball Club hereby exercises its option for the employment of your services under and pursuant to the provisions of paragraph 18 of a certain contract heretofore made with you and bearing date on or about April 28, 1889, and does hereby now employ you under the provisions of said contract and retain your services for the season of 1890, and is now ready and offers to execute the agreement therefore.[82]

Ward notified all Brotherhood members that the letter was meant to intimidate the players and that they should ignore it.

The National League owners next turned to the courts to stop the rebellion. They wanted the courts to pass injunctions that would force the players to play for their National League teams. On January 9, 1890, the New York Giants brought suit against John Montgomery Ward. Ward was represented by ex-judge Henry E. Howland and David Newberger. Judge O'Brien of the New York Supreme Court presided over the case. Joseph Choate, the Giants' lawyer, claimed that baseball was different from any other theatrical entertainment since it required two teams to entertain. The reserve rule was needed, he claimed, to preserve a balance between the teams so that the game would remain competitive and entertaining.[83] Choate also argued that just as the contract obligated Ward to play the 1890 season, it also obligated the Giants to pay him and therefore was not unfair. He went on to say that the reserve rule had been written into all player contracts at the insistence of the Brotherhood since the 1887 season, and that all players had accepted it and were bound to obey it. The club had "the broadest and most unassailable rights to the renewal of contracts."[84] Playing for a club in a new league, he argued, was as much a violation of the reserve rule as playing for another American Association or National League team.[85]

Ward's lawyers argued that there were two distinct problems with the reserve rule. The first was that the rule gave the club complete control over where the team member played and regulated how much money he could make. In addition, the rule did not specify what the players' duties to the club were; consequently, a player could be required to perform an indefinite number of duties for the club. They also argued that although the reserve rule might prevent Ward from playing for a team under the National Agreement, it would not keep him from playing on a team that did not exist when the contract was signed.[86] (See Appendix 5: Complete transcript of Ward's lawyers' argument.)

On January 29, 1890, Justice O'Brien ruled in favor of Ward. In his decision he wrote:

> ... Not only are there no times and conditions fixed, but I do not think it is entirely clear that Ward agrees to do anything further than to allow the right to reserve him upon teams therefore to be fixed. He does not covenant to make a contract for 1890 at the same salary, nor upon the same terms and conditions as during the 1889 season....

The judge did not view the reserve rule as valid because it was both indefinite and uncertain. He went on to say that for a contract to be specifically entered by the court, it must be mutually consented to by both parties.[87] (See Appendix 6: Complete transcript of Judge O'Brien's decision.)

Ward viewed the judge's decision as a great victory for the players. Leaving the courthouse he told a reporter:

> Now that the case has been practically settled, we will go to work and complete our task of organizing the strongest baseball association in the country.... The men who have been brave enough to hold out in spite of the inducements offered in the shape of League gold will reap their reward, and they deserve it....[88]

Judge O'Brien's decision was a great boost to the new league. It encouraged more players to join the movement, and those who were already committed became more confident that their cause could succeed. It also assured owners and potential investors that the courts would not stand in the way of their enterprise.[89]

After the ruling, representatives from the National League and American Association met to discuss its ramifications. They viewed the decision as a setback, not a defeat, and agreed to continue to fight in court to keep their players. It was expected that the National League would lead the battle. They had the most resources and the most to lose from unfavorable court rulings, since the majority of Players' League players came from the National League.[90]

The National League next attempted to keep the Giants' catcher, Buck Ewing, from jumping to the Players' League. This case was heard by Judge Wallace of the United States Circuit Court in New York City. The Giants claimed that their company had invested large amounts of money in land, ballparks, and promotion and that they relied on the reserve rule to maintain stability on their team and to protect their investment. They had thus re-signed Ewing for the 1890 season for $2,000. Judge Wallace ruled against the Giants, calling the reserve rule, "merely a contract to make a contract if the parties can agree and as such is not enforceable against the employee by injunction against entering into other employment."[91] (See Appendix 7: Complete transcript of Judge Wallace's decision.)

The owners made another attempt at using the courts to prevent players from going to the new league in March of 1890. This time Philadelphia tried to restrain William Hallman from playing with any team other than their National League club. Judge Thayer ruled in Hallman's favor. He wrote:

> ... A careful reading of the paragraph discloses that there is nothing whatever contained in it to bind the player to sign another contract ... the failure to designate the exact terms by which he is to be employed renders the contract incomplete, uncertain, and ineffective, and, such being the case, the fault lies with the Philadelphia Base Ball Club, as the contract was drawn up entirely in their interests....[92] [See Appendix 8: Complete transcript of Judge Thayer's decision.]

In several cases, National League lawyers pleaded the English doctrine established in *Lumley vs. Wagner*. In this case the courts had ruled that the law could not compel a specific performance under a personal service contract, but it could keep the party guilty of the contract breach from performing for someone else.[93] The court agreed with this ruling in the case of John Pickett, who had signed a contract to play with Kansas

City in the Western Association and then tried to jump to the Players' League. Judge Arnold of Philadelphia ruled that Pickett could not be forced to play, but he could be barred from playing for Philadelphia. The judge wrote, "There is no reason why base ball players should be treated differently from other persons when they evade their engagements. Managers should not be left entirely at the mercy of their players."[94]

The league's victory over Pickett did not prove to be significant. In every case in which the player had not yet signed a contract, the courts ruled in favor of the players. The judges generally agreed that the reserve rule was one-sided and made players "slaves for life."[95]

While trying to convince the courts that the reserve rule bound the players to their National League teams for the 1890 season, the NL's magnates also brought action against the Players' League's owners under the conspiracy law and tried to get exemplary damages.[96] They claimed that the rival league had tried to "persuade or entice" National League players to violate their contracts for the 1890 season. When the courts ruled in favor of the players and against the reserve rule, the National League owners dropped this suit.[97]

Having lost in the courts, the National League now believed that the baseball war would be won or lost in the sporting press, which was divided on the issue. The three major sporting publications of the period, *The Sporting Life*, *The Sporting News*, and *New York Clipper*, were generally supportive of the Players' League.[98] *The Sporting News*, which had 60,000 subscribers, had long been sympathetic to the players. Editor Al Spink reported that at the root of the trouble was "the mean, niggardly, close-fisted act of the League owners, who had treated the players in a high-handed manner and now squealed to the public."[99] The publication went on to call Ward the "Saint George of Baseball" because he had "slain the dragon of oppression."[100]

F.C. Richter, the editor of the nation's most popular sporting publication, *The Sporting Life*, was a longtime liberal and opponent of the reserve rule.[101] Shortly after the formation of the new league, the publication commended the players' leaders and attacked those who abandoned the movement by writing:

> The leaders of the Players' League have been slandered, libeled, cursed and threatened, but what is the effect? They have borne it all with patience and by their honest, manly actions have elevated themselves in the eyes of the American public. But what of the traitors? Alas! A man who has not enough courage to go ahead when he is in the right, but on the contrary plays his comrades false, is capable of committing any acts which are low, mean and contemptible.[102]

The publication attacked the National League's monopoly, writing:

> The present base ball war is a struggle of the professional players against one of the most tyrannical trusts ever organized in this country — the National League schedule was designed to destroy its rival and maintain its monopoly.

In the same issue, *The Sporting Life* wrote that it believed that the Players' League was the result of years of struggle between players and management. Players had long been blamed for all of the game's ills, while the real "culprits" had been the "unprincipled club owners."[103] When the courts ruled in favor of the players, the paper commended the decisions, explaining "that baseball law and common law will not mix."[104] *The Sporting Life* also extolled the rule changes implemented by the new league and explained that the "games of the Players' League will be the very best expositions of all that real baseball games should be."[105]

The support of the daily papers was divided. As early as 1881, *The New York Mercury* had exhorted players to "rise up in their manhood and rebel."[106] *The New York World, Pittsburgh Dispatch*, and *Chicago Tribune* were also supportive of the players' cause, while *The New York Sun, Star, Tribune*, and *Journal Herald* were supportive of the National League.[107] In many cases, papers were divided on the issue, and often some even changed their position as the season progressed.[108]

Henry Chadwick, the country's best-known baseball writer and author of *Spalding's Baseball Guide*, was generally opposed to the movement. He did write an editorial supporting the players' stand against the reserve rule in April, 1890, but after this he wrote extensively on the virtues of the National League and the ingratitude of the rebellious players. Chadwick echoed the rhetoric of the National League's leaders. He claimed the league had brought stability and integrity to the game and that even the National Agreement was necessary to stabilize the industry.[109] He criticized the players, explaining:

> The men who have been the most unreasonable in their demands ... are men who have come up from the slums, the men who were street loafers and idlers before they began playing ball ... men whose ignorance and loaferism made them a burden on the community and would fall to the same level again were baseball wiped out tomorrow.[110]

Chadwick attacked Ward and his colleagues, claiming that they had forced players to join the Brotherhood by using "terrorism." He also wrote that high salaries, undisciplined players, and demoralizing contract breaking would cause the "first-class patrons" to stay at home.[111]

*The New York Times* was generally supportive of the players' attempts to gain more professional freedom, but it had contempt for what it perceived to be player greed. The paper wrote that National League owners "understood the act of forming trusts and poolmaking precisely as practiced in other business enterprises."[112]

After Judge Thayer's decision, the paper wrote:

> Under the "reserve" clause of the League contract, players have been held by the clubs as so many slaves, to be bought and sold, without any reference to their own wishes, and he who was bold enough to insist on his right to make an engagement in defiance of the club "reserving" him, has been blacklisted and prevented from earning his living as a player anywhere.... Hereafter a player will be worth just what he can get for his services, and the club that is willing to pay for him will secure him. If the Brotherhood does nothing else than it has now accomplished in establishing in a court of law that the slave system of the League cannot be maintained against any player, it has amply justified its existence. [113]

However, several months before this, the paper ridiculed the players, writing:

> The down-trodden baseball player is about the queerest example extant of Labor crushed under the iron heel of Capital. It is quite true that a good deal of money has been made out of him, but it is also true that he has absorbed a very large proportion of it himself, and his present yearning is for all of it.[114]

These sentiments were common in newspapers across the country. Many writers viewed the National League as the game's savior and the rebellious players as ingrates. *The Kansas City Referee* spoke for many when it wrote:

> The men who risked their money, and by their personal exertions and honesty resurrected the game from the mire and elevated it to its present standard are entitled to some consideration. The players, too, whom they have brought into fame and supplied with plenty of the world's goods owe them more than they can ever repay, and for them to be in league with the plotters and wreckers of the great national game is pitiful to contemplate.[115]

Realizing that the press had much influence over the sporting public, and not satisfied that it was giving his league enough support, Spalding took the offensive. The owner attacked writers who sided with the players, claiming they were not properly informed. He contended that those in the press who opposed him were "liars" and "pawns" of the Players' League. Spalding also contended that many writers had been manipulated by the players to help attract capitalists to the new league and keep players loyal to the cause.[116]

To ensure steady media support, Spalding purchased the *Reach Base-*

*ball Guide* in 1889 and Erastus Wiman's *New York Sporting Times* early the following year. Spalding hired O.P. Caylor to be editor of the sporting paper and used the publication as the National League's mouthpiece.[117] Players were attacked regularly, once being described as "drunken knaves who would be idling on street corners but for the opportunity the National League owners opened to them."[118]

Finally, some papers attacked both leagues, cynically believing that the Players' League was not a break from the past and was just a continuation of the baseball trust. Paul Dana of the *New York Sun* wrote in a May, 1890, editorial:

> These baseball leagues are the most highly perfected trusts in this great trust country, the Players' League perhaps being rather more complete in details, though we suppose that there is really no substantial difference between them. Not only are they bound together in an offensive and defensive alliance as regards employees, but any member of the trust is to receive assistance in money from the others if through its individual weakness the circle is in danger of breaking.[119]

Ward realized the influence the press had in the baseball industry and was often available to reporters. He claimed that the press "treated the Players' League fairly," and that the reports on the new league were made in a "manly fashion."[120]

As the season progressed, most newspapers and sports publications gave equal coverage to each league. The general consensus was that the National League was losing the war, but they also reported that the schedule duplication hurt both sides.[121] Although the Players' League got much support, there were also many stories that said the players should not be given too much control or influence in their industry or the game would suffer.[122]

When the season began, both leagues worked hard to gain the public's favor. Most teams gave away thousands of tickets and scheduled numerous promotions to fill the stands. Attendance figures were regularly inflated because teams wanted to show that they were more popular than their crosstown rivals. Some National League owners, like Spalding, eager to expose the exaggerated turnstile counts of their competition, hired agents to count spectators at Players' League games and report these allegedly correct figures to the press. By midsummer the press had grown so disgusted with the attendance chicanery that many papers refused to publish figures for either league.[123]

Most unbiased observers concluded that the Players' League began the season as the more popular league. A poll taken by *The New York World* early in the season showed the Players' League favored by 1,201 to 209.[124]

Players' League opening day crowds were huge. The Pittsburgh team drew 7,000 fans, while its National League rival attracted only 100 in the strong union town. Over 12,000 New Yorkers showed up to watch the home nine play Philadelphia, and several other cities had crowds of over 8,000. After Ward's Brooklyn team beat Boston 3–2 in the season's opener before more than 10,000 fans[125], the captain commented:

> Never in my life have I seen such a reception as was accorded the two clubs in this city yesterday. The streets lined with people, the windows of the large structures, to their very tops, crowded with lookers-on, all anxious to have a peep at the boys, and all waving their hands, caps and handkerchiefs to us in a friendly spirit.[126]

Although both the National League and Players' League had large opening day crowds, in most cases the Players' League teams outdrew National League teams in their respective cities. *The Sporting Life* reported:

> John Montgomery Ward has demonstrated pretty clearly that Byrne's grip on Brooklyn is not what we have all been led to believe after reading Chadwick and Donnelly for the last few months. Everybody expected the intrepid Brotherhood chieftain would have an awful hard time of it over there, but he is drawing well and the patronage is steadily increasing. I honestly expect to see him outdraw the League two to one before September.[127]

As the season progressed, the sporting press covered the battle of the turnstiles almost as closely as it did the games. In mid-May *The Sporting Life* reported that the average Players' League crowd was 3,006 while the National League attracted only 1,564 fans to each contest, down from a 3,039 fan average for all of 1889. The paper estimated that 1,800 spectators per game were needed just for the league to break even, so most teams were already losing money.[128]

By early June, it was almost impossible to get accurate attendance figures, or to determine how many of the people in the stands had actually paid to get in. However, most neutral observers agreed that the Players' League games were better attended than the National League's and that crowds were getting smaller in both leagues. The baseball public had become "disgusted."[129]

By mid-June, *The Sporting Life* reported that the National League's per- game attendance had fallen to 1,488 compared to 2,338 for its rival.[130] However, by August the National League's attendance had stabilized while the fan support for Players' Leagues' continued to dwindle. During the final two months of the season, the new league outdrew its competitor by an estimated 1,638 to 1,526 fans per game, and just one Players' League game in six generated enough revenue to meet expenses.[131] Even the American Association, which did not directly compete with either League's teams, saw a dramatic drop in its attendance, and minor league patronage also declined.[132]

What was clear by midsummer was that the popularity that professional baseball had enjoyed in the 1880s was on the decline and that the public was disgusted with the war. Spalding announced that baseball was "dying out," and he estimated that the combined attendance of the two leagues was less than the National League's of 1889. [133]

Both sides believed that only one league would survive. Spalding realized that the Players' League had higher expenses due to its salaries and stadium costs and consequently could be brought to its knees if its revenues were reduced enough. He thus sought new means to reduce support for his rival.

Like Ward, Spalding viewed the media as an important element in determining which side fans would support. In an attempt to reduce the support given to the new league, the magnate threatened to withhold ads for his sporting goods business in papers that wrote positively of the Players' League.[134] It is difficult to determine how effective these threats were, but there is no doubt that Spalding Sporting Goods and the magnate's numerous other enterprises spent huge sums on advertising, and that most daily and sporting papers would be eager to keep receiving this ad revenue.

The National League also exerted pressure on the business community to support their cause. Generally, National League owners were more entrenched in their cities' economies and had long spent large sums of money at local businesses. There is evidence that some of the league's middle-class constituency was pressured to support it in return for its patronage.[135]

When the Players' League was formed, most observers believed that the National League would not allow its players to return without being punished. Spalding cleverly took the opposite course. In August, the National League announced that all of the "prodigal lambs could return to the fold" without being punished.[136] The Players' League responded by threatening to lure the National League's best players to their league for the 1891 season. Spalding worked behind the scenes to make sure that the opposite happened. Reports were rampant that he had bribed rival players to convince their comrades to return to the National League. Although their is no proof that any Players' League players were on Spalding's payroll, many players were convinced that several stars, including Buck Ewing, were spies for Spalding and out to undermine the movement. Ewing had a close relationship with his former owner, John B. Day, and many believed that he was still loyal to him. Ewing, anxious to maintain the impression of solidarity, said "I'll stick to the Brotherhood as long as it sticks to me." However, doubts persisted when he added "but this three-year contract is so easy to break it will be hard for the Brotherhood to stop me from leaving."[137] Generally, though, Brotherhood players remained loyal during the 1890 season.

There were few problems between players on rival teams. National League president Young encouraged league managers to avoid staying at hotels used by Players' League teams.[138] When the two Brooklyn teams did stay in the same hotel, *The Sporting News* commented, "neither forgot for an instant that he was a gentleman and that they were regarded largely as business rivals."[139]

The National League tried to portray the Players' League competition as an outlaw league whose players were out of control both on and off the field. The league reported that players were often out late drinking and were poorly disciplined when playing.[140] There were occasions when losing Players' League teams pulled their players off the field over a disagreement, but this also happened in the National League.[141]

The Players' League presented a different picture of its league. Ned Hanlon said of the players' behavior, "In my connection with baseball for thirteen years, I have never seen less drinking and a greater determination to avoid anything in act or speech which would injure the organization."[142]

*The Sporting Life* reported that Brotherhood players were remarkably well behaved and explained that this was because they knew that the "eyes of their countrymen were on them."[143] *The Brooklyn Citizen* said of Ward and his fellow players, "Ward has been a captain at all times. The players have been guided by his orders and the greatest friendship exists between all men. Everyone on the team is a gentleman both in appearance and manners." The publication also commented that the league's strict grooming policies made the players appear "professional" and that the National League was in "deplorable condition."[144]

Both the Brotherhood and the Players' League were supported by organized labor. In December of 1889, the A.F.L. endorsed the Players' League and condemned the "iron-clad contracts of baseball." Samuel Gompers ordered the union's committee on boycotts to recommend to members that they attend only Players' League games, and the leader even met with the Players' League's leaders to discuss strategy.[145]

In a January, 1890, *Sporting Life* interview, Gompers explained:

> Laboring men all over the country are in sympathy with the players in this fight.... These gentlemen represent over six hundred thousand

skilled working men in this country, who want to see the players succeed in freeing themselves from League slavery.[146]

That same month, Gompers; A.F.L. vice president P.J. McGuire; vice
president of the Brotherhood of Carpenters and Joiners W.J. Shields; and
James Day, the business agent of Union Number Eight of the Brotherhood
of Carpenters and Joiners all attended a directors meeting of the Philadelphia Players' League Club and extended their support.[147]

At the 1890 Boston A.F.L. convention, resolutions supporting the Players were passed. Similar resolutions were passed by the Amalgamated Association of Iron and Steel Workers, the Brotherhood of Locomotive Firemen,
the Clothing Cutters Assembly of the Knights of Labor, the Central Trades
Council of Western Pennsylvania, the Benevolent Protective Order of Elks,
and the Casters' Protective Union of Boston.[148] The Clothing Cutters
Assembly #2583 of Jersey City endorsed the league and imposed a fine on
members who "attended non-union picnics, parks or baseball grounds."[149]

A Midwestern Knights of Labor leader supported the Players' cause,
explaining:

> The latest subject of discussion among organized laboring men is the
> baseball war now on. It may appear a little singular to outsiders, but a
> peculiar interest is being manifested in the trade union element favor-
> ing this Baseball Brotherhood Movement. The way we look at this
> matter in its present shape is that the Brotherhood is a legitimate
> organization of skilled workmen.... The men are hired on salaries, and
> outside of the oppressive restrictions under which they are placed, they
> are to be as fully recognized as are the skilled workmen of the printing
> craft, the moulder or the carpenter.[150]

Even Chadwick realized the appeal the new league held to organized
labor. He wrote:

> The Brotherhood has added a sympathetic feeling among the labor
> organizations in favor of the striking players, which, though having no
> basis of truth for its creation, nevertheless had its weight. The trade
> unions, as a class, seldom allow judgment or reason to clash with their
> sympathies, and hence we find men who strike against great monopo-
> lies for an increase to enable them to live, joining hands with a class
> who in regard to primary matters, are capitalists themselves in com-
> parison with the regular wage workers.[151]

The National League's Pittsburgh franchise contracted a Knights of
Labor band to play on opening day. However, prior to their performance,
the club was informed by the Musical Protection union that a boycott was
being imposed by the A.F.L., and they could no longer play.

Unions were not the only organizations that supported the movement.
The Massachusetts House of Representatives was canvassed, and its mem-

bers supported the new league over its rival 100 to six. Finally, in a show of sympathy, Yale and Princeton moved their annual baseball game to Philadelphia's Brotherhood Park rather than play on the National League ground.[152]

The players used the rhetoric of labor to describe their cause. A sign on the fence of the Cleveland Players' League park stated "we are the people," and players often referred to each other as "working men" or "comrade." Players who jumped back to the National League were called "scabs" and "deserters."[153] Ward said of these men:

> I do not believe the public has lost all appreciation of honor and manhood and when the next season comes, it will show this fact plainly. A man who violates the most solemn obligation, repudiates his contract and trades upon the good faith of his own comrades is a creature unfit for association with decent men and cannot be trusted to play honest ball.[154]

Many owners were critical of the players for identifying themselves as laborers. Spalding commented:

> The absurdity of classifying professional baseball players earning from three to five thousand dollars for a season ... as overworked and underfed factory operatives of the present day, is one of the most glaring fallacies of the year.[155]

The Players' League foolishly squandered its union support. Players developed a reputation for being dandies. Newspaper accounts often talked of their fur-lined overcoats, silk hats, and expensive cigars—trappings that alienated them from many workers. Its owners craved respectability and middle-class patronage and believed that to attain these, the League would have to remain aloof from labor. Worse, despite their rhetoric, most players never wanted to view themselves as laborers. The majority opposed Sunday ball and a 25-cent admission charge because they equated these with the working class.[156]

These policies hurt the league's relationship with labor. Without Sunday games, and with ticket prices set at 50 cents, most workers could not attend games. Workers realized that this was done to gain the support of society's upper classes. This unwillingness to cater to organized labor was another reason why the league's attendance fell as the season progressed.

The A.F.L. and Knights of Labor both asked Ward to affiliate with them, and both were turned down.[157] In April, 1890, work was being completed on Chicago's Brotherhood Park with union laborers. When the carpenter's union called a strike in the city, the team, desperate to finish the facility in time for the season, employed non-union labor to complete the park. Fights erupted between the strikers and workers, and union support for the team was reduced.[158] Ironically, the league that was branded "socialist" by its rivals helped to destroy itself by being unwilling to identify with the group that it should have felt the most akin to: American labor.[159]

Financial problems mounted for the new league as the season progressed. Despite the fact that it was more popular than its rival, the Pittsburgh franchise was sustaining huge losses and sometimes drew crowds of as low as 130 fans. By May 7, the team owed $8,000 rent, was $65,000 in debt, and had not paid its players in two weeks. The team wanted to stop operations then, but was kept in business when other owners helped to pay its expenses.[160]

That same month the club dropped its ticket price to 25 cents. Many teams protested this, claiming the club did not have the right to do this, but the rate was never changed.[161] The league had hoped to maintain a degree of stability and profitability by dividing receipts evenly, but this was not the case. In July, the Pittsburgh club returned from an Eastern road trip and lamented the fact that they had received only 60 dollars per game, which was hardly enough to cover travel expenses.[162] In spite of these paltry sums, the team changed all of its home games to road contests shortly after this, hoping to increase revenues.[163]

Cleveland and Buffalo also failed to draw well. In July the league decided to try to bolster the Buffalo Club by transferring two pitchers, an infielder, and an outfielder to it from other teams. This may have shown the cooperative nature of the league, but it did little to help the franchise. As midsummer approached, only Boston and Philadelphia were making money, although the league acknowledged that only Buffalo, Cleveland, and Pittsburgh were in the red. Quietly, many of the league's backers were losing their resolve.[164]

The National League also had serious problems. The Pittsburgh franchise came to the brink of bankruptcy. The team, which was probably the worst in either league, often failed to draw 300 people to its games even when it lowered its ticket price to 25 cents to compete with its rival.[165] By July the team owed $1,400 for park rent, $500 in hotel bills, and $1,200 for equipment and newspaper advertising, as well as numerous undisclosed debts.[166] Its situation got so bad that a landlord's warrant of $3,000 was placed in its Recreation Park.[167] The team made it through the 1890 season without being bailed out, but it is doubtful it could have survived the 1891 season with the Players' League still intact.

Throughout the season there were numerous rumors that teams were folding or merging. On August 18, *The New York Times* reported that the Philadelphia Athletics of the American Association and the Philadelphia team of the Players' League were merging. The same day, the paper reported that St. Louis and Louisville of the American Association were going to join the Players' League. The paper also reported that it was likely that the Association would fold, and the Players' League and National League would continue to compete. The paper later reported that the Players' League would likely emerge as the dominant league in the nation.[168]

By July, New York Giants owner John B. Day was almost broke, and a rumor spread that he was going to sell out to the Players' League.[169] To save the franchise, Spalding, John Brush, F.A. Abel (a noted gambler), and Al Reach of Philadelphia purchased more than $60,000 of the team's stock and kept the team solvent.[170] Ward's Brooklyn team was rumored to be moving to Washington, and the shortstop had to issue a statement saying, "The Brotherhood is here to stay." In October the baseball world was shocked when Aaron Stein's National League Cincinnati team was purchased by the Players' League for $40,000. The Players' League planned to combine the best players from the Cincinnati team with those from Buffalo to make one viable franchise.[171] Many thought that the loss of Cincinnati was the beginning of the end for the National League, and had the Giants been allowed to fold, it may have been. Buck Ewing reflected many of the players' sentiments when he explained "with Cincinnati out, the National League cannot last long."[172]

The season continued, with both sides losing huge amounts of money. Spalding said, "Not in the twenty years' history of professional club organizations was there recorded such an exceptional season of financial disaster and general demoralization as characterized 1890. Scarcely a club which entered the lists, either in the major or minor league arena, paid its expenses."[173] Exact data is not available, but the best sources estimate that the Players' League lost at least $400,000, $215,000 of which was for parks, the National League between $200,000 and $300,000, and the American Association $100,000 during the campaign.[174]

Bad weather caused many fans to stay away, and even a fine pennant race between Boston and Brooklyn in the Players' League did not generate much fan interest. (Boston won the race by six and a half games.) Both leagues' bottom lines were hurt when the National League champs refused to meet the Boston squad in a "World Series." The Association's Louisville team and the National League's Brooklyn nine did meet in a postseason series. However, bad weather and low attendance caused the series to be canceled with the series tied at three wins and one tie per team. Most experts agreed that the Players' League Boston team was the best in the nation.[175]

It is doubtful if even a World Series would have saved the 1890 season. To a large extent the conflict had made the American sporting public apathetic toward their national game. *The New York Times* wrote of this apathy:

> It is not merely that the baseball public has divided its interest between the two leagues. In such an affair, a division of interest is a distinction of interest.... The baseball public of 1889 no longer exists.... The "baseball cranks" have disappeared and the baseball public is following them. If the absurd contest between two leagues playing in the same places on the same days continues for another season, the baseball public will be as extinct as the dodo....[176]

The paper went on to say what many had believed for some time. There was one major league too many in the country, and it was inevitable that one would fold or that two would merge. The players had made a just stand, had won in court and proved their manhood, and it was now time to compromise. Without a change in 1891, the "goose that lays the golden eggs" would be destroyed.[177]

As Spalding had predicted, the war would be won by the league that avoided bankruptcy. The magnate explained in mid-May, "It will be a question of bankrolls, and I think we are pretty well-heeled.... The game is dead and the Players' League has killed it. It is not dead, however, for all time. In two years, there will be a keener interest in the sport than ever, but the National League will have the field to itself."[178] Even with the players in revolt and the courts solidly against the reserve rule, Spalding still believed that only with monopoly and complete owner control could the game regain its former luster.

As the season's end approached, *The New York Times* echoed the sentiments of many fans when it wrote:

> It is a potent fact that the season which is now closing has been the most disastrous campaign financially that has ever been known in the history of the national game. Thousands of dollars have been swept away through the war which has ravaged from the beginning to the end of the season, with the outlook no brighter. Neither the National League or the Players' League shows the slightest inclination to give up the fight.... Their obstinacy or persistency was destroying public interest in the greatest of outdoor sports as well as sinking money into a bottomless pit.... The only men benefited by the war were the players as it gave double the usual number employment....[179]

Clearly the 1890 season was a disaster for everyone but the players. They should have realized their fate by observing the changing relationship between the warring capitalists. As the losses mounted and the failure of at least one league became inevitable, the owners became less hostile to each other. Soon the players would understand why. The owners in both leagues were meeting to reach some kind of compromise that would lead to consolidation. However, contrary to the spirit and rules of the new league, its players would not be consulted in any of these proceedings.[180]

The Players' League must be viewed from both the players and owners' perspective. The players revolted because they perceived their National League bosses to be abusing their growing power and reducing the players' wages and freedom. Also, many of these abuses were perceived to be an affront to the players' manliness and honor. This was clearly explained in the league's manifesto, which stated that the National League was out to infringe upon the players' "individual and natural rights." The players saw the fight as both economic and idealistic. They hoped to create an industry where control and profits could be shared, which they believed would lead to prosperity for all.

The players, including Ward, never understood their owners. This was partly because the owners sent ambiguous messages to the players from the league's inception. Ultimately, the capitalists, although not allied with Spalding, were more concerned with profits than justice. This was made clear when owners who began the season saying, "We're with the players out of sympathy for them …" remarked, "We are not in it for sympathy, we're in it for the dust …" at the season's end.[181] Had the owners made this clear from the beginning, it is possible that the league could have defeated its rival.

Ward, the stubborn idealist, convinced the league to put a team in Buffalo and not to change the schedule when the National League copied it. The Players' League magnates should have insisted that such policies were unacceptable and would have to be changed. They should have explained to Ward that they had made large investments in parks, equipment, and players, and that they expected their teams to turn a profit.

The owners should also have anticipated losses for the first year. Clubs should have been required to have more than $20,000 operating capital when the season began, and they should have realized that the baseball rebellion was to be a conflict of attrition and would not result in quick victory. Finally, both players and owners should have seen beyond Spalding's coveted middle-class constituency and sought out the working class by playing Sunday games, selling beer in the parks, and pricing at least some tickets at 25 cents at each park.

Such speculation might be irrelevant. It is possible that the Players' League owners never cared about the long-term success of their league. Perhaps they simply wanted to be involved in the baseball industry and were not concerned with which league they were a part of or how that league was structured. We will never know the owners' ultimate goals, but clearly losing the baseball war did not end the involvement of Players' League owners in the baseball business.

# 9

# Retreat and Defeat: Consolidation

By the end of the 1890 season, it was obvious to the baseball public, players, and owners that dramatic changes would have to be implemented for the 1891 season. As early as July, 1890, papers published unconfirmed reports of consolidation plans in the works.[1] New rumors surfaced almost daily. In August, the *Sporting Life* reported that the Pittsburgh National League and Players' League clubs were about to merge.[2] A month later *The New York Times* reported that Players' League stars Mike Kelly, Buck Ewing, and Jimmy Ryan had signed 1891 contracts with National League teams. The paper also reported that the Players' League would soon merge with the American Association, and this new league and the National League would "work in harmony as they had in the past."[3] At about the same time, the Tri-State League threatened to leave the National Agreement to enter an agreement with the Players' League.[4] Finally in August, *The New York Times* reported that a secret compromise had been reached among the three major leagues. The article claimed that the three leagues would drop their weakest teams and combine into two eight-team leagues. This "conspiracy" report was premature and not accurate, but it was indicative of what was actually going on behind the scenes.[5]

By midseason 1890, there was serious grumbling among Players' League owners. Most had bought into the league to make money, and almost all were losing it. Many owners resented the power of the players and the fact that those who performed poorly could not be released in midseason. They also did not like the fact that players received their salaries no matter how much money a team lost.[6] Owners began to question the concept of a Players' League, and some began to believe that without the controls that the National League had implemented, profits could not be made.

While the new owners questioned the structure of their organization, the National League secretly fought to stay alive. Contrary to what their adversaries believed, many teams in the old league were near bankruptcy and feared that they could not continue in 1891. Although it would not be known until long after consolidation, the National League probably could not have competed for another season against the Players' League.[7]

As early as June, disputes had arisen between Players' League owners. Time and again, Johnson had acted as a mediator and prevented these conflicts from escalating.[8] The great weakness of the Players' League was that when losses mounted, the new league's owners tried to save only themselves, showing little concern for the welfare of the league. The National League, even as many of its teams approached bankruptcy, never lost sight of its goal: the destruction of the Players' League and the return of the old order.[9] As the end of the 1890 season approached, the National League owners began to send friendly signals to their former players. *The New York Times* reported that "not before this season has there been so friendly a feeling between the National League and its deserting players." The Players' League responded with enthusiastic talk about the 1891 season, branded players who signed contracts with National League teams "scabs," and threw them out of the union. The conciliatory rhetoric of the National League worked. It convinced many players that the National League owners had become more respectful of them, and many believed that even if the Players' League failed, they could return to their former league and be treated with dignity.[10]

Allan W. Thurman, the son of an Ohio senator and a minority owner of the Columbus American Association team, initiated the consolidation process.[11] Although not a major figure in the baseball industry, Thurman was friendly with owners in all three leagues and convinced them that as gentlemen and businessmen they should put aside their pride and meet. Spalding, who was still viewed by most National League owners as their leader, had never seen compromise as an option. However, he still agreed to a meeting.[12]

When the players learned of the peace talks, they did not oppose them. Most realized that neither league could withstand another money-losing year like 1890. Ward echoed the views of many players when he told the press:

> I am for peace first, last, and all the time, and stand prepared to do all in my power to bring about that result. It is evident to everybody that war is a losing game, and I guess baseball men, League, Brotherhood, and everybody else, will testify to that statement. Thousands of dollars have been thrown away and it is about time that we cried halt. I told

Mr. Johnson of the Cleveland Club today that it was his duty to look after the interests of the financial men of our organization and at the same time protect the interests of the players who refused League gold and stood by him. We have the most implicit confidence in anything that Mr. Johnson says or does, and we will keep any agreement he sees fit to make.[13]

Ward even proposed creating a new National Agreement that would reduce interleague raiding, create uniform playing rules, and initiate potentially profitable postseason play. He explained that the reserve rule could be replaced by multi-year contracts in order to help maintain the stability that owners desired. All of his proposals were ignored.

On October 10, 1890, National League owners met in New York to hear the peace plan devised by Thurman. Although several plans were reported, it is generally accepted that he proposed that the three leagues be merged into two: a 50-cent league with teams in Boston, Brooklyn, Chicago, Cleveland, New York, Pittsburgh, Cincinnati and Philadelphia and a 25-cent league with teams in Baltimore, Boston, Chicago, Columbus, Philadelphia, St. Louis, Louisville and Washington.[14] In cities where two teams remained, neither the Players' League nor National League team would be required to fold. But in cities where the number of teams was reduced from two to one, the Players' League and National League teams would be consolidated.[15]

The following day representatives from the three leagues secretly met to discuss consolidation. The National League sent Spalding, John B. Day, and Charles Byrne, the Players' League Johnson, Talcott, and Goodman, and the American Association Chris Von der Ahe, Harry Vonderhorst, and Allen Thurman. Noticeably missing were any players.[16] The owners tentatively agreed to Thurman's realignment and consolidation plan, although they proposed to divide the teams up differently from the way he suggested.

One sticking point was what the new league would be called. Players' League owners agreed that their name would have to go, but they did not want one of the new leagues to be called the National. Johnson said, "The Players' League is perfectly willing to make just as many concessions as the National League, but one thing is certain, the leading league cannot be known by the name of either one of the present two.... The Players' League will never accede to a compromise which allows the leading organization to be called the National League." The senior league was reluctant to change its name, but Spalding assured his fellow owners that a compromise could be worked out.[17]

The tone of the meeting was interesting and ultimately helped the

National League to win its victory. Shortly after it started, the committee representing the Players' League apologized to their counterparts for "the condition of affairs" and claimed that they were "grieved" that the Brotherhood players had succeeded in "blocking" things so effectively. Talcott asked what could be done to keep the consolidation process working, and he was told by the National League's representatives, "Don't let the players trample and run roughshod over you." They went on to say that the only way a settlement could be reached was if the players were not involved in the consolidation process.[18] Although Johnson would fight to allow the players to be involved, his fellow capitalists would succeed in keeping them out.

Leaders of all three leagues realized that financial losses had been sustained by everyone in 1890. However, none of the magnates could be sure how severely their rivals had been injured or how willing or able they were to incur future losses. There is some disagreement about who opened their books first. *The Sporting Life* reported the following scenario, and although events may not have unfolded exactly this way, there can be no doubt about the final results of the meeting. After agreeing that changes would have to be made for the 1891 season, Spalding casually inquired about the financial health of the Players' League. He was shocked when its representative opened their books and revealed the extent of their losses. Spalding realized that the Players' League owners were weak, disheartened, and ready to bargain. He maintained his position of strength by cleverly avoiding opening his books, which would have revealed that his league was in even worse financial shape.[19]

Ward and his colleagues did not fear consolidation, because they believed that they would play a direct role in the process. Their League Constitution gave players substantial say in all business decisions, and up to this point they had been treated as the owners' equals. There were also many players who held substantial amounts of team stock. Ward had $3,800 invested in the Brooklyn team, players held $9,500 of New York club stock, and reportedly several teams were as much as 40 percent player-owned.[20]

The players proved to be naïve in two ways. First, they believed that they would be equals in the consolidation process. Secondly, they trusted their owners, believing that they would look out for their interests. Early in the negotiations, when it was not yet clear that the players would be excluded, the Brotherhood leadership notified their owners: "In view of the many rumors current, the members of the Brotherhood of Baseball Players feel it due to you and themselves to extend to you the assurance of their entire confidence in your ability to safely conduct the affairs of the Players' League."[21]

Within the Players' League there was a great deal of dissension. Some owners wanted to sell their teams and be done with baseball, and others wanted to merge with National League and/or American Association teams. Owners also differed on the role that they believed that players should play in the negotiations. Finally, after being pressured by Johnson, the Players' League added Ward, Hanlon, and Arthur Irwin to its negotiations committee, which was to meet with representatives of the other two leagues on October 23.[22]

Spalding and his associates were adamantly opposed to players being involved in the negotiations. The White Stockings owner claimed that only "money men" should meet, and that the addition of players was "an insult to himself and other members of the committee."[23]

On October 23, the committees met at the Fifth Avenue Hotel in New York. When the owners of teams in the Players' League and three player representatives entered the conference room, Spalding refused to begin the proceedings until the players left. The players responded by reminding Spalding that the National Agreement clubs had six representatives and that unless the players were allowed to attend, the Players' League would have only three.[24] Ward became emotional and exclaimed, "Do these gentlemen wish to go on record as saying that the occupation of a ballplayer bars him from business association with respectable men?"[25] Ward reminded Spalding that he too had been a player and said, "Are you willing to place such a stamp of infamy upon the profession of which you were for years a member and to which you owe your start in life?"[26]

The Players' League committee withdrew from the meeting, conferred, and then the three owners returned. They fought for the right of their players to take part in the process, but then foolishly allowed the issue to be put to a vote. The owners voted six to three against allowing the players to participate. Johnson was upset that his colleagues would allow the players to be shut out of the process, but there was little that he could do.[27]

Spalding believed that it was not enough just to keep the players out of the negotiations. For complete victory he would have to drive a wedge between the Players' League owners and players. The more they mistrusted each other and the more each blamed the other for its problems, the more likely the National League could achieve victory.[28]

On October 24, the representatives from the three leagues met in a secret conference. Afterwards, the details of the meeting were leaked to the press, probably by Spalding, and it was reported that the owners of teams in the Players' League apologized for allowing their players to attend the meeting on the previous day. Although the owners denied the story, the result was unavoidable: mistrust between the owners of teams in the Players' League and league's players along with the perception that the league's owners blamed the players for the huge losses of 1890.[29]

By early November, the owners of the Players' League were divided into two camps: one that wanted consolidation at all costs, and another (that included the Philadelphia, Boston, and Chicago franchises) that believed that the league might not have to be terminated. Unable to reach a compromise agreement, the teams began to act independently, each trying to reach the best deal for itself, with no overall league strategy.[30] When it was learned that New York and Brooklyn were about to officially leave the Players' League, the anti-consolidation faction sued to prevent their withdrawal. The courts ruled that the ten-year league agreement was not binding and that teams could leave the league at will.[31] The Players' League then tried to raise enough capital to purchase the teams, but this proved impossible. Consolidation was inevitable.[32]

On November 12, most of the Players' League owners met at the Monongahela House in Pittsburgh. At the meeting, the New York and Brooklyn clubs announced their consolidation with corresponding National League teams.[33] A day later the two Pittsburgh clubs secretly merged. The owners of the city's National and Players' League franchises each controlled one half of the stock in the new team and four of the seven team directors were from the Players' League team.[34] After the loss of these three teams, the other Players' League owners scrambled to make the best deal possible. Chicago sold out to Spalding for $10,000 cash, $15,000 worth of stock in the National League team, and complimentary season passes.[35]

Despite the loss of the four clubs, the remaining owners reassured the players that the Players' League was not dead. A memo was sent to the players saying, "You need have no fear for the success of the organization ... we can assure you that the organization as a whole will remain steadfast and that it will be preserved as such for the coming season ... relying on the loyal players to fill their part, we have confidence in the generous support of the public as in the past."[36]

Up to this point, consolidation had been a relatively simple process because it had only required owners in the same cities to merge their teams. However, Spalding and other league leaders now hoped to move some of the Players' League franchises into the American Association to strengthen this league. To prepare for this, the American Association bought out its Syracuse, Rochester, and Toledo franchises with the intention of replacing them with franchises in more lucrative cities.[37]

Spalding proposed that the Philadelphia Players' League team be admitted into the American Association to replace that league's bankrupt and recently expelled Philadelphia franchise. Philadelphia was the only city to have three major league teams in 1890, and this proved to be disastrous for its American Association franchise. Spalding convinced his fellow National League magnates to allow the Players' League Boston franchise to enter the American Association in spite of the fact that the National League also had a team in this city. Before they allowed this to happen, though, Boston's PL owners had to agree to charge 50 cents admission, return all of its former National League players, and refrain from using the name Boston.[38] Soon after Boston was accepted, Philadelphia was also allowed to join the American Association.

Shortly after the loss of these two teams, the Players' League was officially terminated. All of the previously reserved players were returned to the teams that had held rights to them in 1889. Those reserved players who were not wanted by their old teams were put in the hands of a newly formed national board to be distributed among the weaker NL and Association teams.[39]

The Buffalo and Cleveland Players' League franchises died as a result of consolidation. Buffalo was an anomaly from the beginning. Had it not been for Ward's honor and sense of loyalty to fellow players, White and Rowe, the franchise probably never would have existed. It lacked capital, fan support, and a superior playing facility, and was therefore not attractive to the two remaining major leagues. It is also not surprising that the only Players' League team that was almost exclusively owned by players was not absorbed, and its owners found themselves out of the baseball business.

Johnson's fate was worse. Not only did he own the Cleveland team, but he had put up much of the capital to purchase the National League's near-bankrupt Cincinnati franchise late in the 1890 season. The National League never recognized the sale of the Cincinnati club to Johnson, despite the fact that he paid a large sum for the team. Instead, John Brush, the man who proposed the infamous classification plan, wound up as the team's owner. Cincinnati remained in the National League in 1891.[40] By the time Johnson realized that his cause was doomed, it was too late to sell his Cleveland team. He initially tried to get $45,000 for his club, and the National League made a counteroffer of $25,000. Johnson refused to accept this, claiming that the team had already lost $46,000. The National League responded to this rejection by ignoring him. His franchise folded without Johnson receiving anything for it.[41]

The Players' League may have been dead, but its owners and parks lived on in the National League and American Association. The Boston and Philadelphia teams that were now in the American Association continued to play in their Players' League parks, and Philadelphia's Baker Bowl continued to be one of the best parks in the country until the turn of the century. The National League's newly merged Brooklyn and New York clubs continued to use the superior parks of their defeated rivals, and in 1891, Spalding purchased the larger and better equipped Chicago Players' League Park for his White Stockings to play in.

The American Association's Philadelphia Athletics were now owned by the Wagner brothers, who had previously owned that city's Players' League team. Players' League backers also had stock in the Brooklyn, Boston, Chicago, Pittsburgh, and New York clubs in 1891, although it is impossible to know what percentage of a team's stock was controlled by these capitalists.[42]

Spalding's divide-and-conquer strategy had worked brilliantly. Despite having only six viable franchises at the end of the 1890 season, and by most accounts being in worse financial shape than the Players' League, the National League not only survived the crisis of 1890, it also destroyed its chief rival, absorbed its best facilities and ownership, and emerged stronger than any league in America. *The Chicago Times* reported that the Players' League had "meekly surrendered to the force of arms of A.G. Spalding."[43] Spalding gloated that "The Players' League is deader than the proverbial doornail...,"[44]

By late November, most of the players, including Ward, realized that the Players' League was dead. A "wake" was held at Nick Engles's saloon in New York, and on November 22, secretary Brunell and the league officers in Chicago were evicted from their office for non-payment of rent.[45]

One of the Brotherhood's last official acts was to get assurances from the National League that its members would be treated fairly and that all would be allowed back into the league. Even at this point, many players were naive enough to believe that they were free to sign with the National League or American Association team of their choice.[46]

The National League owners did not accept their victory graciously. They reported that their victory was a triumph for fans, players, and owners because only with the strict controls and regulations of the old order could the game thrive. One owner told the *Sporting Life*:

> The National League and National Agreement are the only salvation of professional baseball. The Brotherhood movement was conceived in treachery, born in mendacity, and has been fostered in credulity ... The cooperative scheme, Ward's pet hobby, which was hailed as the means of emancipation of the down-trodden ball player, has been abandoned, and the player has in reality simply made a change of masters.[47]

The 1891 *Spalding Guide* wrote:

> The only possible system which will yield financial success … is that of having employees in the entire control of the club, leaving the players in the position of paid employees only. Under no other system can the requisite discipline be enforced. The capitalists of the Players' League realized this fact at great financial cost in 1890 and since then the best of them have combined with the National League.[48]

Spalding blamed all of the turmoil of the previous year on "overpaid star players."[49] The Players' League magnates, he claimed "allowed the players to run things to too great an extent. A man may be able to throw curves but know nothing about business."[50]

His league destroyed, Johnson made plans for a new one and sent all of his players a letter explaining the scheme. He admitted that salaries would be cut, but he warned that if the National League regained its monopoly, the players' position would get worse. The National League and many newspapers branded him "wrecker Johnson" and called him an "anarchist" because of his anti-monopoly stance. Even the players lost faith in him, and most ignored his warnings about what would happen after consolidation occurred.[51]

Why did the Players' League fail? It had begun the 1890 season with the best players, the sympathy of organized labor and the sporting public, a more lively brand of ball, new parks, well capitalized ownership, and legal victories. What prevented it from emerging as the dominant league in the nation?

When the season began, the Players' League enjoyed great support from organized labor. Most of this support was squandered, and by the end of the season, organized labor was ambivalent about the conflict. Like its National League counterpart, the Players' League was obsessed with being respected by the middle class, and it did not realize that the time had come to expand the baseball market to include members of the working class. It steadfastly opposed Sunday games and beer sales in the parks and fought to keep teams from lowering ticket prices. This kept workers away and helped to alienate them. It is doubtful that there were enough middle-class fans in most cities to support two teams, so the only hope of success was to destroy their rival. The owners lacked the will to do this, and so failure was inevitable.

Some parks were constructed with non-union labor.[52] In Pittsburgh visiting clubs were transported on the non-union Pittsburgh Transfer Company which was owned by the National League owner William Nimick, rather than on the Excelsior Line, which employed union labor but which was more expensive. By the end of the season, many of the city's union drivers were calling for a Players' League boycott.[53]

Early in the season, Gompers had offered the Brotherhood membership in the A.F.L., but was turned down. This was done despite Philadelphia stockholder J.M. Vanderslice's comment that the A.F.L. "represents over 600,000 skilled workmen ... who want to see the players succeed in freeing themselves from League slavery."[54] Many owners and players had used the rhetoric of class struggle to romanticize the movement, but by summer, this had lost all of its validity, and Gompers would eventually comment that it was a fight of "capital versus capital."[55]

The rhetoric of the National League owners and the shortsightedness of the new league's owners and players both helped to reduce the potential fan base. National League owners red-baited and called the scheme anarchistic and socialistic, and this helped to keep middle-class patrons away. Labor, which should have been driven to the Players' League by such attacks, was alienated and eventually became apathetic.

Until its demise, Ward continued to be the backbone of his league's players. He was a star on the diamond, the players' off-the-field-leader, and the primary intermediary between his league's owners and players. All of these responsibilities put enormous pressure on the shortstop. In addition, Ward's personal life was in disarray. In January, 1890, Helen Dauvray and Ward separated. This was made legal and public in April just as the season was getting under way, and it was reported in both the sporting and theatrical press. Although Ward's unfaithfulness and Helen's desire to return to the stage made this separation inevitable, it did not make it easier on him.[56] Ward never let his feelings be known, but the separation and impending divorce must have distracted such a proud and private man. Newspapers reported that he was "cranky" and "jumpy," although he never admitted that his personal problems were a factor in the league's demise.[57] Without one of their own strong enough to stand up to Spalding and the other owners, the players were at a severe disadvantage.

Even if Ward were able to completely focus on the Players' League, it probably still would have failed. Most of the players involved did not see the conflict in terms of class struggle. To them the new league was a chance to gain more control, freedom, and money, but not worker ownership of their industry. Like many workers of this era, they were craft unionists out for concrete gains and not a revolutionary change in the system. This was evident during the conciliation meetings when they sheepishly allowed themselves to be denied access, even though it was their legal right. Obviously, these players did not believe that as workers they had as much right to representation as the owners.[58] True visionaries would have seen the potential of a baseball world without the National League and the immense possibilities of a Players' League unopposed and structured to divide profits and power with players. The genius of Ward was that he saw this potential, but the genius of Spalding was that he saw his rivals for what they were and realized that with sufficient losses they would run to capital rather than to the new order that Ward dreamed of creating.

Spalding was the perfect general to lead his league through this crisis. He thoroughly believed in the necessity of monopoly to keep baseball alive and was therefore adamant about the destruction of his rival. Immediate losses were acceptable in order to put the game back on its proper footing. Spalding realized that most players were primarily driven by self-interest and that the owners of the Players' League lacked the staying power of those in the National League. He exploited this weakness by matching his rivals' playing schedule.

His most perceptive conclusion was that ultimately the Players' League owners would understand that their natural allies were their fellow owners and not the players. Consolidation would destroy not the Players' League owners, but only their league. Spalding not only defeated his rival, but integrated the vanquished owners into his league and thus infused it with new parks and needed capital.

The Players' League owners were not a loyal lot. The merging of the New York and Brooklyn clubs was done without league approval, and this act ensured the National League the upper hand in any future negotiations.[59] One writer wrote of Johnson's fellow owners after the Players' League folded:

> Had Johnson been treated half as loyally as he treated his associates, the Players' League would today be in the proud place it held October 6 and the National League would have been ready and willing to go into a treaty of peace on very moderate terms.... Johnson is as loyal as the sun is bright.[60]

The players were naïve. Many believed that consolidation was in everyone's best interest. They foolishly trusted the owners when they were told that there would be a modification of the reserve rule, no reprisals, and no player classification plan. More militant workers would never have been so trustful.[61]

Solidarity, a key ingredient in any union's success, was easily broken. Star players like Buck Ewing quickly broke ranks when large contracts were offered to them. Players also lost faith in their cause when several teams were unable to meet their payroll obligations during the season's last weeks. Several players did try to use the New York court system to block the consolidation of the New York teams, but the court ruled against them.[62]

Many argued that the players' on-the-field behavior hurt their cause. Although it is doubtful that they were any more rowdy than their National

League counterparts, the public watched them more closely and perceived some teams to be out of control. Umpires were often treated poorly, and some were accused of allowing too much kicking and backtalk. Teams occasionally walked off the field in protest, and some fans grew sick of the arguments that slowed the game down. Players were also accused of gaining weight, playing drunk, and doing little to inspire fan loyalty.[63] *The Sporting Life* wrote of these problems after the season, explaining:

> The majority (players) gauged the lifting of restraint of discipline as an appeal to rush into excesses whose discovery could but disgust the men who were providing the sinews of war and alienate the public ... There were occasions when some men were better suited for a padded cell than to play ball.

The paper concluded that the Players' League had shown the baseball public that players could not control themselves and therefore needed "the stringent regulations of their former and future employers."[64]

The press became more antagonistic as the season progressed. Even *The New York Times*, a loyal backer, reported:

> ... Well, the Brotherhood men have used plenty of gold this year, and I doubt if they can stand the strain much longer. Then again, I am glad to see that the Brotherhood people admit that they are wreckers. They do this when they say that they are in favor of placing the game on its old basis of popularity, interest, and prosperity. What caused the lack of interest, popularity, and prosperity? Nothing but the Brotherhood wreckers.[65]

Other elements hurt the league's chances. Although a good pennant race developed between Boston and Brooklyn, with Boston eventually winning by a six and a half-game margin, foul weather, apathy, and negative late-season newspaper coverage limited fan support. Also, the National League refused to meet the champion in a "World Series," which would have helped the league to raise needed revenue.[66]

Although the players contributed to their league's demise, they were not the primary reason for its failure. In almost all respects, the league was superior to the senior league, and had its owners had more vision, they would have seen this. For years, the National League had harangued that the reserve rule, National Agreement, and other controls were necessary for success. The Players' League, without these, was stronger than its rival. When all assets are considered, it is possible that all eight of its franchises were solvent at the season's end, while more than half of the American Association and National League teams were near bankrupt.[67]

Despite what Spalding claimed, it was not the players but the owners who were primarily responsible for the league's demise. However, for years after the conflict, the National League would use the Players' League as an example of the folly of giving players too much control. A more accurate assessment would have been that changes in the monopolistic baseball industry could occur only if the owners and players had vision, resolve, and loyalty to each other and their cause.

The players were gullible in their dealings with the owners. In October, the National League announced that it would use a new standard players' contract that would not contain the reserve rule and would require that released players get paid for the entire season.[68] The players viewed this as evidence that the National League was changing and that returning to the fold would not result in a dramatic loss of freedom or money. Ward talked of doing away with the "sales system," and he was told by Spalding that the possibility existed of having players put on the league's conference committee. Of course, Spalding explained, before any of these changes could be made, the two leagues would have to consolidate.[69] Had the players seen beyond the rhetoric and realized the changes that the National League would implement in the years following consolidation, it is doubtful that they would have allowed themselves to be so easily removed from the consolidation process. Their preoccupation with wages and their lack of concern for their role in baseball's management would cost them dearly in the decades following the Baseball War.[70]

Buck Ewing was a star catcher, first baseman, infielder, and outfielder who played on four different teams from 1880 to 1897. Ewing jumped to the Players' League in 1890 and became the manager of the New York team. However, controversy arose when several players accused him of working behind the scenes with A.G. Spalding to undermine the league. He was elected to the Hall of Fame by the Veterans' Committee in 1939 (Library of Congress).

# 10

# *Aftermath: 1891 to 1901*

The destruction of the Players' League and consolidation were not enough for the National League owners. To achieve total victory, they would have to recreate a monopoly similar to the one that existed prior to 1890. To accomplish this, they created a new National Agreement in January of 1891.

The National Agreement of 1891 was designed to regulate the National League, the American Association, and the various minor leagues. It placed restrictions on both players and owners. The reserve rule was the agreement's centerpiece, and each team was allowed to reserve up to fourteen players. A salary minimum of $1,000 was established for the two "major leagues," but with the reserve rule and no outside leagues to compete for players, owners did not have to fear that market forces would drive up salaries. A strict players' code was published, and fines, suspensions, and the blacklist would ensure that players abided by it. To ensure that teams did not have to compete for fans, franchises were not to locate within five miles of another National Agreement member. One provision that did benefit players was that teams could be expelled from any league if they failed to meet their contractual obligations to players.

A national board was created, with broad powers to regulate the entire baseball industry. Although both major leagues had representatives on the board, it was dominated by the National League. The board had the final say in most matters, and no one could appeal its rulings. It established salary limits for all of the minor leagues and determined how much the National League and American Association teams would have to pay to acquire these players. The board also had the power to fine or penalize any player, club manager, or umpire whose conduct was "detrimental to the welfare of the game" or in violation of the letter or spirit of the National Agreement.[1]

The peace between the National League and American Association did not last long. The national board had been given the responsibility of dividing up the players left over from consolidation. Most American Association franchises believed that the two major leagues would each be allowed to reserve fourteen players who had been on a team's roster in 1889 or 1890, and the remaining players would be distributed to National Agreement teams by the board, depending on a franchise's needs. Association owners were angered when the board allowed Pittsburgh and Boston of the National League to sign Louis Bierbauer and Harry Stovey, both of whom had jumped to the Players' League in 1890, but had played for the Association's Philadelphia Athletics in 1889. (Pittsburgh earned the nickname "Pirates" as a result of the acquisition of Bierbauer.) The Association protested the ruling, but the national board, citing a minor technicality, ruled that the players would remain the property of their new National League teams.[2]

American Association clubs were further incensed when many National League teams reserved players who were on their rosters in 1890 and those who had been a team's property in 1889 and then jumped to the Players' League. The senior league even reserved some retired players to prevent them from going to another team as a manager or a coach. This meant that some franchises were reserving as many as thirty-three players in an era when most team rosters consisted of only thirteen or fourteen men. These teams then sold, traded, or released these excess players depending on their needs and the demand for a particular player. The American Association believed that the National League was ignoring the spirit and letter of the National Agreement, was only concerned with its own interests, and could not be trusted. Consequently, it dropped out of the National Agreement in February, 1891.[3]

The year 1891 was a hectic one for players and owners. The courts ruled that since the American Association was not a member of the National Agreement, the reserve clause did not regulate the free movement of players between teams under the National Agreement and the American Association. This free market did not benefit the American Association. The National League had emerged from the confrontation with the Players' League as the strongest league in the nation. It benefited from the merger of Players' League and National League teams, and generally organizations in the senior league were more committed to the baseball industry and better capitalized than teams in the Association.

The Association believed that money would not be the only factor that determined where players chose to play. Its owners claimed that they treated players as "gentlemen" while their rival viewed them as "slaves" and "brutes."[4] They believed that players, smarting from their defeat of

1890 and still craving respect, would flock to the Association. They were wrong! Most players proved to have short memories and went to the team that offered them the most money, regardless of league. Salaries escalated, which hurt the Association more than its rival.

Perhaps the most serious problem that the American Association faced was that there was a tremendous capital and revenue differential between its teams, which reduced the competitive balance of the league. Boston, which had played in the Players' League in 1890 and won the American Association pennant in 1891, had the resources to attract several new stars and to retain the services of their former Players' League stand-outs: Dan Brouthers, Tom Brown, and Hardy Richardson. Second-place St. Louis, which had played in the American Association in 1890, was also well capitalized and was able to keep stars Tommy McCarthy and Jack Stivetts and lure other fine players into the fold. These teams dominated the league in 1891, and most of their competition was out of the pennant race by midsummer. (Third-place Baltimore finished 21 games off the pace.)

This lack of competition and poor weather in some cities helped to keep attendance low, despite the Association's 25-cent admission price, which was half of what the National League charged. The Association attempted to reduce the disparity between rich and poor teams by evenly dividing gate receipts between the home and visiting clubs for all games that were not played on holidays and pooling and equally dividing the Association's holiday earnings. These revenue-sharing measures failed to keep most teams in the black; the Milwaukee and Cincinnati franchises folded midseason, and by the season's end, most clubs were nearly bankrupt. The league had hoped to gain additional money by playing a post-season "world series" against the National League's best club, but its rival refused to meet in such a match, claiming that its teams were not allowed to play teams that were not in the National Agreement.[5]

The American Association went out of business after the 1891 season. Four of its franchises (Baltimore, St. Louis, Washington, and Louisville) were purchased by the National League for $130,000.[6] Spalding rejoiced at the demise of his rival. He claimed that this would lead to a "permanent peace and prosperity." Still the quintessential late 19th-century capitalist, he continued to believe that control and order were all that were necessary for business to be profitable and labor content. As the decade progressed and his monopoly remained unrivaled, the assertion would prove to be wrong.[7]

Not surprisingly, the new twelve-team monopoly was not good for players. In 1890, 24 major league teams competed for America's elite baseball talent and provided approximately 336 on-the-field jobs. By 1892 these

National League owners, circa 1891 (National Baseball Hall of Fame, Cooperstown, N.Y.).

numbers had been cut in half. To help them to pay the huge debt that they had incurred when they purchased the four Association franchises, National League owners wanted to reduce salaries. The National Agreement was updated and made more strict, and with no leagues outside of its jurisdiction, players had no choice but to succumb to its dictates.

Team rosters were reduced from fourteen or fifteen to thirteen. In October, 1891, all players were released even though their contracts ran to November 1. This enabled all clubs to save two weeks' pay. An agreement between all the league's owners prevented teams from bidding for each others' players. The reserve rule, which had long been used to prevent salaries from escalating, was now used to reduce them. An unofficial salary limit of $2,400 and a team payroll cap of $30,000 were established for the 1893 season. Even the provisions of multi-year contracts were ignored. Cincinnati owner John Brush explained that "a contract is not worth the paper it's written on."[8] By 1894, salaries had been reduced at least 40 percent from where they had been in 1890. The $3,000 salary, which had been common prior to 1892, became almost nonexistent in 1893. Many teams had established a $1,800 salary maximum, and rookies were often required to play for as little as $600 per season. This was a dramatic drop from the $2,000 minimum salary of 1889.

Even players who came over from the defunct American Association did not get high salaries as a result of competitive bidding. Instead, the National League divided them up among its twelve franchises. The players could either play for the team to which they were assigned to or quit baseball.

The league did not officially blacklist players who had participated in the revolt of 1890; however, by 1893, only 54 of the 128 men who had played in the Players' League were still employed in the National League. To prevent any further insurrections, a resolution was passed in 1893 that barred from the National League for life any player, official, or manager who worked for a league outside the National Agreement.[9]

Players were treated as children. They were again required to make temperance pledges and submit to management's authority without question. Player trades and sales increased, and the blacklist was used more than ever. Players who were not stars were required to work as ushers, groundskeepers, and ticket collectors before and after games, and they were often released without notice. Individuals who spoke out against such treatment were blacklisted.[10]

Sadly, the defeated players often turned on each other. Rivalries developed between former Players' League players and individuals who had been employed by the American Association or National League in 1890. These rivalries, coupled with the player salary reductions and loss of player control and self-respect, helped to make the game of the 1890s extremely violent.[11] Umpire baiting and "kicking" were regular occurrences at the ballpark, and fights and even riots involving players, fans, and even umpires were not uncommon.[12] Henry Chadwick asked if fans paid to see ball games or "a lot of toughs tripping each other, giving the shoulder, and like action."[13] Bill James, a noted baseball historian, described the game of the 1890s in the following way:

> Dirty; very, very dirty. The tactics of the eighties were aggressive; the tactics of the nineties were violent. The game of the eighties was crude; the game of the nineties was criminal. The baseball of the eighties had ugly elements; the game of the nineties was just ugly.[14]

The monopoly did not result in a strong, centrally organized league. The National Agreement and Constitution did give the league's president substantial power. However, Nick Young, the man who held the office for much of the 1890s, was not able or willing to stand up to team owners who did not want to obey league rules. Most owners were determined to do what they believed would make their teams the most money; consequently, they often ignored league officials.

A schism developed between the National League owners. Many who had previously been involved in the American Association wanted to play Sunday games, sell beer in the parks, and encourage working-class patronage. These men believed that the more violent game was good for business because it would help to attract large numbers of laborers and immigrants. One such owner, St. Louis's Chris Von der Ahe, even paid the fines that his players incurred for fighting or baiting umpires.[15] The more traditional owners still wanted to cater to the middle class and labor elite and thus did not want Sunday games, beer sales, or excessive fighting. Ultimately, the old order lost out, and this resulted in less middle-class and female patronage and generally a more rowdy atmosphere at most ballparks.[16]

Another problem for the league was how to divide revenues. The poorer teams or "little seven"— Baltimore, Brooklyn, Cincinnati, St. Louis, Cleveland, Washington, and Louisville — had forced the league to establish the policy of dividing gate receipts evenly between the home and visiting teams. This angered the richer franchises because they believed that they were subsidizing their poorer counterparts, and league unity was reduced.[17]

The greatest threat to emerge from the postwar consolidation was syndication. When the National League teams merged with or bought out Players' League or American Association teams in 1890 and 1891, many owners gained at least partial control of two or more teams. For example, John Brush owned stock in the Cincinnati and New York teams; Arthur Soden owned one-third of Boston's stock and was also a minority owner of New York; Frank Robison owned both the St. Louis and Cleveland franchises, and even Spalding had a few shares of New York stock in addition to his White Stockings.[18] The men who controlled these "pocket trusts" often used the team in the smaller city to develop players, and as a player reached his peak, he would be transferred to the team in the larger market. In a business where winning should have been a team's only goal, this was an obvious conflict of interest. It generally helped to keep the teams in larger markets on top, while those in smaller cities floundered. The owners saw nothing wrong with this practice even though it influenced the industry much the way they argued free agency would: It helped the richest teams get the best players and win the most games.

Not surprisingly, there was little balance in the National League in the 1890s. During the eight years that the twelve-team league existed, the first-place team had an average winning percentage of .698 while the team at the bottom averaged only .258.[19] Fans often questioned the home nine's loyalty, and their disenchantment increased when poorer, less popular teams would play their "home" games in another park if the owners thought they could make more money.[20]

Lack of competition, rowdy crowds, the recession of 1893 to 1897, and the debt incurred from buying out the American Association franchises all helped to make the 1890s unprofitable years for the National League. Wealthy teams like New York continued to draw over 2,000 fans per game, but losers like Cleveland did not average even 500 patrons per contest in 1897, and by 1899, they attracted fewer than 200 paying customers per game. [21] Even the most successful owners felt the financial strain. Chris von der Ahe and John Day, whose St. Louis and New York franchises had been extremely successful in the 1880s, both went broke. Despite respectable attendance, Day's club lost $32,000 in 1892, and he could not even meet his reduced salary obligations. Von der Ahe had made an estimated $500,000 from baseball in the 1880s, but he could not replicate this success on the field or in his profit/loss statements. His Browns were perennial losers, fans stayed away, and he was forced by his creditors to sell his team in 1899. Although it was obvious that changes were needed in the league's structure, none could be made. Not only could the owners not agree on a solution to their dilemma, but the consolidation agreement of 1892 stated that the framework of the league had to be left intact for ten years, thus making change impossible.[22]

As usual, the owners blamed the players for their financial woes. John Brush, the man who had developed the classification system, believed that the key to improving the league's popularity was to again make it "worthy of confidence and the support of the refined and cultured classes of American citizens." In an attempt to regain their lost middle-class patronage, the league adopted the Brush purification plan in 1898. The plan encouraged players, managers, umpires, club officials, and even fans to submit information and testimony concerning any player who used "obscene, indecent or vulgar language." The league's board of directors heard all accusations and had the power to suspend or expel a player for life from the league if he used excessive vulgarity or swore at a fan. The ruling of the board could not be appealed.[23] The plan did much to anger the players, but it did little to improve attendance.

The National League's problems continued. In December, 1899, the owners agreed to ignore the consolidation agreement and expel Louisville, Cleveland, Washington, and Baltimore primarily because their low attendance was a financial drain on the rest of the league. However, the magnates were so obsessed with monopoly that for the following two seasons the league claimed to control the rights to these cities in order to prevent teams outside the National League from moving there.[24]

In August, 1901, Andrew Freedman, the future owner of the New York Giants and one of the most disliked men in baseball, and John Brush proposed a controversial plan that would have revolutionized the baseball industry. Freedman argued that monopoly was not enough, that to be truly successful, baseball would have to become a trust. He proposed that each National League owner give up control of his club in return for trust certificates. Teams in larger markets, such as the Giants, would get as much as 30 percent of the certificates, while teams in smaller markets, like Pittsburgh, would only get six to eight percent.

Freedman hoped to eventually extend his trust into the sporting goods manufacturing business, the minor leagues, horse racing, and sports-related real estate so that eventually one huge sports trust would dominate the United States. Freedman had the support of half the National League owners, and a fierce battle took place to determine if the plan would be implemented. Interestingly, Spalding opposed it, not for ethical reasons, but because he despised and mistrusted Freedman. (The Chicago owner had proposed a similar plan in 1898 but had received little support.)

Spalding agreed to run for the league presidency in 1901, believing he was the one man who could save the league from Freedman. Freedman's forces wanted to elect Nick Young as National League president. Not only did he support the plan, but Freedman believed that he was weak and could be dominated by the owners who supported the plan. After 25 ballots, the vote remained locked at four to four, and Freedman's supporters left the meeting believing that the voting was over for the day. The wily Spalding then held a 26th ballot and was elected league president four to zero. Freedman fought the validity of the election in court, but to no avail. With Spalding at the helm of the league, the plan was dead.[25]

Many players and writers became disgusted with the National League monopoly and the changes that were occurring on and off the field. Cap Anson, a 22-year National League veteran who had always supported management's policies, grew so fed up that he quit after the 1891 season even though he was still playing well. He explained:

> Baseball as is presently conducted is a gigantic monopoly intolerant of opposition and run on a grab-all-there-is-in-sight basis that is alienating its friends and disgusting the very public that has so long and cheerfully supported it.[26]

*The Sporting Life* in 1900 called the baseball monopoly a "feudal serf system," and that same year even Samuel Gompers, who had been ignored when he tried to help the players in 1890 explained, .." .no salary, however high, could compensate for the degradation of the ball player under the reserve rule ... he becomes a mere human chattel to be bought and sold without the slightest regard for his feelings...." Despite these difficulties, the players did little to resist the owners. Frank Richter of *The Sporting Life* magazine and several players talked of reviving the American Association or the Players' League in 1894, but little came of this. When word of these discussions reached the National League owners, they explained that any player who "deserted" would be blacklisted for life. Players, still smarting from their defeat in 1890 and lacking a leader such as Ward, quietly let the issue die.[27]

John Montgomery Ward continued to play through the 1894 season for Brooklyn and then New York. When he retired, he was the Giants' captain and was still considered to be one of the best players in baseball. In his final season, New York finished in second place, but they won the post-season Temple Cup Series against first-place Baltimore four games to none to claim the league championship. Ward played his final game on October 8 and went one for five.[28]

After he retired, Ward established a law practice in New York that quickly became very successful. He also remained active in baseball. Players frequently visited his office, and he continued to be an outspoken critic of some National League player policies and a proponent of players' rights. On several occasions he represented players who had not been paid their proper wages. In each case, he was able to force the club to pay the player the money that it owed him.[29]

In spite of his support for players and his actions as the leader of the Brotherhood, Ward was respected by many National League owners. He even became friendly with Spalding and corresponded with him regularly. In 1909, John Brush, the man who proposed the classification plan, nominated Ward to be National League president. After several ballots, the vote remained deadlocked at four to four and the magnates were forced to agree on a compromise candidate.[30]

Three years later, Ward and James Gaffney purchased a controlling interest in the Boston Braves, and Ward became the club president. Although he owned the team for less than one season, he proved to be fair but tough. When shortstop Al Bridwell injured himself stepping on a nail prior to the 1912 season, Ward informed him that he would not be paid until he was able to meet his contractual obligations.[31] Ward also sold several players while president, and shortly after he relinquished his interest in the club on August 5, he testified before a congressional committee that he did not believe that baseball should be investigated as an "autocratic trust" because the industry needed to remain organized as it was in order to survive.[32]

After his playing career ended, Ward took up golf and became one of the nation's best amateur players. He won the New Jersey state championship in 1905 and frequently played in important tournaments in the United States and Europe. He was at home with society's upper crust, and it is possible that his association with New York's elite made him less sympathetic to players and more supportive of the baseball industry's owners.

Ward was granted a modification of his divorce decree from Helen Dauvray in the summer of 1903. The change allowed him to remarry prior to her death, and he wed again soon after this. Katherine Waas was willing to accept the domestic role that Ward expected of his wife. Their relationship was warm and peaceful, and their 22 years together were happy. When not on the golf course or practicing law, Ward could often be seen at the ballpark watching his beloved Giants, hunting, fishing, or conducting farm experiments on his 205-acre Long Island estate.[33]

In June of 1900, National League players again attempted to organize. When asked to comment on this, Ward explained, "The players can, through an organization of this kind, do more to help baseball than any other influence ... they can promote a feeling of mutual regard and common interest."[34] This comment shows that even after retirement, the shortstop's attitude toward baseball and organized labor had changed little.

The 65-year-old John Montgomery Ward died on March 4, 1925 after contracting pneumonia while on a hunting trip in Georgia. Katherine Waas was by his side during much of the five days that he fought the illness, and she had his body shipped north for a funeral in West Islip, Long Island. Grantland Rice eulogized Ward, calling him "the greatest competitor this country has ever known."[35] In 1964 he was enshrined in the Baseball Hall of Fame. His plaque in Cooperstown makes no mention of his courageous efforts on behalf of the Brotherhood of Professional Base Ball Players.

After the owners' victory in 1891, Albert Spalding was not a gracious winner. In his 1891 *Baseball Guide*, he mocked the players and their movement by reprinting these laments of a Cleveland player:

> Backward, turn backward, O time in thy rush. Make me a slave again, well-dressed and flush. Bondage come back from the echoless shore. And bring me my shackles I formerly wore....[36]

Later that year he remarked:

> When the spring comes and the grass is green upon the last resting place of anarchy, the National Agreement will rise again in all of its weight and restore America in all of its purity its national pastime — the Great Game of base ball.[37]

In 1901 he gave up the presidency of his team, although he continued as owner. He explained that he did not enjoy the company of the new breed of owners who had come into the league during the 1890s and that he wanted to devote more time and energy to his other personal and business interests. Under his leadership his sporting goods business grew and eventually dominated the world market.

In 1900 he was named the Director of the Section of Sports for the United States at the Paris Olympic games and was awarded the rosette of the Legion of Honor by the French government for his efforts. In 1911 he authored *America's National Game*, a history of baseball, which proved to be quite popular.

Spalding's first wife, Sarah Josephine Kent, died in 1899. One year later, he married Elizabeth Churchill Mayer. They moved to Point Loma, California, where Spalding died of a heart attack in 1915. He was enshrined in Cooperstown in 1939, where his plaque hangs near that of his old rival, John Montgomery Ward.[38]

The reserve rule continued to be the dominant tool used by baseball owners to control players until 1976. Although the game's popularity grew dramatically in the 20th century, baseball players rarely received a fair portion of the wealth they created. The players did form four different unions after the Brotherhood collapsed, but none of them succeeded in altering the player/owner relationship that had existed since the Baseball Rebellion.

In 1966, Marvin Miller, a former attorney for the United Steelworkers of America, became the chief counsel for the Major League Players' Association. Miller believed that major league baseball was a monopoly, and he ridiculed it, saying, "unlike most antitrust conspiracies, this one is written down on paper, even printed." In November, 1975, pitchers Andy Messersmith and Dave McNally claimed that because they did not sign contracts for the 1975 season, they were free to bargain with any team they wished to for the 1976 season. The case went to arbitration, where Miller and Richard Moss, the owner's representative, debated for three days. The owners' argument was similar to the one made by the National League magnates prior to the 1890 season. Moss stated that major league players made far more money than they could in any other industry. He claimed that stability was needed to maintain fan support and that both owners and players benefited from this stability. He also said that owners invested large sums of money to develop major league players and that the reserve rule was necessary to protect this investment.

The arbitration panel consisted of one man chosen by the players, one chosen by the owners, and the impartial Peter Seitz. Seitz had tried to get the parties to reach a compromise prior to the hearing, but the owners refused to bargain, believing that they would win the case. On December 23, 1975, Seitz ruled in favor of Messersmith and McNally and against the reserve rule. The owners responded by firing him and taking the case to court. In March of 1976, their last legal appeal failed, and the owners were forced to deal with Miller and the Players' Association. In July, 1976, a new basic agreement was reached. Miller did not want complete free agency in baseball because he believed this would flood the market with players and not result in a drastic increase in salaries. Instead, players and management agreed that players with six years of major league service could become "free agents" and bargain with any team in baseball. The freedom that Ward and his union had fought for had now, to a large degree, been won.

The owners warned of impending doom for baseball, but instead, the game's popularity soared. Free agency kept baseball in the news year-round and stimulated fan interest. Salaries rose dramatically, but so did attendance and television revenues. During the last fifteen years, numerous new ballparks such as Baltimore's Oriole Park at Camden Yards have been constructed, largely with taxpayer money, and for the most part, these have been enormously popular with fans. These facilities have many modern amenities, but they also have a retro look that reminds fans of the classic ballparks of the early 20th century. In addition, they have a variety of concessions and a large number of luxury boxes, which produce additional revenue.

Despite the successes of the free agency era, there have been problems. Teams in large markets have seen their revenue streams grow at a much more rapid rate than teams in smaller markets. Local and cable television revenues for teams like the New York Yankees are often more than ten times those of teams in markets such as Pittsburgh and Kansas City. These enormous revenues allow these large market teams to lure star players when they are eligible for free agency. Large contracts attained through free agency affect the baseball salary structure in two ways. First, they drive up the costs of players during their fourth through sixth years of service when they are still bound to their team but eligible for salary arbitration. During this process, teams and players each propose a salary, and arbitrators decide which salary a player will receive. They base this decision on the money received by players with similar statistics and years of experience, but the higher overall salaries become, the more salaries proposed by teams and players will increase and the more money arbitration eligible players will receive. In addition, when a player becomes a free agent, his value on the open market is often determined by what has previously been paid for a player of similar ability. Generally, the market price for players is set by large-market franchises, and it is becoming more and more difficult for small-market teams to pay these salaries.

As was often true in the 19th century, baseball has three, not two, competing forces. Owners not only oppose players, but to a growing degree, owners of small-market teams find themselves in opposition to the owners of large-market franchises, and it is the owners of small-market teams who are most inclined to push for salary control measures. Ironically, many of the salary control measures that have been proposed by owners since the advent of free agency — player classification, a salary cap, and the elimination of arbitration so that salaries are set by owners prior to a player becoming a free agent — are similar to those implemented in the 19th century, and modern players view these with the same skepticism as their 19th-century counterparts. This is also one of the main reasons why the player/owner relationship in baseball has been so acrimonious over the last 30 years, and why most collective bargaining sessions have resulted in some kind of work stoppage.

Baseball has always had franchises that were far more successful than their counterparts in other cities. In the 19th century, baseball was enormously popular in St. Louis, Boston, New York, and Chicago, and it still is today. The teams in these cities can prosper under almost any system. In a free market, it is their revenues that will determine the value of players; therefore, they will be able to afford the prevailing salaries. In a controlled market, they will make even more profit since their revenues will remain high and salaries will be deflated. This was also true in the 19th century. In brief, in a free market, teams with the highest revenues generally set labor costs for the entire industry, and often teams in smaller markets cannot generate revenues that are adequate to pay these salaries.

The collective bargaining agreement of 2002 did start to address the small market/large market revenue imbalance. Since the agreement, team salaries over a prescribed level are taxed, and the revenue generated from these taxes is disbursed to lower-revenue franchises. (The salary and tax levels change year to year.) In addition, visiting teams now receive a higher percentage of the gate revenues. Despite these changes, the financial advantage that large-market teams have over small-market clubs is still huge.

If large-market teams have such an enormous financial advantage over small-market teams, why did the Florida Marlins defeat the New York Yankees in the 2003 World Series? The answer to this question may hold the key to the large market versus small market/player versus owner dilemma that plagues major league baseball. The Marlins defeated the Yankees because they had very good players who were also very young.

Baseball players, unlike their counterparts in almost every other profession, enter their prime at a very young age. Most players reach their peak between the ages of 26 and 28 but often earn their highest salaries when they are older and eligible for salary arbitration or free agency. Clearly, once market forces determine the value of the young Marlins, many will be traded or leave the team via free agency.

It is unlikely that players will accept any radical change to this system. However, if the Marlins and other small-market teams could gain access to a larger number of young, talented players, they would have a better chance of succeeding on the field and in the box office. A change that would funnel more young, inexpensive talent to less successful, small-market teams could be implemented through the player draft that takes place each June. Under the current system, teams draft in the reverse order of their win/loss record, and each team selects one player in each round of the draft. However, this system could be altered to funnel more players to the worst teams, which are often in small markets.

Today there are 30 major league franchises. Instead of allowing each team to draft once in each round, the draft could be changed so that in the first three rounds teams 30 to 21 would choose a player, then instead of continuing to team 20, return and allow teams 30 to 21 to draft again and then continue so that teams 20 through 11 draft their first player. At this point the draft would return to team 30 and continue to team one. This would mean that in the first three rounds of the draft the worst ten teams, many of which would be in small markets, would select nine players, while the best ten teams would select only three. The result would be that the less successful teams, which are often not as well financed, would have access to the largest number of talented and inexpensive players. However, once these players became eligible for salary arbitration in year four, or free agency after year six, they could be acquired by large-market teams via trades or free agency. Such a system would not place unacceptable controls on player salaries, but would increase the chances of smaller-market teams acquiring the talented but inexpensive players that are essential to their success. True, this would not immediately help the Marlins because they would be drafting at the bottom after their world championship season, but it would allow them to more quickly rebuild their franchise when it loses its best players. The rationale for this system is clear. Since 1879, owners have been trying to prevent market forces from determining the value of their labor force, and this has often led to conflict with players. Whether the players' rebellion of 1890 or the catastrophic strike of 1994–95, this conflict has almost never been positive for the industry. It is in the best interests of players and owners to develop a system that enables all teams to have a reasonable chance of success on the field and yet still allows for market-determined salaries and reasonable player movement.

Baseball has a long and often troubled history, and the relationship between players and owners has frequently been rancorous. It is not surprising that players advocate a system in which market forces determine their value. However, this has often resulted in instability for their industry, a large amount of player movement, and a competitive advantage for large-market teams. Owners continue to want to regulate their industry and its players much the way their 19th-century counterparts did. The reserve rule dominated the player/owner relationship during most of the 20th century, and although it did stabilize the industry and reduce player movement, it also allowed the owners to underpay players and in many cases ignore their well-being. In many ways, the issues that players and owners struggle to address have changed little since the professional game emerged, and these issues are likely to dominate their relationship for years to come.

Despite these differences between owners and players, baseball is still enormously popular in America. An average of more than 30,000 people attend each major league contest; playoff games almost always sell out; local and national television ratings remain strong, and minor league baseball continues to grow in popularity. Although the game has changed much since Alexander Cartwright's Knickerbockers played on Elysian field and American society has changed even more, baseball is still woven into the fabric of American society like almost no other component of our culture. The game of John Montgomery Ward and Albert Goodwill Spalding is still America's game, and it likely will be for generations to come.

# Appendix 1

# The 1869 Cincinnati Red Stockings

| Player | Craft/ Profession | Baseball Position | Salary |
|---|---|---|---|
| Harry Wright | Jeweler | Centerfield | $1200 |
| George Wright | Engraver | Shortstop | $1400 |
| Asa Brainard | Insurance | Pitcher | $1100 |
| Fred Waterman | Insurance | Third Base | $1000 |
| Charles Sweasy | Hatter | Second Base | $ 800 |
| Charles H. Gould | Bookkeeper | First Base | $ 800 |
| Douglas Allison | Marble Cutter | Catcher | $ 800 |
| Andrew J. Leonard | Hatter | Left Field | $ 800 |
| Calvin A. McVey | Piano Maker | Right Field | $ 800 |
| Richard Hurley | Trade Unknown | Substitute | $ 600[1] |

# Appendix 2

# The First Reserve Agreement: Secret and Unpublished

The undersigned associations, members of the National League of Professional Base-Ball Clubs, do hereby each with the other agree that in contracting with players for 1880 the players named below shall be assigned as follows:

Boston — Snyder, Bond, Burdock, O'Rourke, Sutton
Buffalo — Galvin, Clapp, Richardson, Crowley, Walker
Chicago — Williamson, Quest, Anson, Flint, Hankinson
Cleveland — McCormick, Kennedy, Glasscock, Richmond, Shaffer
Providence — Wright, Start, Hines, Ward, McGeary
Troy — Evans, Caskin, Cassidy, Ferguson, Goldsmith

The said named players assigned above are to be considered and treated as members of their respective Clubs, meaning and intending hereby that the men above as assigned shall be treated in all respects as players engaged and under regular contracts for the season of 1880, to the Clubs to whom they are assigned as above.

— Buffalo, Sept. 30, 1879[1]

# Appendix 3

# Section 18 of the Standard Player's Contract: The Reserve Rule

It is further understood and agreed that the said party of the first part shall have the right to "reserve" the said party of the second part for the season next ensuing the term mentioned on paragraph 2 (commencing on the first day of April, A.D. 1889, and ending on the first day of October A.D. 1889, inclusive) herein provided and said party of the first part upon the following conditions, which are to be taken and construed as conditions precedent to the exercise of such extraordinary right or privilege, *viz*:

I. That the said party of the second part shall not be reserved at a salary less than that mentioned in the twentieth paragraph herein, except by consent of the party of the second part.

II. That the said party of the second part, if he be reserved by the said party of the first part for the next ensuing season shall be one of not more than fourteen players then under contract, that is: that the right of reservation shall be limited to that number of players and no more.[1]

# Appendix 4

# Henry Chadwick's "How the Reserve Rule Helps to Regulate Players' Salaries"

The most difficult problem the League has had to solve, in legislating for the government of the professional fraternity, has been that of how to control and regulate the salaries of players. The club rivalry for the possession of the best players each season, has been, from the very onset, an obstacle to an equitable arrangement of the salary question; and this has led to an increase of club expenses of this kind until the subject became one involving the future existence of even the most wealthy of the League clubs. Within the past year or two this salary question has passed beyond the bounds of a reasonable remuneration for professional service on the ball fields, to the region of exorbitant demands, which, if complied with, would eventually bankrupt the strongest company in the professional arena. From the basis of the rule that "a player's services are to be paid for according to their real value to a club," the question has resolved itself into one in which he is to be regarded as worth all he can get, either by coercion or by reckless competition for his services. All reasonable arguments involving an equitable estimate of a ball player's work on the basis of the relation it bears to that of any other occupation he may be competent to engage in as a means of livelihood, are disregarded. Here is a ball player, who, as a street car driver or conductor, a brakesman, a porter, or an assistant at some ordinary trade in which, at his work as a common day laborer he can only command ten dollars a week for his services, and to earn that has to work laboriously from ten to fifteen hours each day; and yet this self-same individual is taught by unscrupulous or short-sighted rival clubs to believe that he is treated hardly if he is not readily given $2,000 as salary for six months' services as a ball player, in which his work is comparatively a pleasant recreation, requiring but two or three hours of easy work each day. This is the rational view of the situation so far as equity is concerned, in estimating a ball player's real value.

Efforts were made to establish special rates governing the several positions of a club team, so as to regulate the pay according to the work done. But all such efforts failed until the rule reserving eleven men, at a stated minimum salary, was adopted. Up to this point in the history of the question, fancy prices had prevailed in the professional market to an extent which threatened the future existence of the whole professional fabric. It then became a question as to whether the existing stock companies should go on until they were forced into bankruptcy, or by some stringent rule, even if, in a measure arbitrary in its enactment, a stop should be put to the fancy salary abuse. Left to itself, the evil would grow each season and bring down the whole professional structure. It was determined to put a stop to it, and adopt a rule which would preserve even players themselves from fatal results. By reserving eleven men at a salary of not less than $1,000 a season, the clubs placed a barrier to the further progress of the fancy salary business, and besides this they placed themselves on a securer financial footing than it was possible for them to obtain under the old order of things. It will only need another year's trial of the reserve rule to show the few players still opposed to it that it will accrue as much to their future pecuniary benefit as it will to the clubs themselves. The rule which builds up firmer clubs, and which aids their permanent establishment, cannot be otherwise than equally beneficial to the best interests of the club's players. The reserve rule does not lessen the salary of any player, whose marked integrity of character, exceptional ability in his field position, and faithful work in the interest of his club, makes him a valuable man to have in the club team at any salary the financial position of the club can afford to pay; but it simply places a barrier to the reckless competition for the services of men who, outside of the ball field, could not earn a tenth part of the sum they demand for base ball services. It is a defensive law against an abuse which has grown out of an excessive rivalry between individual clubs for certain over-estimated material for their field business.[1]

# Appendix 5

# David Newberger's (Lawyer for the Brotherhood) Argument Against the Reserve Rule

The most important element required to render a contract valid is absent in the contract referred to. It may be said that the payment of the salary mentioned in the contract is a good and sufficient consideration; but this is very much in doubt. The extraordinary privilege of which the party of the first part is to avail himself must first of all be one which is legal and binding. If there was no valid consideration moving from the party of the first to the party of the second, then it is not binding. As for the payment of the salary for the performance of work by the party of the second part, I doubt very much whether it would be held that this payment, or any agreement to pay it, would constitute a sufficient consideration to validate the clause. Is the clause sufficiently definite as to the meaning of the word "reserve"? It is silent as to what is expected to be done with the party of the second part. The party of the second part might be called upon to fulfill any menial position in the club. It might be claimed that it would be held as a substitute, or it might be claimed under this extraordinary clause of the contract that the party of the first part, might require him to do many things foreign to his employment and prejudicial to him as a professional: and it therefore would certainly be difficult just how to say from an examination of this contract when and where the possibilities liable and likely to arise from so vague, indefinite, and meaningless a clause might end, and anything which might be claimed by the parties of the first part within and without the range of human possibility could be stated by them to be covered by this clause.

For these reasons the clause is invalid and not binding, and the party of the second part, whoever he may be, in my judgment is at liberty to accept employment under any conditions he may choose and whenever he pleases.[1]

# Appendix 6

# *Judge O'Brien's Decision Allowing John Montgomery Ward to Play in the Players' League*

One of the principal questions discussed on the argument was as to the meaning of this word "reserve" as used in the contract. On the part of the plaintiff it is claimed that the meaning of this word is clear and unambiguous, requiring no explanation, being used in its ordinary sense of "to hold, to keep for future use." The defendant, on the other hand, claims that this word, which was not a new one to the parties, has a history. That it had always been used in a particular sense, and in order to ascertain that meaning, reference must be had to the history of the word. That if resort is had to such history it will result in a construction to be given to the contract which shall determine that when the defendant accorded the right to reserve his services that it was not thereby meant that he was absolutely pledged or bound to plaintiff, but that his services were reserved to the exclusion of any other member of the league of baseball clubs. It is sufficient to say that, whether we have regard to the history of the word as used in the various contracts or give it its ordinary and well-accepted meaning, we shall arrive at the same conclusion as to the meaning of the word adverse to the defendant's contention and in favor of the meaning given to it by the plaintiff.

Not only are there no terms and conditions fixed, but I do not think it is entirely clear that Ward agrees to do anything further than to accord the right to reserve him upon terms thereafter to be fixed. He does not covenant to make a contract for 1890 at the same salary, nor upon the same terms and conditions as during the season of 1889. The failure of the existing contract to expressly provide the terms and conditions of the contract to be made for 1890 either renders the latter indefinite and uncertain, or we must infer that the same terms and conditions are to be incorporated in the one to be enforced, which necessarily includes the reserve clause, for no good reason can be suggested. If all the others are to be included, why should this be omitted? Upon the latter assumption the want of fairness and of mutuality, which are fatal to its enforcement in equity, are apparent, as will be seen when we consider to what extent under such circumstances each of the parties is bound.

It will thus be seen that I do not fully concur in the claims made by the plaintiff that the probability of finally succeeding is of the strongest and most certain kind. Upon either one or both of the grounds considered, but principally upon the ground that the contract is indefinite and uncertain, does there arise a serious doubt as to the plaintiff's being accorded on the trial the relief asked for.

While, therefore, I think that this is not a case in which a preliminary injunction should be granted, it is proper that the rights of the parties should be determined by a trial before the ball season begins, and to that end an application made, I shall assist in securing a speedy trial, upon which a final and deliberate judgment upon the rights of the parties can be pronounced.[1]

# Appendix 7

# *Judge Wallace's Decision on Buck Ewing and the Reserve Rule*

The promise of a baseball player to reserve himself for a particular club for a given season would hardly, without more, convey any definite meaning of the understanding of the parties. It certainly would not bind him to submit to any special rules or regulations respecting the performance of his services not expressly consented to, or not to be necessarily implied from the nature of the employment and the situation of the contracting parties. If it had been the meaning of the contract to allow for a second season upon the same conditions as those for the first season, that intention could have been easily and unequivocally expressed. As it is, it is left wholly to implication, unless the "right to reserve" is a term having a definite and specific signification.

The right of reservation is nothing more or less than a prior and exclusive right as against the other clubs to enter into a contract securing the player's services for another season. Until the contract is made which fixes the compensation of the player and the other conditions of his service there is not definite or complete obligation upon his part to engage with the club; he agrees that he will not negotiate with any other club, but enjoys the privilege of engaging with the reserving club or not, as he sees fit. Read with this understanding the clause in question by which the privilege of reserving the defendant is given to the club expresses definitely the terms of the option.

As a coercive condition which places the player practically in a situation where he must contract with the club that has reserved him or face the probability of losing any engagement for the ensuing season, it is operative and valuable to the club. But as the basis for an action for damages

184

if the player fails to contract or for an action to enforce specific performance, it is wholly nugatory.

It follows that the act of the defendant in refusing to negotiate with the club for an engagement for the season of 1890, while a breach of contract is not the breach of one which the plaintiff can enforce.[1]

# Appendix 8

# *Judge Thayer's Ruling on William Hallman and the Reserve Rule*

If this case depended upon the question of jurisdiction invoked by the plaintiff, and if all the facts alleged by either side existed, there would not be the slightest doubt concerning the justice of granting an injunction. But inquiry into the facts presented reveals a different condition of affairs from that alleged. On October 21, 1889, the plaintiff received a written notice requiring him to sign a contract similar to that of 1888, which, of course, included the eighteenth paragraph, as follow: "It is further understood and agreed that the said party of the first part shall have the right to 'reserve' the said party of the second part for the season next ensuing the term mentioned in Paragraph 2, herein provided, and the said party of the first part." This request Hallman refused to comply with, and on that refusal the case rests.

A careful reading of the paragraph discloses that there is nothing whatever contained in it to bind the player to sign another contract. All that it enacted was that the club should have the privilege of reserving him for another year. But upon what terms? It would have been easy for them to have said in the contract, "Upon the same terms as the preceding year," but they omitted to do so.

The fact is that Paragraph 18 does not make any contract whatever, but only stipulates that Hallman shall sign a subsequent contract. The failure to designate the exact terms by which he is to be employed renders the contract incomplete, uncertain, and ineffective, and, such being the case, the fault lies with the Philadelphia Baseball Club, as the contract was drawn up entirely in their interests. If it were true, as claimed by counsel for the plaintiff, that the contract binds him to sign a similar contract each ensuing year, it is then apparent that he must sign so long as it may suit his employers.

In Paragraph 17 of the contract it is stated that they have the right to discharge a player at ten days' notice for any cause, and by this, in conjunction with their reading of Paragraph 18, Hallman has sold himself for life to them at a salary of $1,400 a year. He has no further hold on them than a ten days' notice and is at their mercy. Sick or well, at home or 2,000 miles abroad, he may be cast off with this ten days' notice. It is perfectly apparent that such a contract is so unfair and lacking in mutuality that no court of equity would lend itself to its enforcement. If the Philadelphia Ball Club did not want or insist on his signing a contract, including the eighteenth paragraph, they should have left it out of the notice which they sent to him requesting his signature. They did not leave it out, and it is now too late to alter it. The demurrer against the granting of an injunction is therefore sustained, and the costs of the suit are placed on the defendants.[1]

# Notes

## Introduction

1. Kevin Cook, "1989 Baseball Preview," *Playboy*, May 1989, p. 153.

## Chapter 1

1. Jack Selzer, *Baseball in the Nineteenth Century: An Overview* (Manhattan, Kansas: Ag Press, 1986), p. 3.
2. Warren Goldstein, *Playing for Keeps: A History of Early Baseball* (Ithaca, New York: Cornell University Press, 1989), pp. 11–12; Robert F. Burk, *Never Just a Game: Players, Owners, and American Baseball to 1920* (Chapel Hill: University of North Carolina Press, 1994), p. 3.
3. Harold Seymour, *Baseball: The Early Years* (New York: Oxford University Press, 1960), p. 16; Burk, pp. 4, 6.
4. *Ibid.*, pp. 6–7; Selzer, p. 4.
5. *Ibid.*, p. 3; Burk, p. 22.
6. Ted Vincent, *Mudville's Revenge: The Rise and Fall of American Sport* (New York: Seaview Books, 1981), p. 16; Bryan Di Salvatore, *A Clever Base-Ballist: The Life and Times of John Montgomery Ward* (New York: Pantheon Books, 1999), p.83.
7. Goldstein, p. 84; Burk, p. 23.
8. Seymour, p. 24.
9. Selzer, p. 3.
10. Vincent, p. 88.
11. David Quenton Voight, *American Baseball: From Gentleman's Sport to the Commissioner System* (Norman: University of Oklahoma Press, 1966), p. 15.
12. *Ibid.*, p. 15.
13. Goldstein, p. 84.
14. Seymour, pp. 51–52.
15. *Ibid.*, p. 29.
16. Vincent, p. 122.
17. Goldstein, p. 103.
18. *Ibid.*, p. 107.
19. Peter Levine, *A.G. Spalding and the Rise of Baseball: The Promise of American Sport* (New York: Oxford University Press, 1985), pp. 10–11.
20. Seymour, p. 57.
21. Goldstein, p. 99.
22. Selzer, p. 7.
23. Voight, p. 19.
24. Selzer, p. 7.
25. Voight, p. 41.
26. Mark Alvarez, *The Old Ball Game* (Alexandria, Va.: Redefinition, Inc., 1990), pp. 102–113; Di Salvatore, p. 87; Burk, p. 46.
27. Seymour, p. 59.
28. Goldstein, p. 112.
29. Vincent, p. 14.
30. *Ibid.*, p. 131.
31. Selzer, p. 7.
32. Voight, pp. 20–21.
33. Goldstein, p. 97.
34. *Ibid.*, p. 149.
35. Selzer, p. 8.
36. Goldstein, p. 90.
37. Steven Riess, "Professional Baseball and American Culture in the Progressive Era: Myths and Realities" (Ph.D. dissertation, University of Chicago, 1974), p. 13.
38. Alvarez, pp. 107–113.
39. Bill Mooney, "The Tattletale Grays," *Sports Illustrated*, October 14, 1974, pp. E6-E8.
40. Alvarez, pp. 107–113.
41. Selzer, p. 8.
42. Survey of Sporting Press, 1871–1876.
43. Vincent, pp. 129–130.

## Chapter 2

1. William Hulbert file, National Baseball Library, Cooperstown, New York; Burk, p. 51.
2. Daniel Okrent and Harris Lewine, eds., *The Ultimate Baseball Book* (Boston: Houghton Mifflin Co., 1981), p. 12.
3. Levine, *A.G. Spalding and the Rise of Baseball*, pp. 23–25; Voight, p. 63.
4. *Ibid.*, p. 63.
5. Seymour, p. 76; Nick Salvatore, *Eugene V. Debs: Citizen and Socialist* (Chicago: University of Illinois Press, 1982), p. 56.
6. Selzer, p. 10.
7. Seymour, p. 81.
8. Selzer, p. 10; Mooney, p. 74.
9. Voight, p. 65.
10. Seymour, p. 81.
11. Levine, p. 24.
12. Albert Spalding file, vol. I, National Baseball Library, Cooperstown, New York; Henry Chadwick file, vol. II, National Baseball Library, Cooperstown, New York.
13. Seymour, p. 190.
14. Levine, p. 24.
15. Seymour, p. 82.
16. Okrent and Lewine, p. 12.
17. Henry Chadwick, ed., *Spalding's Base Ball Guide and Official League Book for 1890* (Chicago: A.G. Spalding and Bros., 1890), p. 8.
18. Seymour, p. 191.
19. Levine, p. 51.
20. Henry Chadwick, ed., *Spalding's Base Ball Guide and Official League Book for 1889* (Chicago: A.G. Spalding and Bros., 1889), pp. Survey.
21. Seymour, p. 91; Reiss, p. 344.
22. Reiss, p. 344.
23. Seymour, p. 207.
24. *Ibid.*, p. 328.
25. Henry Chadwick, ed., *Spalding's Base Ball Guide and Official League Book for 1884* (Chicago: A.G. Spalding and Bros., 1884), pp. Survey.
26. Seymour, p. 328.
27. Reiss, p. 22.
28. *Sporting News*, May 13, 1883.
29. Levine, p. 51.
30. *Saint Louis Post-Dispatch*, May 19, 1883.
31. Vincent, pp. 105–106.
32. Reiss, p. 209.
33. Vincent, p. 114.
34. Reiss, p. 203.

35. *Ibid.*, p. 203.
36. *Ibid.*, pp. 351, 360.
37. *Ibid.*, pp. 351, 360; Seymour, p. 327.
38. *New York Clipper*, December 25, 1875; Voight, p. 52.
39. Vincent, p. 134.
40. Levine, p. 24.
41. Seymour, p. 104.
42. Vincent, p. 135.
43. Voight, p. 74.
44. Daniel M. Pearson, *Baseball in 1889: Players vs. Owners* (Bowling Green, Oh.: Bowling Green State University Popular Press, 1993), pp. 86, 153; Mooney, p. E6-E8.
45. Voight, p. 66.
46. Selzer, p. 18.
47. Goldstein, pp. 151–152.
48. Seymour, p. 67.
49. Henry Chadwick, ed., *Spalding's Base Ball Guide and Official League Book for 1880* (Chicago: A.G. Spalding and Bros., 1880), p. 45; Seymour, p. 67
50. Vincent, pp. 146–149.
51. *Sporting News*, April 30, 1876.
52. Okrent and Lewine, p. 15.
53. Voight, p. 69.
54. Seymour, p. 135.
55. Selzer, p. 13; Pearson, pp. 38–39.
56. *Sporting News*, August 4, 1888.
57. Vincent, p. 114.
58. Voight, pp. 125–126.
59. Henry Chadwick, ed., *Spalding's Official Base Ball Guide and Official League Book for 1891* (Chicago: A.G. Spalding and Bros., 1891), p. 38.
60. Selzer, p. 15; Seymour, pp. 100, 101, 148, 364; Joseph L. Reichler, ed., *The Baseball Encyclopedia: The Complete and Official Record of Major League Baseball*, seventh edition (New York: Macmillan, 1988), pp. Survey; Burk, pp. 57–58; Frederick Ivor-Campbell, Robert L. Tiemann, Mark Rucker, eds., *Baseball's First Stars* (Cleveland: The Society for American Baseball Research, 1996), p. ix.
61. Selzer, p. 10.
62. Seymour, p. 94.
63. *Reach's Official American Association Base Ball Guide: 1891* (Philadelphia: A.J. Reach Company, 1891), p. 145.
64. Burk, pp. 92–93; Voight, p. 130.
65. *Ibid.*, p. 130; Levine, p. 37; Vincent, p. 70; Seymour, p. 119; Selzer, p. 12; Di Salvatore, pp. 45, 91, 144–145.
66. Voight, p. 220.
67. Levine, p. 37; *Sporting News*, August 31, 1889.

68. Henry Chadwick, ed., *Spalding's Base Ball Guide and Official League Book for 1878* (Chicago: A.G. Spalding and Bros., 1878), p. 50.
69. Seymour, p. 208–209.
70. Levine, p. 56; Seymour, p. 202.
71. Seymour, p. 86.
72. Spalding file, vol. I.
73. *Ibid.*
74. Seymour, pp. 202–203.

## Chapter 3

1. Chadwick, *Spalding's Base Ball Guide for 1880*, p. 22.
2. Selzer, pp. 6–7.
3. Henry Chadwick, ed., *Spalding's Base Ball Guide and Official League Book for 1876* (Chicago: A.G. Spalding and Bros., 1876), pp. Survey.
4. Henry Chadwick, ed., *Spalding's Base Ball Guide and Official League Book for 1877* (Chicago: A.G. Spalding and Bros.,1877), pp. Survey; Seymour, p. 82; Survey of *Spalding Guides*, 1876–1879.
5. Chadwick, *Spalding's Base Ball Guide for 1878*, pp. Survey.
6. *Ibid.*, pp. Survey.
7. Seymour, p. 108.
8. Selzer, p. 15.
9. Vincent, p. 190.
10. *Sporting News*, August 11, 1888; Levine, p. 40; Seymour, p. 170; Reichler, pp. Survey.
11. Chadwick, *Spalding's Base Ball Guide for 1880*, p. 24.
12. *Ibid.*, p. 45.
13. Chadwick, *Spalding's Base Ball Guide for 1884*, pp. 41–43.
14. *Ibid.*, pp. 12, 41–43; Seymour, p. 106; Burk, 243.
15. Chadwick, *Spalding's Base Ball Guide for 1884*, pp. 44–45.
16. Chadwick, *Spalding's Base Ball Guide for 1891*, p. 93.
17. Chadwick, *Spalding's Base Ball Guide for 1890*, pp. 12–13.
18. Goldstein, p. 113.
19. Henry Chadwick, ed., *Spalding's Base Ball Guide and Official League Book for 1881* (Chicago: A.G. Spalding and Bros., 1881), pp. 14–15.
20. Henry Chadwick, ed., *Spalding's Base Ball Guide and Official League Book for 1882* (Chicago: A.G. Spalding and Bros., 1882), pp. 26–27.

21. *Sporting News*, October 20, 1888.
22. Chadwick, *Spalding's Base Ball Guide for 1890*, pp. 12–13.
23. Levine, p. 42; Chadwick, *Spalding's Base Ball Guide for 1884*, pp. 44–45; Chadwick, *Spalding's Base Ball Guide for 1882*, p. 26.
24. Levine, p. 30.
25. Chadwick, *Spalding's Base Ball Guide for 1891*, p. 206; Chadwick file, vol. II.
26. *Sporting News*, May 21, 1936; Voight, p. 70.
27. Henry Chadwick, ed., *Spalding's Base Ball Guide and Official League Book for 1883* (Chicago: A.G. Spalding and Bros., 1883), p. 24.
28. Vincent, p. 186; Voight, p. 174; Burk, p. 90.
29. *Sporting Life*, August 1, 1886; *Sporting Life*, August 8, 1886.
30. Fred Pfeffer file, National Baseball Library, Cooperstown, New York.
31. Chadwick, *Spalding's Base Ball Guide for 1880*, p. 87.
32. Chadwick, *Spalding's Base Ball Guide for 1890*, p. 27.
33. *Reach's Base Ball Guide: 1891*, p. 144; Chadwick, *Spalding's Base Ball Guide for 1880*, p. 88; *Reach's Official American Association Base Ball Guide: 1890* (Philadelphia, PA: A.J. Reach Company, 1890), p. 26; Lee Lowenfish and Tony Lupien, *The Imperfect Diamond: The Story of Baseball's Reserve System and the Men Who Fought to Change It* (New York: Stein and Day Publishers, 1980), p. 31; Okrent and Lewine, p. 16.
34. Chadwick, *Spalding's Base Ball Guide for 1883*, p. 95.
35. Chadwick, *Spalding's Base Ball Guide for 1882*, p. 29.
36. Vincent, pp. 186–187; Voight, p. 106.
37. Chadwick, *Spalding's Base Ball Guide for 1882*, p. 26.
38. Chadwick, *Spalding's Base Ball Guide for 1883*, p. 24.
39. Chadwick file, vol. II.
40. Arthur Bartlett, *Baseball and Mr. Spalding: The History and Romance of Baseball* (New York: Farrar, Straus and Young, Inc., 1951), p. 205.
41. *Sporting Life*, November 28, 1888; Levine, p. 58; Di Salvatore, p. 262.
42. Seymour, pp. 125, 129, 130, 224.
43. *Sporting Life*, November 28, 1888.
44. *Ibid.*
45. *Sporting Life*, December 5, 1888.
46. *Sporting Life*, November 28, 1888.
47. *Sporting News*, May 21, 1936.

48. Chadwick, *Spalding's Base Ball Guide for 1880*, pp. 50–51; Burk, pp. 71–72; Di Salvatore, pp. 156–157, 165.
49. Seymour, pp. 98–100.
50. Chadwick, *Spalding's Base Ball Guide for 1883*, p. 24.
51. Chadwick, *Spalding's Base Ball Guide for 1880*, pp. 50–51; Seymour, p. 100.
52. Seymour, p. 139.
53. *Ibid.*, p. 143.
54. Voight, p. 123; *New York Clipper*, November 12, 1881.
55. *Reach's Base Ball Guide: 1890*, pp. 116–119.
56. *Ibid.*, p. 120.
57. Chadwick, *Spalding's Base Ball Guide for 1883*, p. 32; Seymour, pp. 139–140.
58. Chadwick, *Spalding's Base Ball Guide for 1890*, pp. 9–10.
59. Levine, pp. 51–52; Chadwick, *Spalding's Base Ball Guide for 1883*, pp. Survey; Chadwick, *Spalding's Base Ball Guide for 1884*, pp. Survey.
60. Chadwick, *Spalding's Base Ball Guide for 1883*, pp. 58–60.
61. Levine, p. 52; Chadwick, *Spalding's Base Ball Guide for 1890*, p. 147.
62. Chadwick, *Spalding's Base Ball Guide for 1882*, pp. League Constitution.
63. Chadwick file, vol. II.
64. Chadwick, *Spalding's Base Ball Guide for 1883*, pp. 58–61.
65. Seymour, pp. 146–147.
66. Selzer, p. 15.
67. Seymour, pp. 169–170; Henry Chadwick, ed., *Spalding's Base Ball Guide and Official League Book for 1886* (Chicago: A.G. Spalding and Bros., 1886), pp. Survey.
68. *Sporting Life*, 1887; Albert Spalding file, vol. II, National Baseball Library, Cooperstown, New York.
69. Seymour, p. 147; Vincent, p. 150; *Reach's Base Ball Guide: 1890*, pp. 8–9; Chadwick, *Spalding's Base Ball Guide for 1890*, pp. 151–152; Albert Spalding file, vol. VI, National Baseball Library, Cooperstown, New York.
70. Levine, p. 56; *Sporting Life*, June 8, 1887.
71. *Sporting Life*, August 1, 1886; *Sporting Life*, August 8, 1886.
72. Spalding file, vol. VI.
73. Chadwick, *Spalding's Base Ball Guide for 1880*, p.83.
74. Seymour, pp. 105–106.
75. Chadwick, *Spalding's Base Ball Guide for 1886*, pp. Survey.

76. Levine, p. 53.
77. Mark Alvarez, "The Brotherhood Rebellion," *Sports Heritage*, July/August 1987, pp. 15–23; Survey of National League Constitutions: 1876–1887.

## Chapter 4

1. Alfred D. Chandler Jr., *The Visible Hand: The Managerial Revolution in American Business* (Cambridge: The Belknap Press of Harvard University Press, 1977), p. 484.
2. David Montgomery, *The Fall of the House of Labor: The Workplace, the State, and American Labor Activism 1865–1925* (Cambridge: Cambridge University Press, 1987), p. 214; Chandler, p. 202.
3. Bruce Laurie, *Artisans Into Workers: Labor in Nineteenth Century America* (New York: Hill and Wang, 1989), pp. 113–115.
4. Chandler, p. 484.
5. Montgomery, p. 47.
6. Jeremy Brecher, *Strike* (Boston: South End Press, 1972), p. XXI.
7. Montgomery, p. 184.
8. *Ibid.*, pp. 251, 254.
9. David Montgomery, *Workers' Control in America: Studies in the History of Work, Technology and Labor Struggles* (New York: Cambridge University Press, 1979), p. 26.
10. Levine, p. 26.
11. Brecher, p. 21.
12. Chandler, p. 317.
13. David Gordon, Richard Edwards, and Michael Reich, *Segmented Work, Divided Workers: The Historical Transformation of Labor in the United States* (Cambridge: Cambridge University Press, 1982), pp. 94–95.
14. Chandler, p. 319.
15. *Ibid.*, pp. 278, 319, 485.
16. *Ibid.*, pp. 316, 319, 423–424.
17. Seymour, p. 190.
18. Gordon, Edwards, and Reich, p. 91.
19. Laurie, p. 86.
20. Gordon, Edwards, and Reich, p. 67.
21. Laurie, p. 78.
22. Gordon, Edwards, and Reich, p. 3.
23. Laurie, p. 103; Pearson, pp. 13–14, 68.
24. Montgomery, *Workers' Control in America*, p. 17.
25. *Ibid.*, p. 15.
26. Gordon, Edwards, and Reich, pp. 115, 125.
27. Laurie, p. 176.

28. *Ibid.*, p. 176.
29. Salvatore, p. 66.
30. Laurie, p. 178.
31. *Ibid.*, p. 183.
32. Montgomery, *Workers' Control in America*, pp. 23–24.
33. Brecher, p. 25.
34. Laurie, pp. 142, 174.
35. *Ibid.*, p. 149.
36. Brecher, p. 28.
37. Laurie, pp. 150–151.
38. *Ibid.*, p. 155.
39. Salvatore, pp. 27–29, 43.
40. *Ibid.*, pp. 27, 43.
41. *Ibid.*, p. 138.
42. Montgomery, *The Fall of the House of Labor*, pp. 287, 425.
43. Salvatore, pp. 19, 47, 48.
44. *Ibid.*, pp. 48, 58.
45. Montgomery, *The Fall of the House of Labor*, pp. 204, 209.
46. Laurie, p. 185.
47. Salvatore, p. 25.
48. Montgomery, *The Fall of the House of Labor*, p. 250.
49. Salvatore, p. 61.
50. Tim Keefe file, National Baseball Library, Cooperstown, New York. Pearson, pp. 72, 77.
51. Salvatore, p. 24.
52. *Sporting Life*, April 12, 1890.
53. Brecher, p. 33.
54. *Ibid.*, p. 69.
55. Gordon, Edwards, and Reich, p. 67.
56. Montgomery, *The Fall of the House of Labor*, p. 90.
57. Salvatore, pp. 97, 156.

## Chapter 5

1. Goldstein, pp. 24–25.
2. *Ibid.*, p. 114.
3. *Ibid.*, p. 121.
4. *Ibid.*, p. 118.
5. *Ibid.*, p. 23.
6. Survey of Sporting Press, 1865–1876.
7. Goldstein, pp. 25, 31; Survey of Sporting Press, 1865–1876.
8. *New York Times*, March 10, 1872.
9. Montgomery, *Workers' Control in America*, p. 11; Vincent, pp. 140–145.
10. Seymour, p. 118.
11. Montgomery, *The Fall of the House of Labor*, p. 27.
12. Voight, p. 293.
13. *Sporting News*, July 21, 1888.

14. Voight, p. 170; Survey of *Spalding's Base Ball Guides*: 1880–1889.
15. Vincent, p. 181.
16. Reiss, p. 253; Survey of Players' Letters, National Baseball Library, Cooperstown, New York.
17. Vincent, pp. 181–184.
18. Seymour, p. 118.
19. Vincent, pp. 183–185.
20. Fred Pfeffer file.
21. Reiss, p. 248.
22. *Sporting Life*, January 23, 1892.
23. Reiss, p. 251.
24. Voight, p. 171.
25. Seymour, p. 336.
26. Lowenfish and Lupian, p. 40–43.
27. Reiss, p. 22.
28. Voight, pp. 85, 175, 176.
29. *Sporting News*, August 4, 1888.
30. Frank H. Brunell, ed., *Players' National League Base Ball Guide for 1890* (Chicago: W.J. Jefferson Print, 1889), p. 11.
31. Voight, p. 285.
32. Seymour, p. 164.
33. Vincent, p. 154.
34. *Ibid.*, p. 104.
35. *Ibid.*, p. 182.
36. Voight, p. 172.
37. *Sporting Life*, July 18, 1888; *Sporting Life*, July 25, 1888.
38. *Sporting Life*, February 26, 1890.
39. Seymour, pp. 202–204.
40. Goldstein, pp. 144, 146; Survey of Sporting Press, 1880–1888.
41. Montgomery, *The Fall of the House of Labor*, pp. 113–115.
42. Goldstein, p. 140.
43. Spalding file, vol. I.
44. Chadwick, *Spalding's Base Ball Guide for 1890*, p. 59.
45. Bill James, *The Bill James Historical Baseball Abstract* (New York: Villard Books, 1986), pp. Survey.
46. Chadwick, *Spalding's Base Ball Guide for 1890*, p. 59.
47. *Ibid.*, pp. 11–12.
48. Brecher, p. 46.
49. Reiss, p. 22.
50. Voight, pp. 282–283.
51. *Chicago Tribune*, July 30, 1882.
52. Chadwick, *Spalding's Base Ball Guide for 1891*, p. 89.
53. Vincent, p. 185.
54. Levine, p. 24.
55. Herbert Gutman, *Work, Culture, and Society in Industrializing America: Essays in*

*American Working Class and Social History* (New York: Vintage Books, 1977), p. 53.

56. Chadwick, *Spalding's Base Ball Guide for 1884*, p. 97.

57. Henry Chadwick, ed., *Spalding's Base Ball Guide and Official League Book for 1893* (Chicago: A.G. Spalding and Bros., 1893), p. 97.

58. Salvatore, pp. 72–77.

59. Jonathan Prude, *The Coming of Industrial Order: Town and Factory Life in Rural Massachusetts, 1810–1860* (New York: Cambridge University Press, 1983), pp. Survey.

60. Laurie, p. 185; Montgomery, *The Fall of the House of Labor*, p. 204.

61. Goldstein, pp. 30–35, 76.

62. Reiss, p. 7.

63. Voight, pp. 25–32; Goldstein, p. 45.

64. *Ibid.*, pp. 60–61, 79.

65. Seymour, p. 89; Voight, pp. 289–291.

66. *Ibid.*, pp. 287–288; Pearson, pp. 21–22; Burk, pp. 73–74, 128.

67. Survey of Sporting Press, 1863; Pearson, pp. 21–22; Burk, pp. 73–74, 128.

68. Voight, pp. 71, 80.

69. Goldstein, p. 36.

70. Voight, p. 175.

## Chapter 6

1. Seymour, p. 345.

2. *Ibid.*, pp. 347–348.

3. *New York Times*, October 15, 1889.

4. Voight, p. 220.

5. Peter Levine, ed., *Baseball History: An Annual of Original Baseball Research: Volume II* (Westport, CT: Mechler Books, 1989), p. 94.

6. Chadwick, *Spalding's Base Ball Guide for 1890*, p. 119.

7. Reiss, p. 9; *Reach's Base Ball Guide: 1890*, pp. 3–4; Brunell, p. 16; Burk, p.73.

8. Levine, *Baseball History*, p. 94; *Sporting Life*, January 8, 1890; *Chicago Times*, December 18, 1892.

9. Chadwick, *Spalding's Base Ball Guide for 1890*, pp. 21–30; *Reach's Base Ball Guide: 1890*, p. 11.

10. *Ibid.*, p. 7.

11. Okrent and Lewine, p. 17; *Sporting Life*, August 1, 1886; *Sporting Life*, August 8, 1886; *Sporting News*, August 4, 1886.

12. Seymour, p. 221.

13. *Sporting Life*, August 1, 1886; *Sporting Life*, August 8, 1886; *Sporting News*, August 4, 1886; Di Salvatore, pp. 176–177.

14. Preston Orem, *Baseball from the Newspaper Accounts: 1890* (Altadena, Calif.: Presdon D. Orem, 1967), p. 446.

15. Brunell, p. 7.

16. Orem, p. 446.

17. *Sporting News*, August 4, 1886; *Sporting Life*, August 1, 1886; *Sporting Life*, August 8, 1886.

18. *Ibid.*

19. *Ibid.*

20. *Ibid.*

21. John Montgomery Ward, *Base-Ball: How to Become a Player* (Philadelphia: Athletic Publishing Co., 1888), p. 31; *Sporting Life*, August 1, 1886; *Sporting Life*, August 8, 1886; *Sporting News*, August 4, 1888; Di Salvatore, pp. 146–147.

22. Ward, *Base-Ball: How to Become a Player*, p. 31.

23. Bartlett, pp. 201–202.

24. *Sporting Life*, September 28, 1887; *Sporting Life*, November 9, 1887.

25. *Sporting Life*, August 24, 1887.

26. *Sporting Life*, September 14, 1887; *Sporting Life*, November 9, 1887.

27. Survey of Sporting Press, 1887–1888.

28. Brunell, p. 9.

29. *Sporting Life*, November 9, 1887; *Sporting Life*, September 14, 1887.

30. *Sporting Life*, September 28, 1887.

31. *Ibid.*

32. *Sporting Life*, October 19, 1887.

33. *Sporting Life*, September 28, 1887.

34. *Ibid.*

35. *Sporting News*, December 16, 1887; *Sporting Life*, December 14, 1887; *Sporting Life*, December 21, 1887.

36. *Sporting News*, December 16, 1887; *Sporting Life*, November 23, 1887; *Sporting Life*, August 15, 1886; *Sporting Life*, December 14, 1887; *Sporting Life*, December 21, 1887.

37. Brunell, pp. 3–4.

38. *Sporting Life*, November 23, 1887.

39. Ward, *Base-Ball: How to Become a Player*, p. 32.

40. Orem, p. 446.

41. Spalding file, vol. VI.

42. *Sporting Life*, March 9, 1912; *Sporting Life*, March 16, 1912.

43. *Sporting Life*, January 8, 1890.

44. Orem, p. 446.

45. *Sporting Life*, November 28, 1888.

46. Okrent and Lewine, p. 17.

47. Cynthia Bass, "The Making of a Baseball Radical," *The National Pastime* (Fall, 1982): pp. 63–66; Lowenfish and Lupian, p. 32.

48. Brunell, p. 4.
49. Seymour, pp. 224–225.
50. Bass, p. 65.
51. *Sporting Life*, January 8, 1890.
52. *Sporting News*, April 3, 1972; Pearson, pp. 144, 150, 158, 173, 183, 223–224; Burk, p. 99; Chadwick, *Spalding's Base Ball Guide for 1890*, p.119; Reiss, p. 9; *Reach's Base Ball Guide: 1890*, pp. 3–4; Brunell, p. 16; Levine, *Baseball History*, p. 94; *Sporting Life*, January 8, 1890; *Chicago Times*, December 18, 1892.
53. Survey of Sporting Press, 1887–1890.
54. *Sporting Life*, January 22, 1890.
55. Seymour, pp. 126–127.
56. *Ibid.*, p. 225.
57. Bill James, *The Baseball Book 1990* (New York: Villard Books, 1990), p. 143; Lowenfish and Lupian, p. 34.
58. *Ibid.*, p. 31; John M. Ward, "Is the Base-Ball Player a Chattel?," *Lippencott's Magazine*, August, 1887, pp. 310–319.
59. Chadwick, *Spalding's Base Ball Guide for 1890*, pp. 10–11; Orem, p. 446; Chadwick, *Spalding's Base Ball Guide for 1889*, p. 11; Spalding File, vol. VI; Burk, pp. 103–104.
60. Survey of Sporting Press, 1888–1889; Chadwick, *Spalding's Base Ball Guide for 1889*, pp. 11–12.

## Chapter 7

1. Levine, *A.G. Spalding and the Rise of Baseball*, p. 3.
2. *Ibid.*, p. 9.
3. *Ibid.*, pp. 13, 16.
4. Levine, *A.G. Spalding and the Rise of Baseball*, pp. 3, 17.
5. *Ibid.*, p. 13; Reichler, p. 2,155.
6. Levine, *A.G. Spalding and the Rise of Baseball*, p. 21.
7. *Ibid.*, pp. 28–29, 70.
8. *Sporting Life*, September 28, 1887.
9. Chadwick, *Spalding's Base Ball Guide for 1893*.
10. Chadwick, *Spalding's Base Ball Guide for 1890*, pp. 14, 15, 31.
11. Levine, *A.G. Spalding and the Rise of Baseball*, pp. 68–70, 146.
12. Seymour, p. 352; Pearson, p. 66.
13. Alvarez, "The Brotherhood Rebellion," p. 16.
14. Voight, p. 217; Di Salvatore, p. 225.
15. Levine, *A.G. Spalding and the Rise of Baseball*, p. 83.
16. Voight, pp. 217–218.

17. Levine, *A.G. Spalding and the Rise of Baseball*, p. 93.
18. Seymour, p. 352.
19. John M. Ward file, National Baseball Library, Cooperstown, New York; Letter from John M. Fleming, nephew of John Ward, December 30, 1963, Ward file; Letter from Winifred Watson, cousin of John Ward, February 20, 1964, Ward file; Di Salvatore, pp. 23, 29, 42.
20. Ward file.
21. Marvin Lee, "Strike Four! You're Out!," *Town and Gown*, April 1978; Di Salvatore, 94.
22. Alvarez, "The Brotherhood Rebellion," p. 15; Di Salvatore, p. 41.
23. *Ibid.*, p. 15; Ward file; Di Salvatore, pp. 56–57.
24. Ward file; Lee.
25. Ward file; Reichler, p. 2,211.
26. Lee; Reichler, Survey; Di Salvatore, pp. 118, 133.
27. Letter from Robert Tiemann, Chairman of Nineteenth Century Committee, Society for American Baseball Research.
28. Okrent and Lewine, p. 14.
29. Bass, pp. 63, 64; Di Salvatore, pp. 136, 141.
30. Notes of Mark Alvarez, Librarian; Society for American Baseball Research, author of numerous books and articles on nineteenth century baseball.
31. *Ibid.*; *Sporting Life*, March 2, 1912; *Sporting Life*, March 16, 1912; Alvarez, "The Brotherhood Rebellion," p. 15.
32. Lee Lowenfish, "The Later Years of John M. Ward: Is a Ballplayer Barred from Business Association with Respectable Men?" *The National Pastime* (Fall 1982), p. 67; Ward file.
33. *Ibid.*
34. Lowenfish and Lupien, p. 28; Ward file; Di Salvatore, p. 237.
35. Ward, *Base-Ball: How to Become a Player*, p. 25 and Survey.
36. Phone conversation, Columbia University Law School, New York, Liz Hydes, Director of Alumni Relations, March 14, 1991; Di Salvatore, pp. 181–182.
37. Ward file; *Sporting News*, November 24, 1888; Alvarez, "The Brotherhood Rebellion," p. 15.
38. *Sporting Life*, January 22, 1900.
39. *Sporting Life*, October 19, 1887; Di Salvatore, pp. 196, 236.
40. Survey of Sporting Press, 1888–1890; Di Salvatore, pp. 328–338.

41. Ward file; Di Salvatore, pp. 10, 131.
42. *Sporting Life*, June 14, 1890.
43. *Sporting Life*, July 27, 1887.
44. *Sporting News*, September 15, 1888; *Sporting News*, September 22, 1888.
45. Orem, p. 488; Di Salvatore, p. 191.
46. Ward, *Base-Ball: How to Become a Player*, p. 31.
47. *Ibid.*, p. 26.
48. *Ibid.*, p. 27.
49. Bass, pp. 64–65.
50. Bartlett, p. 204.
51. Bass, pp. 63–65; Survey of Sporting Press, 1887–1889.
52. *Sporting Life*, February 6, 1915; Ward file.
53. Albert Spalding file, vol. V, National Baseball Library, Cooperstown, New York.
54. Ward file.
55. Vincent, p. 195; *Sporting Life*, July 20, 1887.
56. *Ibid.*; Vincent, p. 195.
57. Bass, p. 64–65; Ward File.
58. *Sporting Life*, January 8, 1890.
59. Vincent, p. 195.
60. Bass, pp. 64–65.
61. Ward, "Is the Base-Ball Player a Chattel?," pp. 310–319.

## Chapter 8

1. Brunell, p. 3.
2. Vincent, p. 190.
3. Voight, p. 155; Brunell, p. 3.
4. *New York Times*, January 17, 1890.
5. Lowenfish and Lupien, p. 31.
6. *Ibid.*; Pearson, p. 11.
7. *Sporting Life*, January 22, 1890; Pearson, pp. 44, 52; Di Salvatore. pp. 148–150.
8. *Sporting Life*, January 8, 1890; Pearson, pp. 44–52.
9. *Sporting Life*, May 24, 1890.
10. Chadwick, *Spalding's Base Ball Guide for 1890*, p. 26.
11. Fred Pfeffer file; Burk, p. 101.
12. Brunell, p. 9; Di Salvatore, pp. 263, 265; Pearson, 51.
13. Chadwick, *Spalding's Base Ball Guide for 1890*, p. 30.
14. Survey of New York Giants' Box Scores, June 21, 1889-July 8, 1889; Survey of Sporting Press, 1889.
15. *Kansas City Star*, February 18, 1969.
16. Brunell, p. 4.
17. Seymour, pp. 226–227.
18. Chadwick file, vol. IV.
19. Orem, p. 447.
20. Vincent, p. 197.
21. Orem, p. 447; *Sporting Life*, June 28, 1890.
22. Henry Chadwick file, vol. IV, National Baseball Library, Cooperstown, New York; Reiss, p. 110.
23. Orem, p. 447.
24. Chadwick file, vol. II; Reiss, p. 103; Orem, p. 448.
25. *Ibid.*, p. 448; Lowenfish and Lupien, p. 35; Ward File.
26. James, *The Baseball Book 1990*, p. 143; *Sporting Life*, June 7, 1890.
27. Chadwick, *Spalding's Base Ball Guide for 1890*, p. 10.
28. Vincent, p. 194.
29. Seymour, p. 228; Bartlett, pp. 208–209.
30. Spalding File, vol. II; Vincent, p. 198; Orem, pp. 449–450.
31. Brunell, p. 5.
32. *Reach's Base Ball Guide: 1890*, p. 16.
33. Seymour, p. 228; Orem, p. 247.
34. *Reach's Base Ball Guide: 1890*, p. 17.
35. Vincent, p. 194; *Sporting Life*, June 14, 1890; *Reach's Base Ball Guide: 1890*, p. 17.
36. *Sporting Life*, February 5, 1890.
37. Vincent, p. 196; *Sporting Life*, June 7, 1890.
38. *Reach's Base Ball Guide: 1890*, p. 17.
39. Orem, p. 448.
40. Edward Talcott file, National Baseball Library, Cooperstown, New York.
41. *New York Times*, November 7, 1889.
42. Orem, p. 447; Brunell, p. 5; Burk, p. 110.
43. *Reach's Base Ball Guide: 1890*, pp. 40–42; Bartlett, pp. 209–212; Pfeffer file.
44. *Sporting Life*, April 12, 1890.
45. Brunell, pp. 97–99.
46. James, *The Baseball Book 1990*, p. 152; *Sporting Life*, March 5, 1890; *Sporting Life*, March 12, 1890.
47. James, *The Baseball Book 1990*, p. 145; *New York Times*, March 23, 1890.
48. James, *The Baseball Book 1990*, pp. 144, 149, 152.
49. *Reach's Base Ball Guide: 1890*, p. 17; *Sporting Life*, May 31, 1890.
50. *Ibid.*; James, *The Baseball Book 1990*, p. 146.
51. Keefe file; James, *The Baseball Book 1990*, p. 150.
52. *Sporting Life*, February 26, 1890; James, *The Baseball Book 1990*, p. 150.

53. Chadwick, *Spalding's Base Ball Guide for 1890*, p. 24.
54. Lowenfish and Lupien, pp. 33, 43.
55. James, *The Baseball Book 1990*, p. 144.
56. *New York Times*, March 23, 1890.
57. *Sporting Life*, April 5, 1890.
58. *Sporting Life*, May 31, 1890.
59. *Sporting Life*, May 24, 1890.
60. *Reach's Base Ball Guide: 1890*, p. 14; Bartlett, p. 209.
61. *Sporting Life*, February 12, 1890; *Sporting Life*, March 26, 1890; Brunell, p. 99.
62. *New York Times*, January 11, 1890; *New York Times*, January 14, 1890.
63. *Sporting Life*, March 5, 1890.
64. *Sporting Life*, January 8, 1890.
65. Vincent, pp. 202–203.
66. Levine, *A.G. Spalding and the Rise of Baseball*, pp. 60–62; *New York Clipper*, November 23, 1889.
67. *Sporting Life*, January 8, 1890.
68. *New York Times*, February 5, 1890.
69. Chadwick, *Spalding's Base Ball Guide for 1890*, pp. 14–16.
70. *Sporting Life*, May 31, 1890.
71. Bartlett, p. 209; Chadwick, *Spalding's Base Ball Guide for 1890*, pp. 14–18.
72. *Sporting Life*, May 31, 1890.
73. Levine, *A.G. Spalding and the Rise of Baseball*, pp. 60–63; Chadwick, *Spalding's Base Ball Guide for 1890*, pp. 28–31.
74. Vincent, p. 202.
75. Reichler, pp. 162–163.
76. James, *The Baseball Book 1990*, p. 144.
77. *Sporting Life*, September 27, 1890.
78. *Sporting Life*, February 26, 1890.
79. Chadwick, *Spalding's Base Ball Guide for 1891*, p. 66.
80. *Sporting Life*, May 31, 1890.
81. *New York Times*, October 22, 1889.
82. *New York Times*, October 29, 1889.
83. *New York Times*, January 10, 1890.
84. *New York Times*, January 17, 1890; Chadwick, *Spalding's Base Ball Guide for 1890*, p. 18.
85. *New York Times*, November 13, 1889.
86. *New York Times*, December 16, 1889; *New York Times*, January 7, 1890.
87. *New York Times*, January 29, 1890.
88. *Sporting Life*, February 12, 1890.
89. *Ibid.*
90. *Sporting Life*, February 5, 1890.
91. *New York Times*, March 27, 1890.
92. *New York Times*, March 16, 1890.
93. Seymour, pp. 236–237.
94. *Sporting Life*, May 3, 1890.

95. *Reach's Base Ball Guide: 1891*, p. 3; *Sporting Life*, March 26, 1890.
96. *Sporting Life*, March 12, 1890.
97. *New York Times*, March 9, 1890.
98. Lowenfish and Lupien, pp. 44–48; Vincent, p. 198; Survey of Sporting Press, 1890.
99. Seymour, pp. 232, 350.
100. Okrent and Lewine, p. 14.
101. Seymour, p. 232.
102. *Sporting Life*, January 15, 1890.
103. *Ibid.*
104. *Sporting Life*, April 12, 1890.
105. *Sporting Life*, May 31, 1890.
106. Ward file.
107. Vincent, p. 198.
108. Survey of Available Newspapers, 1890.
109. *Sporting Life*, April 5, 1890.
110. Chadwick file, vol. II.
111. Seymour, p. 231; Albert Spalding file, vol. III, National Baseball Library, Cooperstown, New York.
112. *New York Times*, March 4, 1890.
113. *New York Times*, March 17, 1890.
114. *New York Times*, December 13, 1889.
115. *Sporting Life*, January 1, 1890.
116. Chadwick, *Spalding's Base Ball Guide for 1890*, pp. 15–16, 24.
117. Voight, p. 162.
118. Ward file.
119. *Sporting Life*, May 31, 1890.
120. Brunell, p. 5; *Sporting Life*, January 22, 1890.
121. *Sporting Life*, June 14, 1890.
122. Spalding file, vol. II.
123. Ned Hanlon File, National Baseball Library, Cooperstown, New York; Levine, *A.G. Spalding and the Rise of Baseball*, p. 61; Bartlett, pp. 215–216; Lowenfish and Lupien, p. 44; *New York Clipper*, August 16, 1890.
124. Vincent, pp. 199–200.
125. Orem, pp. 488–490; *Sporting Life*, April 26, 1890.
126. *Ibid.*
127. *Ibid.*; *Sporting Life*, June 7, 1890.
128. *Sporting Life*, May 17, 1890.
129. *Sporting Life*, June 14, 1890; *Sporting Life*, May 10, 1890; Survey of Sporting Press, summer 1890.
130. *Sporting Life*, June 14, 1890.
131. Vincent, p. 209; Seymour, pp. 237–238; *Reach's Base Ball Guide: 1891*, p. 7.
132. Orem, p. 516.
133. James, *The Baseball Book 1990*, pp. 150–151.

134. Voight, pp. 161–163.
135. Vincent, pp. 209–211; Levine, *A.G. Spalding and the Rise of Baseball*, p. 45.
136. *New York Times*, August 11, 1890.
137. *Ibid.*
138. James, *The Baseball Book 1990*, p. 154.
139. *Sporting Life*, May 17, 1890.
140. *Sporting Life*, May 24, 1890; *Reach's Base Ball Guide: 1891*, pp. 6–7.
141. James, *The Baseball Book 1990*, p. 154.
142. *Sporting Life*, June 14, 1890.
143. *Sporting Life*, June 21, 1890.
144. *Sporting Life*, March 12, 1890; *Sporting Life*, May 31, 1890.
145. Vincent, p. 200.
146. *Sporting Life*, January 22, 1890.
147. *Ibid.*
148. *Sporting Life*, January 15, 1890; *Sporting Life*, May 10, 1890.
149. Vincent, p. 201.
150. *Ibid.*, p. 201.
151. *Sporting Life*, April 12, 1890.
152. *Ibid.*
153. *Sporting Life*, November 16, 1887; *Sporting Life*, May 10, 1890.
154. *Ibid.*
155. Chadwick, *Spalding's Base Ball Guide for 1891*, p. 40.
156. *Sporting Life*, June 28, 1890.
157. Seymour, pp. 232–233.
158. *Sporting Life*, April 26, 1890.
159. Vincent, p. 207.
160. James, *The Baseball Book 1990*, p. 145.
161. *Sporting Life*, May 3, 1890.
162. Hanlon file.
163. James, *The Baseball Book 1990*, p. 145.
164. Orem, pp. 493–497; *Sporting Life*, July 12, 1890.
165. *Sporting Life*, June 14, 1890.
166. *New York Times*, July 3, 1890.
167. *Sporting News*, May 10, 1890.
168. *New York Times*, August 18, 1890.
169. *Sporting News*, July 19, 1890.
170. Seymour, p. 238; *Sporting Life*, July 5, 1890.
171. *New York Times*, October 3, 1890; Seymour, p. 238; *New York Times*, September 20, 1890.
172. *New York Times*, September 26, 1890.
173. Chadwick, *Spalding's Base Ball Guide for 1891*, p. 15.
174. Orem, p. 516.
175. Lowenfish and Lupien, p. 47; *New York Times*, October 3, 1890; *New York Times*, November 24, 1890; *Reach's Base Ball Guide: 1891*, p. 21.
176. *New York Times*, May 31, 1890.
177. *Ibid.*
178. *Sporting Life*, May 17, 1890.
179. *New York Times*, October 6, 1890.
180. Orem, pp. 496, 516–517.
181. *New York Times*, October 3, 1890.

## Chapter 9

1. *New York Times*, July 3, 1890.
2. *Sporting Life*, August 16, 1890.
3. *New York Times*, September 1, 1890.
4. *Sporting Life*, August 16, 1890.
5. *New York Times*, August 17, 1890.
6. *Sporting Life*, June 14, 1890.
7. Lowenfish and Lupien, p. 49; Survey of newspapers, June-October, 1890.
8. *Sporting Life*, December 27, 1890.
9. Allan Thurman file, National Baseball Library, Cooperstown, New York.
10. *New York Times*, August 11, 1890.
11. Orem, p. 516.
12. Thurman file.
13. *New York Times*, October 10, 1890.
14. Orem, p. 517; Di Salvatore, pp. 308–309.
15. *Reach's Base Ball Guide: 1891*, p. 8.
16. Orem, p. 517.
17. *Sporting Life*, October 18, 1890; Orem, p. 517; *Sporting Life*, October 11, 1890.
18. Talcott File; *Sporting Life*, October 25, 1890.
19. Alvarez, "The Brotherhood Rebellion," pp. 15–23.
20. Orem, p. 519; James, *The Baseball Book 1990*, p. 149.
21. Orem, p. 519.
22. Alvarez, "The Brotherhood Rebellion," pp. 15–23.
23. *Sporting Life*, November 22, 1890.
24. Orem, p. 521.
25. Lowenfish, pp. 67–69; Vincent, p. 214.
26. *Ibid.*, p. 214.
27. *Ibid.*, p. 214; *Sporting Life*, October 25, 1890; Albert Johnson file, vol. I, National Baseball Library, Cooperstown, New York.
28. *Sporting Life*, November 8, 1890.
29. Orem, p. 522.
30. *Ibid.*, p. 523.
31. *New York Times*, January 7, 1891.
32. Orem, p. 524.

33. *New York Times*, November 22, 1890; Alvarez, "The Brotherhood Rebellion," pp. 15–23.

34. Orem, p. 524.

35. *New York Times*, November 14, 1890.

36. Orem, p. 526.

37. Seymour, p. 245.

38. Seymour, pp. 245–248.

39. *Reach's Base Ball Guide: 1891*, p. 9.

40. Tiemann, phone conversation, February 12, 1991.

41. Albert Johnson file, vol. II, National Baseball Library, Cooperstown, New York.

42. Tiemann, phone conversation.

43. Levine, *A.G. Spalding and the Rise of Baseball*, p. 64; *Chicago Times*, December 28, 1890.

44. *Chicago Herald*, November 23, 1890.

45. James, *The Baseball Book 1990*, p. 153; Vincent, p. 216.

46. *Sporting Life*, November 15, 1890.

47. *Sporting Life*, December 27, 1890.

48. Chadwick, *Spalding's Base Ball Guide for 1891*, p. 13.

49. Chadwick, *Spalding's Base Ball Guide for 1891*, p. 16.

50. Orem, p. 527.

51. *New York Times*, December 20, 1890.

52. Vincent, pp. 210–211.

53. *Sporting Life*, May 3, 1890.

54. Vincent, p. 210.

55. *Sporting Life*, April 7, 1900.

56. *Sporting Life*, April 19, 1890.

57. James, *The Baseball Book 1990*, p. 151.

58. *New York Times*, October 23, 1890.

59. *Reach's Base Ball Guide: 1891*, p. 7.

60. Johnson file, vol. II.

61. Vincent, pp. 215–216.

62. *New York Times*, January 7, 1891.

63. James, *The Baseball Book 1990*, p. 153; Orem, p. 496; *Sporting Life*, November 8, 1890; *Sporting Life*, November 15, 1890.

64. *Ibid.*

65. *New York Times*, October 3, 1890.

66. Survey of Sporting Press, July-October, 1890.

67. James, *The Baseball Book 1990*, p. 152; Vincent, p. 212.

68. *Sporting Life*, October 11, 1890.

69. *Sporting Life*, December 20, 1890.

70. *New York Times*, October 14, 1890.

## Chapter 10

1. Chadwick, *Spalding's Base Ball Guide for 1891*, pp. 50–54.

2. *Reach's Base Ball Guide: 1891*, p. 10; Chadwick, *Spalding's Base Ball Guide for 1891*, pp. 49, 58, 59.

3. Seymour, p. 256–259; *Reach's Base Ball Guide: 1891*, p. 10; Di Salvatore, p. 123.

4. Seymour, pp. 256–259; Selzer, p. 14.

5. Reichler, p. 170 and Survey; Voight, p. 152; Selzer, p. 14; Spalding file, vol. III; Di Salvatore, p. 341.

6. Seymour, pp. 265–266; Voight, p. 152.

7. Okrent and Lewine, p. 20; Spalding file, vol. III.

8. Seymour, pp. 265–272.

9. *Ibid.*, p. 271; Voight, p. 247; Di Salvatore, p. 360; Vincent, p. 217.

10. *Ibid.*, p. 217.

11. *New York Times*, January 6, 1891.

12. Voight, pp. 187–188; Spalding file, vol. VI.

13. Seymour, p. 289.

14. James, *The Historical Baseball Abstract*, p. 38.

15. Voight, p. 187.

16. Montgomery, *The Fall of the House of Labor*, p. 174; Seymour, pp. 295–296.

17. Voight, p. 230.

18. Seymour, p. 304.

19. *Ibid.*, p. 299.

20. Selzer, pp. 23–25.

21. *Ibid.*, p. 22; Voight, p. 232.

22. Seymour, p. 300; Di Salvatore, p. 137.

23. Henry Chadwick,ed., *Spalding's Base Ball Guide and Official League Book for 1898* (Chicago: A.G. Spalding and Bros., 1898), pp. 195–198.

24. Seymour, p. 305.

25. Mark Alvarez, "The Abominable Owner," *Sports Heritage*, November/December, 1987, pp. 43–47.

26. Selzer, p. 23; Reichler, p. 712.

27. *Sporting Life*, April 7, 1900; Pearson, pp. 187, 204; Burk, p. 126; Di Salvatore, p. 366.

28. Ward file.

29. Lowenfish, p. 68.

30. *Sporting Life*, March 2, 1912; Ward File.

31. Ward file; letter from John Ward, April 25, 1912.

32. Ward file; letters from John Ward, March 2, 1912 and April 12, 1912; Lowenfish and Lupien, pp. 51–52.

33. Ward file; Di Salvatore, p. 391.

34. *New York Times*, June 22, 1900.

35. Ward file; *New York Tribune*, March 5, 1925; Di Salvatore, pp. 397–398.

36. Chadwick, *Spalding's Base Ball Guide for 1891*, p. 44; Vincent, p. 216.
37. Levine, *A.G. Spalding and the Rise of Baseball*, p. 65; *Chicago Herald*, November 23, 1890.
38. Dumas Malone, ed., *Dictionary of American Biography: Vol. XVII* (New York: Charles Scribner's Sons, 1935), pp. 420–421.
39. Lowenfish and Lupien, pp. 17–22.

## Appendix 1

1. Seymour, p. 57.

## Appendix 2

1. First Reserve Agreement, made available by the Society for American Baseball Research.

## Appendix 3

1. National League Constitution: 1881; Survey of Standard Players' Contracts; *New York Times*, September 24, 1889.

## Appendix 4

1. Chadwick, *Spalding's Base Ball Guide for 1884*, pp. 41–43.

## Appendix 5

1. *New York Times*, December 16, 1889.

## Appendix 6

1. *New York Times*, January 29, 1890.

## Appendix 7

1. *New York Times*, March 27, 1890.

## Appendix 8

1. *New York Times*, March 16, 1890.

# Bibliographic Note

Both primary and secondary sources were used in the writing of this book. The secondary sources that were utilized were the works of reputable labor and sports historians. Almost all of these sources contained extensive notes which were examined carefully. I avoided using "popular" sports histories, which are usually primaily concerned with on-the-field activities and almost never provide sources for the information used. Although numerous primary sources were used, I relied most heavily on the annual *Spalding Base Ball Guide, The New York Times, The Sporting Life, The Sporting News, The New York Clipper,* the *Henry Chadwick* and *Albert Goodwill Spalding Files,* the numerous files from the National Baseball Library in Cooperstown, New York, and Preston Orem's *Baseball from the Newspaper Accounts: 1890. The New York Times* had an extensive and informative sports section in the 1880s and 1890s and is indexed. *The Sporting Life* was one of several sports weeklies published in the last decades of the nineteenth century. It is generally viewed by scholars and the librarians at the National Baseball Library as the most informative and accurate of the sports weeklies; consequently, I relied on it more than the other weekly publications. The Hall of Fame files are located in the National Baseball Library, Cooperstown, New York. Each file contains numerous newspaper and sporting press accounts of a particular player or owner as well as letters, etc. Often this material is not dated and it is impossible to tell from where the information came. I read the material in numerous files and tried to use only material that was dated and identified. However, sometimes material that was not dated and identified was used. The librarians at the National Library assured me that this was accepted practice in doing baseball research and that when the files were created, every effort was made to include only articles from reliable sources in the files. I also used material from the files of Mark Alvarez and Robert Tiemann. Both of these men are authorities on 19th-century baseball, and they reviewed all of the material that I borrowed and assured me that they believed all of it to be accurate.

# Bibliography

## Books

Alvarez, Mark. *The Old Ball Game*. Alexandria, Va.: Redefinition Inc., 1990.

Bartlett, Arthur. *Baseball and Mr. Spalding: The History and Romance of Baseball*. New York: Farrar, Straus and Young, Inc., 1951.

Brecher, Jeremy. *Strike*. Boston: South End Press, 1972.

Brunell, Frank W., ed. *Players' National League Base Ball Guide for 1890*. Chicago: W.J. Jefferson Print, 1889.

Burk, Robert F. *Never Just A Game: Players Owners and American Baseball to 1920*. Chapel Hill: University of North Carolina Press, 1994.

Chadwick, Henry, ed. *Spalding's Base Ball Guide and Official League Book for 1876*. Chicago: A.G. Spalding and Bros., 1876. The following editions of *Spalding's Base Ball Guide* were used: 1877, 1878, 1880, 1881, 1882, 1883, 1884, 1886, 1889, 1890, 1891, 1893, 1898.

Chandler, Alfred D. *The Visible Hand: The Managerial Revolution in American Business*. Cambridge, Mass.: Belknap Press of Harvard University Press, 1977.

Di Salvatore, Brian. *A Clever Base-Ballist: The Life and Times of John Montgomery Ward*. New York: Pantheon Books, 1999.

Dworkin, James. *Owners versus Players: Baseball and Collective Bargaining*. Boston: Auburn House, 1981.

Einsten, Charles, ed. *The Third Fireside Book of Baseball*. New York: Simon and Schuster, 1968.

Frisch, Michael, and Daniel Walkowitz, eds. *Working Class America: Essays in Labor, Community, and American Society*. Chicago: University of Illinois Press, 1983.

Goldstein, Warren. *Playing for Keeps: A History of Early Baseball*. Ithaca, N.Y.: Cornell University Press, 1989.

Gordon, David; Richard Edwards and Michael Reich. *Segmented Work, Divided Workers: The Historical Transformation of Labor in the United States*. Cambridge, England: Cambridge University Press, 1982.

Gutman, Herbert. *Work, Culture, and Society in Industrializing America: Essays in American Working Class and Social History*. New York: Vintage Books, 1977.

Gutman, Herbert, and Donald Bell, eds. *The New England Working Class and the New Labor History*. Chicago: University of Illinois Press, 1987.

Ivor-Campbell, Frederick; Robert Tiemann, and Mark Rucker, eds. *Baseball's First Stars*. Cleveland: Society for American Baseball Research, 1996.

James, Bill. *The Baseball Book 1990*. New York: Villard Books, 1990.

_____. *The Bill James Historical Baseball Abstract*. New York: Villard Books, 1986.

Laurie, Bruce. *Artisans into Workers: Labor in Nineteenth Century America*. New York: Hill and Wang, 1989.

Levine, Peter. *A.G. Spalding and the Rise of Baseball: The Promise of American Sport*. New York: Oxford University Press, 1985.

_____, ed. *Baseball History: An Annual of Original Baseball Research: Volume II*. Westport, Conn.: Meckler Books, 1989.

Lowenfish, Lee, and Tony Lupien. *The Imperfect Diamond: The Story of Baseball's Reserve System and the Men Who Fought to Change It*. New York: Stein and Day, 1980.

Malone, Dumas, ed., *Dictionary of American Biography: Vol. XVII*. New York: Charles Scribner's Sons, 1935.

Montgomery, David. *The Fall of the House of Labor: The Workplace, the State, and American Labor Activism*. Cambridge: Hill and Wang, 1989.

_____. *Worker Control in America: Studies in the History of Work, Technology, and Labor Struggles*. New York: Cambridge University Press, 1979.

Okrent, Daniel, and Harris Lewine, eds. *The Ultimate Baseball Book*. Boston: Houghton Mifflin, 1981.

Orem, Preston. *Baseball from the Newspaper Accounts: 1890*. Altadena, Calif.: Preston Orem, 1967.

Pearson, Daniel M. *Baseball in 1889: Players vs. Owners*. Bowling Green, Ohio: Bowling Green State University Press, 1993.

Prude, Jonathan. *The Coming of Industrial Order: Town and Factory Life in Rural Massachusetts, 1810–1860*. New York: Cambridge University Press, 1983.

*Reach's Official American Association Base Ball Guide: 1890*. Philadelphia: A.J. Reach Company, 1890.

*Reach's Official American Association Base Ball Guide: 1891*. Philadelphia: A.J. Reach Company, 1891.

Reichler, Joseph, ed. *The Baseball Encyclopedia: The Complete and Official Record of Major League Baseball*, 7th ed. New York: Macmillan, 1988.

Salvatore, Nick. *Eugene V. Debs: Citizen and Socialist*. Chicago: University of Illinois Press, 1982.

Selzer, Jack. *Baseball In the Nineteenth Century*. Manhattan, Kansas: Ag Press, 1986.

Seymour, Harold. *Baseball: The Early Years*. New York: Oxford University Press, 1960.

Staudohar, Paul D., ed. *Diamond Mines: Baseball and Labor*. Syracuse, N.Y.: Syracuse University Press, 2000.

Taylor, Frederick W. *The Principles of Scientific Management*. New York: W.W. Norton, 1911.

Vincent, Ted. *Mudville's Revenge: The Rise and Fall of American Sport*. New York: Seaview Books, 1981.

Voight, David Quenton. *American Baseball: From Gentleman's Sport to the Commissioner System*. Norman: University of Oklahoma Press, 1966.

Ward, John M. *Base-Ball: How to Become a Player*. Philadelphia: Athletic Publishing Co., 1888.

## Dissertations

Riess, Steven. "Professional Baseball and American Culture in the Progressive Era: Myths and Realities." Ph.D. Dissertation, University of Chicago, 1974.

## Magazines

Alvarez, Mark. "The Brotherhood Rebellion." *Sports Heritage*, July/August 1987, pp. 15–23.
____. "The Abominable Owner." *Sports Heritage*, November/December 1987, pp. 43–47.
Cook, Kevin. "1989 Baseball Preview." *Playboy*, May 1989, pp. 152–166.
Lee, Marvin. "Strike Four! You're Out!" *Town and Gown*, April 1978.
Mooney, Bill. "The Tattletale Grays." *Sports Illustrated*, October 14, 1974, pp. E6–E8.
Ward, John M. "Is the Base-Ball Player a Chattel?" *Lippencott's Magazine*, vol. XL, August 1887, pp 310–319.

## Journals

Bass, Cynthia. "The Making of a Baseball Radical." *The National Pastime* (Fall, 1982): pp. 63–66.
Lowenfish, Lee. "The Later Years of John M. Ward: Is a Ballplayer Barred from Business Association with Respectable Men?" *The National Pastime* (Fall, 1982): pp. 67–69.

## Newspapers

*Chicago Hearld*, 1890
*Chicago Times*, 1890
*Chicago Tribune*, 1882
*Kansas City Star*, 1969
*New York Tribune*, 1925
*New York Times*, 1872–1900
*Saint Louis Post-Dispatch*, 1883

## Sporting Press

*New York Clipper*, 1875–1890
*Sporting Life*, 1885–1915
*The Sporting News*, 1876–1972

## Hall of Fame Files

Chadwick, Henry, vols. II and IV, National Baseball Library, Cooperstown, New York.
Galvin, Jim, National Baseball Library, Cooperstown, New York.
Glasscock, Jack, National Baseball Library, Cooperstown, New York.
Hanlon, Ned, National Baseball Library, Cooperstown, New York.
Hulbert, William, National Baseball Library, Cooperstown, New York.

Johnson, Albert, vols. I and II, National Baseball Library, Cooperstown, New York.
Keefe, Tim, National Baseball Library, Cooperstown, New York.
McAlpin, Edward, National Baseball Library, Cooperstown, New York.
Mills, Abraham, National Baseball Library, Cooperstown, New York.
Pfeffer, Fred, National Baseball Library, Cooperstown, New York.
Spalding, Albert, vols. I–VI. National Baseball Library, Cooperstown, New York.
Talcott, Edward, National Baseball Library, Cooperstown, New York.
Thurman, Allan, National Baseball Library, Cooperstown, New York.
Ward, John M., National Baseball Library, Cooperstown, New York.
Young, Nicholas, National Baseball Library, Cooperstown, New York.

## *Letters*

Fleming, John M. nephew of John Ward, December 30, 1963. Ward file.
Watson, Winifred, cousin of John Ward, February 20, 1964. Ward file.
Various Letters from John M. Ward. Ward file.
Tieman, Robert, Chairman of Nineteenth Century Committee, Society for American Baseball Research.

## *Interviews*

Hydes, Liz. Columbia University Law School, New York. Interview, March 14, 1991.
Tieman, Robert. Chiarman of Nineteenth Century Committee, Society for American Baseball Research. Interview, February 12, 1991.

## *Miscellaneous*

Alvarez, Mark librarian, Society for American Baseball Research and author of numerous books and articles on nineteenth century baseball. Notes.

# Index

Numbers in *bold italics* refer to photographs.